Evangelicalism
& the Future
of Christianity

ALISTER
M^cGRATH

INTERVARSITY PRESS
DOWNERS GROVE, ILLINOIS 60515

This U.S. edition published in the United States of America by InterVarsity Press, Downers Grove, Illinois, with permission from Hodder & Stoughton, London, England.

InterVarsity Press® is the book-publishing division of InterVarsity Christian Fellowship®, a student movement active on campus at hundreds of universities, colleges and schools of nursing in the United States of America, and a member movement of the International Fellowship of Evangelical Students. For information about local and regional activities, write Public Relations Dept., InterVarsity Christian Fellowship, 6400 Schroeder Rd., P.O. Box 7895, Madison, WI 53707-7895.

ISBN 0-8308-1694-1

Printed in the United States of America ♾

Library of Congress Cataloging-in-Publication Data

McGrath, Alister E., 1953-
    Evangelicalism and the future of Christianity/Alister McGrath.
      p.   cm.
    Includes bibliographical references.
    ISBN 0-8308-1694-1
    1. Evangelicalism. 2. Evangelicalism—History.
    3. Christianity—20th century. I. Title.
    BR1640.M41994
    280'.4'09—dc20   94-23846
                                        CIP

17	16	15	14	13	12	11	10	9	8	7	6	5	4	3	2
09	08	07	06	05	04	03	02	01	00	99	98	97	96	95	

Acknowledgments

The origins of this book lie in a series of lectures given at Moore College, Sydney, in May 1993. I am deeply indebted to the hospitality of the Moore College faculty and students and to their response to these lectures. The material relating to evangelical spirituality represents an adaptation of the St. Antholin Lecture given at Central Hall, Westminster, London, in June 1993. I have also drawn on material originally presented in the 1992 Anderson Lectures at McGill University. Some of the remaining material was first presented in various forms at Oxford University; Wheaton College, Illinois; China Graduate School of Theology, Hong Kong; and Ridley College, Melbourne. Once more, I am most grateful to those audiences for their comments and suggestions, and I have endeavored to incorporate them into the text where possible. I myself remain responsible for all errors of fact or interpretation.

My greatest debt is to the faculty and students of Wycliffe Hall, Oxford, who for the past ten years have provided me with an outstanding environment in which to live, teach, think and write. They have taught me more than I can ever hope to express adequately.

Introduction

In 1804 the young English poet William Wordsworth penned words that captured a sense of optimism and hope among the youth of Europe. The French Revolution had shattered the tired old political framework of Europe, sweeping away its outdated tradition-bound practices and beliefs and opening the way to a bright new future. A new dawn seemed to be at hand, promising to usher in an era of hope and opportunity.

> Bliss was it in that dawn to be alive,
>
> But to be young was very heaven![1]

Wordsworth's feelings were echoed by many young people throughout Western Europe. Here, at long last, was something new, something *liberating*, which a repressed and disillusioned youth could embrace. The future seemed to belong to them.

That need for an inspirational vision remains as strong in the modern world. Marxism provided students of the 1960s and 1970s with a powerful vision of a transformed future. Political realism and intellectual respectability seemed to flow together to fire the hearts and minds of a generation of young people who were earnestly searching for a cause to give meaning and dignity to their lives, and ultimately to the world. Theodor Adorno and others provided what seemed to be a solid intellectual basis to a refashioned Marxism, grounded in the experience and aspirations of student communities. Today that vision, so powerful in its day, is seen to be tired and deluded. It is yesterday's vision for yesterday's people.

The Christian vision of the future now seems increasingly to belong to evangelicalism, which is coming more and more to constitute the mainstream of American Protestant Christianity,[2] to the intense irritation of others who believe that they ought to have pride of place. Some regard this development with a mixture of disbelief and resentment: how could such a movement come to gain so great an influence within the churches? Others regard it as the salvation of Christianity in the West, giving a new dynamism and purpose to a church that increasingly seemed to have lost its way.

Evangelicalism is a high-octane faith that seems set to continue its upswing into the next millennium. In a 1990 survey of the five hundred fastest-growing Protestant congregations in the United States, 89 percent were found to be evangelical.[3] Scarcely any part of the world has remained untouched by the global renaissance of evangelicalism. Even Latin America, traditionally regarded as a stronghold of Roman Catholicism, is now expected to become numerically dominated by various forms of evangelicalism by the year 2025.[4]

In Europe, evangelicalism has had a lesser impact and is often regarded as an English-language movement. The Church of England, to give one obvious example, has been deeply affected, especially during the last two decades, by a resurgent evangelicalism within its ranks.[5] The election of a younger and hitherto unknown evangelical bishop, George Carey, as archbishop of Canterbury was seen by the British quality press as a symbol of the new confidence and strength of evangelicalism within the English national church. For reasons such as these, the future of Christianity seems to belong to the movement. Young people are attracted to it, partly on account of its inherent spiritual and growing intellectual appeal and partly on account of the sense of well-being and optimism within its ranks.

The inspirational nature of the evangelical vision is now being supplemented by the forging of increasingly rigorous theological foundations, and its intellectual credibility has been enhanced by the growing number of academic theologians within its ranks. Head and heart are being brought together in a movement that is looking forward to the future with a sense of expectancy and anticipation. It is an exciting time for evangelicals to be alive; to be young is more wonderful still. The future seems to beckon to evangelicalism, inviting it to advance and mature still further.[6]

But will it? By the time of Wordsworth's death in 1850, the French Revolution was but a distant memory. Its legacy was political instability and a climate of suspicion within a Europe that had been shattered by the forces it had unleashed. The hopes and aspirations that had been pinned on its success lay in tatters. The same Marxism that had been adopted with such enthusiasm and commitment by students in the early 1970s collapsed in 1989, the fall of the Berlin Wall a potent public symbol of its death. A movement that seemed to hold the future in its hands lay fallen in the dust of a vengeful history, which had found no place for it. Will evangelicalism go the same way? Will a movement that today seems to hold such promise for the future of Christianity become an irrelevance tomorrow?

Perhaps it will. Nobody can say. But what can be said is this. Evangelicalism can never afford to take its recent successes and achievements for granted. There is evidence of weakness and complacency within its substantial ranks[7] and, above all, a lack of willingness to look into the future and plan for what may lie there. Evangelicalism stands under the judgment of God, as a movement to which much has been given and from which much is demanded. It needs to look to its roots and foundations, continually asking how its gifts may be related to the needs of Christ's church and the furtherance of his gospel.

I write this book as a committed yet critical evangelical. I have no hesitation in describing myself as an evangelical or in affirming the central beliefs and attitudes of the movement. I became a Christian at Oxford University in 1971 through the influence of the Oxford Inter-Collegiate Christian Union and was nourished by the writings and speaking ministries of leading British evangelicals, including Michael

Green, James Packer and John Stott. If I can be said to owe my Christian origins to anyone or anything human, it is to evangelicalism.

Yet, as I shall relate later in this work, eventually I found myself going through a sustained crisis of confidence in evangelicalism, partly on account of the low esteem in which it was held in academic circles. After a period of wrestling with the immense agenda of liberalism at both Oxford and Cambridge, during which I was confronted with issues many evangelicals choose to ignore, I found myself appreciating and valuing my evangelical heritage all the more. My intellectual wanderings during this "wilderness period" served to bring home to me how spiritually and intellectually *satisfying* evangelicalism is; they also taught me that there is a real need for evangelicalism to engage with internal and external issues that in the past (and for understandable reasons) it largely chose to disregard.

For the last ten years I have taught Christian theology at the leading evangelical theological college of the Church of England—Wycliffe Hall, Oxford—and become increasingly familiar with the agenda and issues facing evangelicalism in its English context. As honorary vice president of the Universities and Colleges Christian Fellowship, the British branch of the International Fellowship of Evangelical Students, I have become deeply involved in issues relating to student Christianity. As research professor of systematic theology at Regent College, Vancouver, I have had the privilege of teaching and learning from a highly motivated international group of students at this pioneering North American evangelical lay graduate school of theology. And as consultant editor of the leading evangelical publication *Christianity Today,* I have the privilege of being able to contribute to the discussion of the major issues facing Christianity, especially in its evangelical forms, both in North America and in its global context. In all of these matters, I have become increasingly convinced that evangelicalism holds the key to the future of Western Christianity.

I have no vested interest in making this judgment. When I make a mistake, I say so. I have no hesitation in acknowledging that I made such a mistake during the period 1976-1982, when I went through a protracted liberal phase in which I reacted against evangelicalism, treating it (as I and others were encouraged to do by our professors) as an academically insignificant and spiritually spurious movement, espoused only by immature and insecure people with deficient mental processes. Yet the more I thought about the liberal project, and the more I wrestled with its agenda and approaches, the more I felt that it was academically vulnerable and spiritually inadequate. Its pastoral weaknesses became especially evident to me during a three-year period as a pastor in Nottingham (1980-1983), in which I came to realize that liberalism had little to offer in the midst of the harsh pastoral realities of unemployment, illness and death.[8] My increasing familiarity and involvement with every aspect of evangelicalism since 1982 has caused me to affirm its validity; had this not been the case, I would have had no difficulty in admitting so fully and publicly.

My concerns lie elsewhere. Evangelicalism has considerable attractions and strengths; it also has its darker side. While this book is concerned to explore the history, identity and strengths of evangelicalism, it also aims to identify its weaknesses. I happen to believe that those weaknesses can be corrected and that the outcome of such a process of correction will be enriching both to evangelicalism and to Christianity as a whole. Yet evangelicalism has been reluctant to acknowledge its darker side, giving the impression that it will listen to none save its friends.

The reader of this work will thus encounter criticisms of evangelicalism that some may find wounding or distressing. It is not my intention to wound or distress anyone; however, it would be naive to think that some of the issues I shall raise will not disturb some of my readers. Yet evangelicalism has now gotten past the stage when it needs to be defensive about everything. Its survival seems assured; its next task is to get itself into shape for expansion and consolidation. It needs to ask itself some hard questions before it moves further.

My belief, which will be stated and justified throughout this work, is that evangelicalism will gain the intellectual and spiritual high ground within Western Christianity during the next generation—but it will do so only after a thorough shakeout, in which some of its less desirable and theologically dubious aspects have been purged and the necessary attention paid to its emerging weaknesses. Evangelicalism needs to shed its ghetto mentality and become more involved with the real world as it prepares to expand still further.

This book is thus written in the profound conviction that evangelicalism has a vital and continuing role to play in the century ahead, coupled with a growing suspicion that the movement is failing to do justice both to its own intellectual and spiritual birthright and to the *evangel*—the good news of Jesus Christ—from which it takes its name and on which it must take its stand. It is an attempt to stimulate discussions within the worldwide evangelical community by drawing attention to the present and potential strengths of the movement as well as to a few of its present weaknesses. What is here said *needs* to be said. I have, however, tried to say it as gently and as sensitively as I could, in the belief that today's weaknesses can be addressed and eliminated, perhaps even becoming tomorrow's strengths. I consider this to be particularly the case with evangelical spirituality, a weakness that I believe will be resolved within a generation, perhaps even during my lifetime.

The present volume is concerned to explore some issues of major importance confronting evangelicalism as a religious movement within global Christianity, rather than as a theological system that merits being taken seriously by the academy. This book is not, and does not pretend to be, a work of scholarship. It is written by a committed evangelical for an evangelical readership that needs to discover its own history, learn from the errors of the past and face up to the challenges of the future.

For this reason, the present book is not concerned with detailed theological analysis, full documentation of sources or the studied detachment that is the hallmark of academic scholarship; I shall attempt to provide these in a book due to be published two years from now, *The Intellectual Foundations of Evangelicalism* (InterVarsity Press). In that work I shall set out and defend the intellectual coherence of evangelicalism in a postmodern and postliberal world, with the agenda of the academy firmly in mind. Evangelicalism has already ensured its continuing presence within the churches; its next frontier is the academy. The present book, however, is written for an evangelical readership, on the basis of the shared assumptions of the movement.

Any attempt to understand evangelicalism must begin with considered reflection on the history and identity of the movement. For this reason, the opening chapters of this work deal with these issues, to which we may turn immediately.

1

THE EVANGELICAL
RENAISSANCE

E VANGELICALISM IS ONE OF THE POWERHOUSES OF THE MOD-
ern Christian church in the Western world. Time and time
again, people—especially young people—put their discovery of
the vitality and excitement of the gospel down to the witness
of evangelicalism. In an increasingly secular age, evangelism is of decisive importance in reaching out beyond the bounds of the church
and bringing men and women the good news of Jesus Christ. There
is a growing realization that the future existence and well-being of the
churches depends on a determined and principled effort to proclaim
the gospel. Evangelicalism, once regarded as marginal, has now become mainline, and it can no longer be dismissed as an insignificant
sideshow, sectarian tendency or irrelevance.[1] It has moved from the
wings to center stage, displacing others once regarded as mainline,
who consequently feel deeply threatened and alienated. Its commitment to evangelism has resulted in numerical growth, where some
other variants of Christianity are suffering from severe contraction.

These trends have been widely noted by both Christian and secular
observers of the global religious scene. Evangelicalism is generally
accepted as being well on its way toward becoming a major constit-

utive element of global Christianity. Yet this new awareness of the importance of evangelicalism has not been accompanied by a deepening understanding of the origins, nature and distinctives of the movement. Even among evangelicals there is often an alarming lack of awareness of their own family history. It is therefore of considerable importance to establish what evangelicalism is, sketching at least the contours of the movement, and to attempt to understand both its enormous attraction and its darker side.

Knowing the Family History

I recall once hearing a lecture in southern California given by a Kiowa Apache Indian, a Native American from the Oklahoma region. His theme was discovering one's identity through the history of one's people. He told his audience how he learned the story of his people while he was still a young boy.

One day, just after dawn, his father woke him and took him to the home of an elderly Kiowa woman. He left him there, promising to return to collect him that afternoon. All that day the woman told this young boy the story of the Kiowa people. She told him of their origins by the Yellowstone River and how they then migrated southward. She told him of the many hardships they faced—the wars with other Native American nations and the great blizzards on the winter plains. She told him of the glories of the life of the Kiowa nation—the great buffalo hunts, the taming of wild horses and the skill of the braves as riders. Finally she told him of the coming of the white man and the humiliation of their once-proud nation at the hands of horse soldiers who forced them to move south to Kansas, where they faced starvation and poverty. Her story ended as she told him of their final humiliating confinement within a reservation in Oklahoma.

The lecturer told us how, shortly before dark, his father returned to collect him. "When I left that house, I was a Kiowa," he declared. He had learned the story of his people. He knew what his people had been through and what they stood for. Before learning the family history, he had been a Kiowa in name only; now he was a Kiowa in reality.

Evangelicals tend not to know their family history. They are often unfamiliar with the great struggles that evangelicalism has gone through in the past—its victories and its defeats. They are unaware of a small galaxy of writers, thinkers, preachers, pastors and ordinary believing Christians who went before them and prepared the way. Through ignorance of that history, they are liable to repeat the mistakes of the past—the evangelical infighting, for example, that came close to extinguishing the movement in the 1920s and early 1930s. Knowing one's family history is one way of avoiding past errors and preparing to face the future. As Woody Allen quipped, "History repeats itself. It has to. Nobody listens the first time round."

As evangelicalism gains further ground in the Western churches and beyond, it becomes ever more prone to make the mistakes that could send it spiraling into irreversible decline. Its hard-won victories could easily be undone by a new generation of evangelicals who unknowingly repeat the errors of the past.

But knowing the family history is not simply about avoiding mistakes. It also allows us to appreciate the attraction of evangelicalism and discover what it is about the evangelical approach to Christianity which has such a powerful appeal to so many people. Many younger evangelicals are unaware of what led to the emergence of evangelicalism as a leading force in global Christianity. Many just assume that it has always been like this. It certainly has not! Knowing and learning from the family history is one way of making sure that evangelicalism will continue to have a secure place in the future of Christianity.

The Historical Roots of Evangelicalism

The term *evangelical* dates from the sixteenth century, and it was first used to refer to Catholic writers who wished to revert to more biblical beliefs and practices than those associated with the late medieval church. Research tells us that attitudes toward the personal appropriation of salvation and the spiritual importance of the reading of Scripture which would now be called "evangelical" emerged in Italian Benedictine monasteries during the late fifteenth century.[2] Similarly,

19

scholars of the later Italian Renaissance have identified a major spiritual movement, which became particularly important among the Italian aristocratic laity in the 1520s, that emphasized a personally appropriated salvation.[3] Through an obvious lack of familiarity with Christian spirituality, earlier scholars of the movement used the inappropriate (though related) term *evangelism* to refer to it. It is clear that it is an early form of evangelicalism, the emergence of which can be paralleled throughout Europe during this period.

One of the most important features of the late Renaissance was the growth of lay religion throughout Western Europe and laypeople's demands for a form of Christian spirituality that would be of direct relevance to their personal spiritual concerns. It must be remembered that much medieval spirituality was developed by monastic writers and was intended to be read within a monastic context. There was an urgent need for the evolution of forms of the Christian faith that related to the spiritual needs and concerns of the laity.[4] Martin Luther's doctrine of justification, with its emphasis on the faith and assurance of the individual, proved to meet the needs of at least some such people.[5]

It is known that such evangelical attitudes were not initially regarded as a threat by ecclesiastical authorities; indeed, they were even welcomed in some areas as making an overdue and needed contribution to the renewal of the spiritual vitality of a tired church. The Italian church in particular was deeply and positively affected by the emergence of evangelicalism during the 1530s. Several cardinals of the period were profoundly influenced by evangelical attitudes, and they did not regard this as inconsistent with their senior positions within the church. It was only in the mid-1540s that an increasingly anxious church, alert to the growing threat posed by Northern European Lutheranism, condemned such attitudes as destabilizing, and evangelicalism fell into official disfavor. The church authorities had become convinced that to be an *evangelical* was to be a *Lutheran*—and hence to be anti-Catholic.

While I have considerable admiration for Luther, both as a person and as a theologian, I cannot fail to note this negative aspect of his impact: the identification of evangelicalism and Lutheranism led to the rejection of the former along with the latter. The criticism of a specific form of evangelicalism was thus extended to evangelicalism in general.

The term *evangelical* was especially associated with the 1520s, when the French term *évangélique* and the German *evangelisch* begin to feature prominently in the controversial writings of the early Reformation. In the 1530s the term *Protestant* became more significant; increasingly this came to be understood simply as "anti-Catholic." However, it must be appreciated that this term was imposed on evangelicals by their Catholic opponents and was not of their own choosing. *Protestant* referred originally to the "protest" of the six princes and fourteen south German cities at the second Diet of Speyer (1529) against the rescinding of the religious freedom guaranteed by the first Diet of Speyer three years earlier. Despite the popular mythology surrounding the origins of the term, the "protest" in question was not against Rome, nor even against the theology of the pre-Reformation church, but against the outcome of a specific form of political intrigue in southern Germany.

By the middle of the seventeenth century, the term *Protestant* had become generally accepted, and it gradually displaced the older term *evangelical*. But the word *evangelical* is regularly encountered in seventeenth-century English works of devotion, both Puritan and Anglican, with the general sense of "being grounded in the gospel," as in John Owen's studied definition of assurance as "a gracious evangelical persuasion of acceptance" or his reference to the Word of God as containing "sacred, evangelical, fundamental truths."[6] At this stage the term does not seem to have been used to denote a particular theological stance, and it was used by writers as diverse ecclesiologically as the high-church bishop Jeremy Taylor and the congregationalist divine John Owen.

In the German language, for historical reasons, the term *evangelisch* has now become more or less equivalent to "Protestant" and has lost at least a large measure of its original meaning; the somewhat clumsy neologism *evangelikal,* clearly derived from the English original, is now used increasingly by German evangelical writers to denote a specifically "evangelical," rather than a more general "Protestant," outlook.[7] In French the term *évangélique* has a long history of use to refer to evangelical (as opposed to Protestant) outlooks; however, the term *évangélisme* is now becoming increasingly accepted as the normal French term to refer to this movement.[8] This confusion has not happened in English, on account of a deliberate decision to prevent it from taking place. Since the 1940s there has been a determined, and largely successful, effort on the part of the English-speaking heirs of the Reformation to recover the older term and rehabilitate it.

The deliberate decision to use the term *evangelical* to refer to the form of Christianity to be discussed in this work dates from 1942. The formation of the National Association of Evangelicals (NAE) in the United States represented a carefully weighed and considered move to distinguish "evangelicals" from "fundamentalists," partly on account of the growing pejorative associations of the latter term and partly on account of an increasing recognition of the failures of the movement that it designated. There was a need for a reappraisal and a fresh start. The term *evangelical* was chosen to designate the new movement, but initially nobody seemed to like the word very much. For a start, it had British roots. More worryingly, it was seen as being outdated, recalling an earlier period in Christian history which many felt was passé. Yet as time went on, it became clear that Flaubert himself could not have chosen a better *mot juste.* It pointed to a "theology of retrieval" in which the heritage of the evangelical past could legitimately be reappropriated. By the early 1960s, both the term and the agenda associated with it had achieved widespread acceptance.

Evangelical is thus the term chosen by evangelicals to refer to themselves, as representing most adequately the central concern of the movement for the safeguarding and articulation of the *evangel*—the good news of God which has been made known and made possible in Jesus Christ. *Protestant* too easily implies a preoccupation with a system of church government (such as presbyterianism), which can come to overshadow more important concerns relating to the gospel itself. Evangelicalism refuses to allow any matter of church government to take precedence over the gospel itself; the term *evangelical,* by placing emphasis on this gospel, conveys both the focus and the substance of the movement. All else is deliberately subordinated, as a matter of principle, to this central theme.

Significant Movements

In one sense, then, evangelicalism recognizes only one normative historical source—the gospel of Jesus Christ, as this is proclaimed in the New Testament and anticipated in the Old. Yet evangelicalism also has historical roots in the sense that there have been significant movements in Christian history that have prepared the way for it and on whose resources it may draw. Several such movements may be recognized, and this complex mutual interaction of sources has led to a number of tensions within modern evangelicalism. Three major sources may be noted.

1. The magisterial Reformation.[9] The mainstream Reformation, often referred to in the literature as the "magisterial Reformation" on account of its positive attitude toward the magistracy and existing power structures, is a major source and reference point for modern evangelicalism. The Reformers Martin Luther (1483-1546) and John Calvin (1509-1564) demonstrated a passion for the reformation of the structures, doctrine and spirituality of the church along more biblical lines. Their intellectual coherence, pastoral concern and practical wisdom ensured that the emerging churches of the Reformation were endowed with an academically credible and pastorally relevant outlook that would be firmly grounded in Scripture. The Reformation remains a focus and defining point of reference for evangelicalism today, as it seeks to ensure that the central themes of the Reformation—such as the doctrine of justification by faith alone and the Scripture principle—remain deeply embedded in the evangelical consciousness.

Nevertheless, the Reformation cannot be allowed to dominate the horizons of evangelicalism. As its name suggests, the sixteenth-century movement was concerned with the "reformation" of the Christian church. Its agenda centered on the need to reform an existing church in a settled Christian cultural context. The issue of evangelism—that is, reaching into a non-Christian context in order to gain converts— never became important for Luther or Calvin. Their horizons were dominated by the need to alter existing church structures. Even the program of "the evangelization of France," which was of major significance to Calvin from 1555 to the end of his life,[10] is to be understood as the attempt to persuade *Catholic* Christians to become *evangelical* Christians. Calvin considered the Catholic Church of his day to be Christian; the problem was that it was an unreformed, and hence unacceptable, version of Christianity. Evangelization was *not* understood primarily to mean converting individuals from a secular culture.[11] The Reformation did not address the issue of evangelism in the modern sense of the term, so evangelicalism is obliged to extend the agenda of the Reformation in this respect.

2. Puritanism. The impact of Puritanism on evangelicalism has been considerable. Even John Wesley (1703-1791), whose theological Arminianism placed him at some distance from the more Reformed approach of writers such as John Owen (1616-1683), was sufficiently impressed by the Puritan tradition to include many of their writings in his influential *Christian Library.*[12] Indeed, there are excellent reasons for supposing that the English evangelical revivals of the eighteenth century built directly on the foundations laid by Puritanism in the previous century.[13]

Although Puritanism is often represented as a somewhat cerebral and moral movement, concerned for good theology and morals, it must be pointed out that recent scholarship has drawn attention to the Puritan emphasis on a "religion of the heart." A deep concern for spirituality is now recognized to have been integral to the movement.[14] Despite the distinguished presence of the movement within English evangelicalism of the seventeenth century, it is generally thought that Puritanism reached its spiritual and intellectual zenith in the ministry and writings of the American Jonathan Edwards (1703-1758).

3. Pietism. During the second half of the seventeenth century, many German Lutherans became alarmed at the spiritual state of their church.[15] It was doctrinally orthodox; nevertheless, it seemed to lack spiritual warmth and any obvious signs of the joyful presence of Christ in its corporate life. Lutheran orthodoxy had become an intellectual system that was appreciated in the mind but did little to warm the heart. Pietism was a response to this. It placed considerable emphasis on a personally appropriated faith, which was understood as a "re-born" and "personal" living relationship with Christ rather than the passive assent to the creeds it discerned as underlying nominal faith.[16] The phrase "a living faith" came to be used to refer to this personal and intimate relation with Christ. The writings of August Hermann Francke (1663-1727) are an especially important witness to this trend,[17] and they had a major impact in the University of Halle in the eighteenth century.

Pietism, which began in Germany during the seventeenth century, had its greatest influence in England in the century that followed. John Wesley's Aldersgate experience, in which he felt his heart to be "strangely warmed" while he listened to a reading of Martin Luther's preface to Romans, is an excellent illustration of the Pietist emphasis on the positive place of experience in the Christian life. The great eighteenth-century awakening now generally known as the Evangelical Revival, had a deep impact on English religion. Although Pietism lacked the intellectual rigor of Calvinism and could easily lapse into little more than a personal devotion to Jesus, its passion for a living, personal spiritual experience gave it a popular appeal that in the eyes of many was of greater importance. It has often been pointed out that the fiercely antireligious French Revolution (1789) took place in a nation untouched by any form of Pietism and thus able to dismiss Christianity as an irrelevant and oppressive force. To put it simply, Pietism made the gospel relevant to the ordinary believer.

Other contributing sources could be listed. For example, the vigor-ously antitraditional approach of radical Reformers, such as Menno

Simons (1496-1561) and Balthasar Hubmeier (c. 1485-1528), has had an impact on a number of evangelical writers and has encouraged the development of separatist attitudes. The forms of revivalism that flourished in the United States before the emergence of fundamentalism in the 1920s should also be noted. Nevertheless, the three sources identified above have constituted the main fountainheads of evangelical thinking and offered frameworks through which the New Testament may be read and interpreted.

The Cultural Factor

It is important to appreciate, however, that while these three streams merge, as contributories, to form a single flux in modern evangelicalism, their mingling produces eddies and vortices. Like great rivers cascading at their point of juncture, their merger causes tension and disruption. The resulting flux is greater; yet it is also more disturbed, with a number of disagreements and debates featuring prominently within the evangelical heritage. This inherent theological and spiritual tension is supplemented by additional factors, including the cultural contexts in which evangelicalism finds itself.

The origin of this cultural tension needs to be understood. Although evangelicalism had its origins in the later European Renaissance, especially in France, Germany and Italy, it appears to have consolidated itself in England and North America. One major contributing factor to this development was the rise of Puritanism, which gained considerable influence in both England and North America during the early seventeenth century. Puritanism, as we noted above, is of particular interest and importance, as it appears to have brought together both the intellectual rigor of the Reformed tradition, deriving from Calvin and his followers, and an emphasis on the experiential aspects of the Christian life which in a number of respects anticipated Pietism. Some of the Puritans forced out of England by the repressive religious policies of Charles I settled in the American colonies, which thus soon became centers of Puritanism. As a result, evangelicalism emerged and developed primarily within an English-speaking context.[18]

While evangelicalism remained confined to well-defined (and related) geographical and cultural contexts, such as North America and England, the cultural factor remained of limited importance. To put it crudely, evangelicals were almost all white.[19] However, as evangelicalism began to expand into Asian and African contexts in the late nineteenth and early twentieth centuries, and as it became increasingly aware of its own black constituency in the United States, differences began to emerge in relation to cultural issues. The issue of the application of the gospel to cultures has become of major importance in global evangelicalism. Differences between American and East Asian, or English and East African, evangelicals often reflect deep-seated cultural differences rather than fundamental differences concerning the gospel itself. The importance of such disagreements must not be overestimated. They exist, but are not seen as identity-giving. There is, to use Wittgenstein's helpful term, a clear "family resemblance" among the various types and styles of evangelicalism.

One such disagreement in North America in the 1920s led directly to the emergence of a distinctive form of evangelicalism known as fundamentalism. In view of the importance of this development, I will consider it in more detail.

Evangelicalism and Fundamentalism

Fundamentalism is both one of the most influential and one of the most detested movements in the modern world. The rise of Islamic fundamentalism in particular has contributed significantly to the negative, anti-intellectual associations of the term. Fundamentalist tendencies are now well established within Protestant, Roman Catholic, Hindu, Jewish and Islamic contexts. It is not a specifically Christian, or even a specifically Protestant, phenomenon. In what follows, however, I will restrict my comments to Christian Protestant fundamentalism and use the term *fundamentalist* to refer to this specific movement, whose relationship to evangelicalism requires particular comment.

In 1910 the first of a series of twelve books appeared from a small

American publishing house. The series was unremarkably entitled The Fundamentals.[20] By a series of historical accidents, the term *fundamentalist* took its name from this series of works. Fundamentalism arose as a religious reaction within American culture to the rise of a secular culture.[21] Despite the wide use of the term to refer to religious movements within Islam and Judaism, the term originally and properly designates a movement within Protestant Christianity in the United States, especially during the period 1920-1940. Initially the term *fundamentalism* was devoid of the overtones of obscurantism, anti-intellectualism and political extremism now associated with it. Yet these were not long in developing.

Fundamentalists at first saw themselves simply as returning to biblical orthodoxy. This point was recognized at the time by Kirsopp Lake (1872-1946), a leading British modernist writer who specialized in the field of New Testament and patristic studies. In his *Religion of Yesterday and Tomorrow* (1926), which advocated a form of religion based on individual human perceptions and experience rather than revelation, Lake wrote as follows:

> It is a mistake often made by educated men who happen to have but little knowledge of historical theology, to suppose that fundamentalism is a new and strange form of thought. It is nothing of the sort; it is the partial and uneducated survival of a theology which was once universally held by all Christians. . . . The fundamentalist may be wrong; I think he is. But it is we who have departed from the tradition, not he, and I am sorry for the fate of anyone who tries to argue with the fundamentalist on the basis of authority. The Bible and the *corpus theologicum* of the church is on the fundamentalist side.[22]

Lake, writing at the time of the emergence of fundamentalism as a distinctive movement, recognizes the continuity between its basic ideas and the historical witness of the Christian church.

Yet the modernist context in which the fundamentalist protest took place inevitably had an influence in shaping the movement's response to the challenges facing it. In consequence, it is not correct to regard the movement simply as a return to older positions, although aspects of fundamentalist teachings may indeed be discerned in the writings of classic Reformed orthodoxy and in those of members of the Old Princeton School such as Benjamin B. Warfield (1851-1921) and Charles Hodge (1797-1878). As James Davison Hunter points out, fundamentalism cannot be equated with "a basic unaltered orthodoxy":

> Orthodoxy as a cultural system represents what could be called a "consensus through time"—more specifically, a consensus based upon the ancient rules and precepts derived from divine revelation. Its authority and legitimacy derive from an unaltering continuity with truth as originally revealed—truth in its primitive and purest expression. *Fundamentalism is orthodoxy in confrontation with modernity.*[23]

This point has been emphasized by Martin E. Marty, the distinguished student of modern American Christian thought. He writes, "The fundamental theological feature of modern fundamentalisms which are religious is oppositionalism. Fundamentalism in any context takes form when members of already conservative or traditional movements experience threat."[24]

In at least one sense, fundamentalism is a deliberate and considered reaction to developments in the twentieth century, and it is thus, in one sense of the word, thoroughly "modern." It was from its outset, and has remained, a countercultural movement, using central doctrinal affirmations as a means of defining cultural boundaries. Whereas most nineteenth-century forms of American evangelicalism were culturally centralist, committed to engaging with culture in order to transform it through the gospel,[25] the fundamentalist reaction against "modernity" carried with it, as part of its religious package, a separatist attitude to culture. Certain central doctrines (most notably the absolute, literal authority of Scripture and the premillennial return of Christ) were treated as barriers, intended as much to alienate secular culture as to give fundamentalists a sense of identity and purpose.[26]

The emphasis on the premillennial return of Christ is of special significance. This view has a long history, but it never attained any great importance prior to the nineteenth century. It is not found in the writings of a group of theologians of major importance to fundamentalism, such as Charles Hodge, B. B. Warfield and J. Gresham Machen (1881-1937).[27] The idea was brought to North America by John Nelson Darby (1800-1882). Although it served as the intellectual foundation of Darby's program of separation from existing denominations, nobody seems to have paid much attention to it. Then the controversies of the 1920s erupted. Suddenly separatism and its intellectual underpinning in dispensationalist premillennialism were found to have a new appeal. Moreover, fundamentalism appears to have discerned in the idea an important weapon against liberal Christian ideas of a kingdom of God on earth to be achieved through social action. "Dispensationalism," especially of a premillenarian type, became an integral element of fundamentalism.

A siege mentality became characteristic of the movement; fundamentalist communities viewed themselves as walled cities, or (to evoke the pioneer spirit) circles of wagons, defending their distinctives against an unbelieving culture.[28] "Oppositionalism," to use Marty's clumsy but illuminating term, became a leading characteristic of a fundamentalist *mentalité*.

The negative consequences of this polarization can be seen especially from the painful history of the Presbyterian Church in the United States earlier this century.[29] In 1922 an ill-tempered controversy broke out, which is widely regarded as having marked the beginning of the spiral of numerical decline within that church, laid the foundations of schism and ultimately caused a radical loss of theological vision that eroded the church's distinctiveness within the American situation. The row centered on whether traditional doctrines should be modified in the light of modern scientific and cultural knowledge.

On May 21, 1922, Harry Emerson Fosdick preached a polemical sermon entitled "Shall the Fundamentalists Win?" One hundred and thirty thousand copies of the sermon, rewritten by a skilled public relations expert and funded by John D. Rockefeller Jr., were circulated. A vigorous riposte soon followed. Clarence Edward Macartney

entitled his reply "Shall Unbelief Win?" The situation rapidly polarized. Toleration and compromise proved impossible. Presbyterians
were forced to decide whether they were, to use the categories of the
protagonists, "unbelieving liberals" or "reactionary fundamentalists."
The church was shattered. There were other options and saner voices;
yet the climate of opinion made it impossible for them to gain a
hearing. "Oppositionalism" led to the issue being perceived in crystal-
clear terms: either an unbelieving culture would win or victory would
go to the gospel. There were no alternatives.

Conservatives soon discovered that there seemed to be nothing they
could do to retard the influence of modernist thinkers such as Fosdick
in their denominations. The slide into modernism seemed inexorable.
This led to a growing demand within fundamentalist circles for separation from allegedly corrupt denominations. If it proved impossible
to reform a denomination from within, the only course open was to
break away from the denomination and form a new, doctrinally pure,
church body. The separatist approach went back to the dawn of American Protestantism: Roger Williams (c. 1604-1684), founder of Rhode
Island, had been a leading proponent of a pure, separatist church. He
argued that the Church of England was apostate and that any kind
of fellowship with it was a serious sin. Yet Williams was also a vigorous defender of religious freedom, establishing Rhode Island as a
model of toleration.[30]

These attitudes, generally minus the emphasis on toleration, ree-
merged within fundamentalism over the period 1920-1940. Indeed, for
some fundamentalist writers the only way of safeguarding the "fundamentals of faith" was to separate. George Marsden comments on this
development as follows:

> By the 1930s, when it became painfully clear that reform from
> within could not prevent the spread of modernism in major north-
> ern denominations, more and more fundamentalists began to make
> separation from America's major denominations an article of faith.
> Although most who supported fundamentalism in the 1920s still
> remained in their denominations, many Baptist dispensationalists

and a few influential Presbyterians were demanding separatism. Yet the question was far from settled in the 1930s and 1940s.[31]
The fundamentalist war against modernity led to a closed, cautious and defensive attitude on the part of fundamentalists toward what they regarded as a secular culture and largely apostate churches. Separatism seemed the only way ahead. If culture and mainline denominations could not be converted or reformed, there was no option but to become a voice in the wilderness.

It is important to note that the separationist strategy was a response to a specific set of historical circumstances and that it had not been seen as an integral, necessary or implied element of "evangelicalism" until that point in history. The evolution of the separationist strategy resulted from the perception that nothing was to be gained from remaining within the mainline denominations. The overriding criterion employed in arriving at this conclusion was the need to establish a believing orthodoxy. In the 1920s it seemed increasingly clear to fundamentalists that the orthodox cause was lost beyond salvage within the Northern mainline denominations; separation was the only viable option. But had historical circumstances been different, separationism would not have been advocated.

These developments led to a significant polarization within evangelicalism, which continues to this day. As Francis Schaeffer points out, various forms of modernism managed to gain control of mainline denominations by taking over their bureaucracies and seminaries. Evangelicals adopted two different strategies in this respect: some chose to leave and found distinctively evangelical denominations, while others chose to remain within increasingly liberal denominations and attempt to reform them from within. As Schaeffer remarks, with obvious sadness, evangelical fought evangelical, rather than liberal:

> The periodicals of those who left tended to devote more space to attacking people who differed with them on the issue of leaving than to dealing with the liberals. Things were said that are difficult to forget even now. Those who came out refused at times to pray with those who had not come out. Many who left broke off all

forms of fellowship with true brothers in Christ who had not left. Christ's command to love one another was destroyed. What was left was frequently a turning inward, a self-righteousness, a hardness.[32] Sadly, this pattern would emerge time and time again within evangelicalism, as the sometimes vicious and wounding struggle within English evangelicalism over the same issue in the 1960s would demonstrate. Evangelicalism can be very good at self-righteousness, when it ought to be concerned with Christian love.

One of the most significant results of the shakeup within the Presbyterian Church in the United States, noted above, was the departure of four members of the Princeton Theological Seminary faculty to form Westminster Theological Seminary, Philadelphia.[33] Convinced that Princeton had abandoned its commitment to the "old theology," J. Gresham Machen and three Princeton colleagues (including Cornelius van Til) became the nucleus of the faculty of the new seminary, dedicated to maintaining the tradition from which Princeton now seemed to have departed. They took with them some of the seminary's most promising students, including Carl McIntyre and Harold J. Ockenga, both of whom proved to be of considerable significance to the development of evangelicalism. By separating from Princeton, Machen and his colleagues believed that they could reclaim the classical evangelical heritage that Princeton seemed to them to be abandoning in its rush to embrace modernism.

Princeton had long been established as a center of academic excellence for conservative evangelicalism of a Reformed character. In the nineteenth century the seminary had been dominated by the likes of Hodge and Warfield. Yet its evangelical affiliation came under scrutiny and was eventually broken. Machen saw in this a depressingly familiar pattern—"the same old story, so often repeated, of an institution formerly evangelical that is being made to drift away by insensible degrees from the gospel it was founded by godly donors to maintain."[34]

"Oppositionalism" rapidly proved, however, to be of limited value in constructing a movement to face the future. Those who demanded separation from apostate denominations found that their agreement did not always extend beyond this short-term agenda, and their unstated and unresolved differences soon came to the surface once they attempted to chart out a positive program of their own.

An example of this development is associated with Machen himself. It centers on the formation of the Independent Board for Presbyterian Foreign Missions in 1933, set up in response to his perception that the official Presbyterian Board of Foreign Missions failed to do justice to the uniqueness of Christianity.[35] Those who joined him shared this sentiment; as time proved, they shared little else. Divisions over other issues, such as strict Calvinism versus dispensationalism, soon emerged. Machen was ousted as its president in 1936, and, worn out by the arguments and dissent within a supposedly "doctrinally pure" body, died within months. By the time of his death in January 1937, the board had virtually ceased to exist in anything but name.[36]

Despite this weakness, separatism continued to be of defining importance to a generation of fundamentalists. In September 1941 Carl McIntyre announced the formation of the American Council of Christian Churches. This organization was designed to be a separatist counterpart to the mainline Federal Council of Churches (founded in 1908), which McIntyre regarded as little more than a hotbed of liberal and modernist agitation.[37]

There were parallels to these developments outside the United States around the same time; however, they lacked the intensity of the American experience. As historian David Bebbington comments, fundamentalist controversies existed in Britain during the period between the world wars, but they were "storms in a teacup when compared with the blizzards of invective that swept contemporary America."[38] A similar pattern emerges within the Canadian context, where fundamentalist attitudes had a strictly limited impact in shaping the Christian response to the drift of Canadian culture away from its Christian moorings.[39] Similarly, Australian evangelicalism has been relatively little influenced by fundamentalist trends, whereas what might be termed "classic Protestantism" or "conservative evangelicalism" has been of major importance since World War I, especially in the city of Sydney.[40]

Despite its many apparent successes, most historians regard fundamentalism as never having recovered its credibility from the Scopes "monkey trial" of 1925.[41] In May 1925, John T. Scopes, a young high-school science teacher, fell foul of a recently adopted statute that prohibited the teaching of evolution in Tennessee's public schools. The American Civil Liberties Union moved in to support Scopes, while William Jennings Bryan served as prosecution counsel.[42] The trial proved to be the biggest public relations disaster of all time for fundamentalism. Bryan, who had billed the trial as a "duel to the death" between Christianity and atheism, was outmaneuvered by the celebrated agnostic attorney Clarence Darrow. The legal move was as simple as it was brilliant: Bryan was called to the stand as a hostile witness for the defense and interrogated concerning his views on evolution. Bryan was forced to admit that he had no knowledge of geology, comparative religions or ancient civilizations, and he showed himself to have hopelessly naive religious views.

In the end, Bryan succeeded in winning the trial in the courtroom; Scopes was fined one hundred dollars. But a much greater trial was taking place in the nation's newspapers, in which Bryan was declared to be unthinking, uneducated and reactionary. Fundamentalism might make sense in a rural Tennessee backwater, but it had no place in sophisticated urban America. In particular, the journalist and literary critic H. L. Mencken (to whom Sinclair Lewis later dedicated *Elmer Gantry*) successfully portrayed fundamentalists as intolerant, backward and ignorant dolts who stood outside the mainstream of American culture.

From that moment onward, fundamentalism became as much a cultural stereotype as a religious movement. It could not hope to win support among educated and cultural elites within mainline Protestantism. The damage inflicted would never be undone. It was only with the emergence of a new form of evangelicalism after World War II that momentum and credibility were regained.

But how did this new form of evangelicalism emerge? The story of the emergence of the "new evangelicalism" is one of the most important episodes in modern Western church history; it deserves to be told in some detail.

The Public Emergence of Evangelicalism in the United States

It is beyond doubt that there has been an evangelical renaissance in the West since World War II.[43] One of the most distinctive features of this "new evangelicalism" has been its recovery of the vision of the gospel as something that transforms culture as well as saving souls. If the separatist vision traced its roots back to Roger Williams, the "new evangelicalism" saw itself as resuming the agenda set by John Winthrop (1588-1649), the first Puritan governor of Massachusetts, who sought to build a Christian civilization on the basis of the gospel. It was imperative that evangelicalism engage culture, with the ultimate objective of bringing it captive to Christ.

In many ways the "new evangelicalism" that began to emerge in the 1940s sought to return to the approach of the mainstream of the Reformation, rather than the separatist mentality of the radical Reformation, often still referred to as Anabaptism. In terms of the history of the Reformation, separatism is a specifically Anabaptist, rather than a universally evangelical, position. That reformers such as Luther operated outside the Catholic Church is undeniable; it is equally undeniable that this was not their preferred option.

Luther's vision of "reformation" was that of reform and renewal *from within* the church. It cannot be stated too often that he did not *choose* to separate from the medieval church; he was kicked out of it and *forced* to undertake a program of reform from outside that church. Even as late as 1519, well after his epoch-making discovery of the "righteousness of God," Luther wrote: "If, unfortunately, there are things in Rome which cannot be improved, there is not—nor can there be!—any reason for tearing oneself away from the church in schism. Rather, the worse things become, the more one should help her and stand by her, for by schism and contempt nothing can be mended."[44]

Schism was *forced on,* not *chosen by,* Luther.

Separatism was thus an option that sixteenth-century evangelicals were obliged to accept, rather than one that they themselves would have chosen. The leading Luther scholar Heinrich Bornkamm summarizes the situation as follows:

> Luther was excluded from his church because of his criticism of the theology and the ecclesiastical conditions of his time. It was *his* church from which he was excluded, for it was for no other church that he uttered his fervent pleadings and prayers and his painful laments and angry indictments. Everything he did and said and wrote was not against it, but for it, for its sake, not in order to establish a new church. It was because *his* church, the Roman Church of that time, excluded him that an inner reform, which had often taken place before, became something new, outside of the hitherto existing church.[45]

The mainline Reformation vision was thus that of reform within a church rather than the creation of a new church. As Luther put it, there could be no justification for separatism; for by schism nothing was resolved. Even once separation became inevitable,[46] Luther remained hopeful that it would be merely temporary and that a reconciliation might take place in his lifetime, with his reforming agenda being taken with the seriousness it deserved.

Up to the early 1940s, it was an approach more typical of the radical than the mainstream Reformation which gained the ascendancy among American evangelicals dissatisfied with developments within mainline Protestantism. Like Anabaptism in the sixteenth century, fundamentalism withdrew from what it regarded as a corrupt society and an apostate church. This is not to say that fundamentalism deliberately and consciously decided to appropriate ideas drawn from the sixteenth-century radical Reformation. Rather, the approaches that fundamentalists adopted, whether they were aware of it or not, were more typical of the radical than of the mainline Reformation. Anabaptism affirmed the need for believers to separate from a godless society and form communities of the committed faithful.[47] The same trend can be seen at many other points in Western religious history—for example, among Baptist communities in seventeenth-century London. Yet the rise of fundamentalism in the United States during the 1920s saw this separatist tendency reach its zenith. The doctrinally pure chose to separate from those who were deemed impure.

In his influential study *Christ and Culture,* H. Richard Niebuhr characterized this stance as "Christ against Culture."[48] Although Niebuhr finds this model primarily in the period of the early church (especially Tertullian), monasticism and later writers such as Tolstoy, it is clear that one of the unacknowledged targets of his critique of countercultural trends is the Anabaptist tradition within American Christianity. It is not correct to say that Anabaptism in any way *caused* the emergence of fundamentalism, as there is no evidence of any serious awareness among fundamentalists of the distinctiveness of Anabaptism at this point. Nevertheless, the similarities caused some alarm to many modern Anabaptist writers, who reacted with dismay to any perception of a link between themselves and fundamentalism.[49]

But in the 1940s a new option became possible—recovering an approach more typical of the mainline than of the radical Reformation, with the distinctively world-affirming and culture-embracing vision of evangelicalism. There are strong parallels here between fundamentalism and postexilic Judaism, which insisted that the only way of maintaining holiness and distinctiveness was through separation; the more affirmative and engaging style of Jesus Christ was taken up by neo-evangelicals, taking their cue from the mainstream Reformers, who saw this as an authentically Christian means of bringing the good news to the world.[50]

The emergence of evangelicalism as a distinctive option, avoiding the weaknesses of both fundamentalism and modernism, dates from the period immediately following World War II, and it is especially associated with the figures of Billy Graham (b. 1918) and Carl F. H. Henry (b. 1913). Both of these Christian leaders became disillusioned with fundamentalism, but for different reasons.

Henry argued that fundamentalists did not present Christianity as a worldview with a distinctive social vision, but chose to concentrate on only one aspect of the Christian proclamation. As a result, an impoverished and reduced gospel was presented to the world, radically defective in its social vision. Fundamentalism was too otherworldly and anti-intellectual to gain a hearing among the educated public, and it was unwilling to concern itself with exploring how Christianity relates to culture and social life in general. The seventy-five pages of his *The Uneasy Conscience of Modern Fundamentalism* (1947)—the "manifesto of neo-evangelicalism," in the words of Dirk Jellema—sounded a clarion call for *cultural engagement* on the part of evangelicals.[51] This book does not represent a critique of fundamentalism from the standpoint of later evangelicalism; it is an essay in fundamentalist self-criticism, in which Henry—writing as a fundamentalist—expresses considerable misgivings concerning the directions the movement has taken and its failure to achieve its intended goals. As Millard J. Erickson pointed out, it had become increasingly clear that fundamentalism had totally failed to turn back the rising tide of modernism, that it had not achieved any significant impact on the thought world of its day and that it had spurned the social problems of its time.[52]

Initially, the term *new evangelicalism* was used to refer to this third force in North American Protestantism; gradually, as the movement gained acceptance and ceased to be "new," this was displaced by the simpler and more economical term *evangelicalism*. The movement was distinguished by its stalwart defense of orthodox Christian faith, backed up by solid theological scholarship, and by its commitment to the social application of the gospel message.[53] Francis Schaeffer points out that the term *evangelical* came to be used

> with the connotation of being Bible-believing without shutting one's self off from the full spectrum of life, and in trying to bring Christianity into effective contact with the current needs of society, government and culture. It had a connotation of leading people to Christ as Savior, but then trying to be salt and light in the culture.[54]

Schaeffer himself contributed significantly to this new mood within evangelicalism, publishing a series of widely read books dealing with the relation of the gospel and culture.[55]

So important was Henry to the development of this new style of evangelicalism that he deserves to be discussed in more detail.[56] Carl Ferdinand Howard Henry was born in New York City on January 22, 1913. His parents sent him to a local Episcopalian church, apparently seeing this as ensuring social respectability without any awkward demands for personal religious commitment. After his confirmation, Henry dropped out of church life and began a career as a cub reporter for various local newspapers. Everything changed on June 10, 1933, when he fell into a three-hour conversation with a Christian friend. As a result of this, Henry had a conversion experience and joined a Baptist congregation on Long Island. Reappraising his life's priorities, he enrolled at Wheaton College in 1935, attracted both by its academic reputation and by the emphasis placed on the rational dimension of faith by its president, J. Oliver Buswell. He subsequently went on to study, and then teach, at the Northern Baptist Theological Seminary in Chicago, which had been founded in response to the increasingly modernist direction being taken by the University of Chicago Divinity School.

The year 1947 marked a turning point in Henry's life. *The Uneasy Conscience of Modern Fundamentalism* appeared, setting out his anxieties concerning the weaknesses of fundamentalism, and that same year witnessed his invitation to join the faculty of the newly founded Fuller Seminary in Pasadena.[57] A series of influential works followed, in which Henry established himself as a formative influence and guide for the rapidly expanding and developing evangelical movement in North America. *Remaking the Modern Mind* (1948), *Giving a Reason for Our Faith* (1949), *The Protestant Dilemma* (1949) and *The Drift of Western Thought* (1951) gave a sense of direction and intellectual rigor to the emerging movement. By the early 1950s Henry was firmly established as a leading architect of evangelical thought.[58]

His early work as a journalist received a new lease on life when he was invited by Billy Graham and L. Nelson Bell to give editorial leadership to a journal then being launched. As editor in chief of

Christianity Today from 1956 until 1968, Henry established the profile, shared concerns and credibility of the new evangelicalism, leading to such major global ventures as the 1966 World Conference on Evangelism as well as a series of publications dedicated to the consolidation of the evangelical renaissance then emerging within North America and beyond.

Billy Graham is also of considerable importance to the shaping of the "new evangelicalism." Although Graham was initially associated with the fundamentalist wing of American Protestantism, he gradually found himself disenchanted by its rigidity in relation to his burgeoning evangelistic ministry. In 1956 the popular fundamentalist magazine *Christian Life* published an article entitled "Is Evangelical Theology Changing?"[59] It argued that the old guard was committed to the slogan "Ye should earnestly contend for the faith," whereas the new generation preferred "Ye must be born again." A heated controversy resulted. Three months later the same journal published an interview with Graham, in which he declared that he was "sick and fed up" with such controversies and wanted to get on with preaching the gospel.[60] For Graham, "oppositionalism" had become a barrier to the preaching of the gospel.

The growing alienation of Graham from fundamentalism had been publicly demonstrated when he accepted an invitation in 1955 to hold a crusade in New York City. The invitation came from a coalition of Christian churches, many of which were not fundamentalist. By the time the crusade opened to massive publicity in the spring of 1957, fundamentalism seemed to be something of the past. *Christianity Today* and the Graham crusades became the icons of the "new" evangelicalism, which displaced the old.

It must be appreciated that evangelicalism, in the modern sense of the term, is a postfundamentalist phenomenon. It arose in reaction to the perceived deficiencies of fundamentalism. While it is unquestionably true that evangelicalism picked up and developed many insights deriving directly from the Reformation, Puritanism and Wesleyanism, the fact remains that the impetus to retrieve these great evangelical

41

traditions came from a conviction that fundamentalism had failed at every level—social, scholarly and spiritual.

As a result of such developments, evangelicalism began to emerge as a movement of major public importance in the United States in the 1950s. The full public recognition in America of the new importance and public visibility of evangelicalism is generally thought to date from the early 1970s. The crisis of confidence within American liberal Christianity in the 1960s was widely interpreted to signal the need for the emergence of a new and more publicly credible form of Christian belief.[61] In 1976 *Newsweek* magazine informed the United States that its citizens were living in the "Year of the Evangelical," with a born-again Christian, Jimmy Carter, as their president. The result was an unprecedented media interest in evangelicalism,[62] even if the outcome of that interest was not always positive.

Some writers have persisted in applying the outdated and totally inappropriate label *fundamentalism* to evangelicalism, with polemical intentions that parallel those of some fanatical right-wing politicians who brand anything that hints at social concern as "communist." As the Canadian scholar Clark Pinnock points out, *fundamentalist* has come to be "more often than not a word of contempt, a theological smear-word." This is certainly the case with James Barr's abusive and polemical book *Fundamentalism* (1977),[63] which fails to make the necessary distinction between fundamentalism and evangelicalism. As Pinnock observes, "The people Barr is sharply and vehemently criti-cizing, the British evangelicals, do not like the term being applied to them because they are not, in fact, fundamentalists."[64] Some twenty years ago historian Richard Quebedeaux complained of the uncritical and hostile tendency of "mainstream ecumenical liberalism to lump together with pejorative intent all theological conservatives into the worn fundamentalist category."[65] The use of the term *fundamentalist* in this context is tired, outdated and must now also be deemed to be politically incorrect.

More significantly, the kinds of criticisms that Barr directed against his "fundamentalist" opponents were already widely current within evangelicalism at this time. As Carl Henry himself scathingly remarked, evangelicals did not need Barr to tell them that "fundamentalist preaching is often exegetically shallow, that fundamentalism uncritically elevated certain prudish traditions to scriptural status . . . and that many fundamentalists tend to appropriate selected bits of non-evangelical scholarship rather than to initiate creative studies."[66] Barr's deeply flawed work failed to distinguish between fundamentalism and its evangelical critics, satisfying only those sufficiently ill-informed to be unable to distinguish them yet sufficiently prejudiced to dislike each with an equally uncritical vigor.

Happily, a new and more positive attitude toward evangelicalism is beginning to emerge within mainstream Christian circles. An excellent example is provided from the recent writings of one of the most important liberal Christian theologians of today, David Tracy of the University of Chicago. In his earlier writings Tracy tended to dismiss anyone who was critical of modernity as "fundamentalist." Yet Tracy now recognizes that it is as simplistic as it is inaccurate to suggest that approaches to Christianity must be either "fundamentalist" or "modernist." In his recent writings he draws a distinction between a "neo-conservative revival" and fundamentalism, declaring that the former "sees through the emptiness of the present and the poverty of the modern subject." Here is a theology of retrieval, of rediscovery, which "knows that a present without past memory and tradition is self-illusory and . . . sees the folly of the Enlightenment's wholesale attack on the very concept of tradition." While continuing to insist that "fundamentalism cannot be taken as an intellectually serious option," Tracy declares that "the non-fundamentalist version of anti-modernity . . . merits not merely human but full intellectual respect . . . as in conservative evangelical but not fundamentalist Christians."[67] This clear distinction between "fundamentalists" and "conservative evangelical Christians" is to be welcomed, as representing a somewhat overdue recognition by the academy that evangelicalism represents a distinctive, viable and *intellectually respectable* Christian option in its own right.

What has been said thus far might convey the impression that evangelicalism is primarily an American phenomenon. This is not entirely the case, although the considerable influence of American writers, speakers, journals and publishing houses must be acknowledged. To illustrate the global nature of evangelicalism, let's pause to consider its evolution in England since World War II.

Evangelicalism in Postwar England

Prior to World War II, evangelicalism was a despised minority presence within the English church.[68] Hensley Henson (1863-1947), bishop of Durham, famously dismissed the movement as "an army of illiterates, generalled by octogenarians." With exceptions as honorable as they were few, the movement was characterized by an anti-intellectual defensiveness, nourished by a separatist mentality. "Evangelicals inclined to the view that they were excused culture, scholarship and intellectual exercise on religious grounds and they felt exonerated from loving God with their minds. It was all part of their 'backs-to-the-wall' attitude."[69]

The isolation and numerical weakness of the movement led to what many now regard as an unhealthy passion for uniformity within the movement, with those who stepped out of line, even on matters of relative rather than absolute importance, being branded as traitors or compromisers. Although the movement honored Scripture, it perhaps fostered the impression that no biblical truth could be permitted to be expressed in any terms other than those inherited from the Reformation or Charles Simeon and that there was nothing to be learned from Scripture that evangelicals did not already know. It was not until the 1950s that things began to change—decisively.

Why? Part of the explanation of the rapid growth in evangelicalism lies in developments within England itself which owe little, if anything, to what was happening in North America. Although it initially seemed that the intellectual and ecclesiastical leadership of English evangelicalism might pass into the hands of liberal evangelicals such as Stephen C. Neill and Max Warren, a new generation of more conservative evangelicals emerged to displace them. E. J. H. Nash organized Christian camps at Iwerne Minster, aimed at "top boys from top schools," which laid the nucleus for a new generation of evangelical thinkers and leaders.[70] The Tyndale Fellowship for Biblical Research laid the foundations for a new generation of evangelical biblical scholars. The Inter-Varsity Fellowship (now the Universities and Colleges Christian Fellowship) extended its ministry in student circles, providing both intellectual and pastoral support for those of evangelical views. Its publishing house, Inter-Varsity Press (IVP), issued a series of "pocket books" providing reasoned and scholarly defenses of evangelical positions.[71]

But it is generally agreed that one of the most important factors, if not *the* most important factor, was the personal ministry of John R. W. Stott, who was appointed rector of the central London church of All Soul's, Langham Place, in 1950, when he was only twenty-nine years old. His impact on a rising generation of evangelical students through his speaking and writing, though universally acknowledged, cannot easily be measured. If the remarkable growth of English evangelicalism can be attributed to any one person, it is to Stott. Stott's parish-based ministry gave evangelical clergy and ordinands throughout England a new awareness of the possibilities open to them. Monthly "guest services" provided opportunities for Christians to bring their friends along to hear the gospel preached and subsequently to join "nursery groups" that explained and explored the Christian faith. It was not long before these ideas were being replicated in evangelical parishes throughout the country.

Yet the impact of developments in the United States must also be noted. It was not long before the influence of the "new evangelicalism" began to be felt elsewhere in the English-speaking world. England happens to be a case in point. Billy Graham, perhaps the most publicly visible representative of this new evangelical style, became a well-known figure in English society. Initially he was unknown to anyone in England. Yet this changed dramatically through the astonishing impact of his three-month crusade at Harringay Arena in 1954, which, with the benefit of hindsight, can be seen as one of a series of turning points for British Christianity since World War II.[72] Evangelism became a major issue, was talked about extensively by the British public and captured the imagination of many younger evangelicals. The obvious emotional appeal of Graham's style of evangelism (criticized by some as lacking intellectual weight and substance) was supplemented by a vigorous appeal by leading British preachers such as D. Martyn Lloyd-Jones to ground Christian faith firmly on Scripture. The rise of the Puritan and Westminster Conferences, associated with Lloyd-Jones and James I. Packer, gave added intellectual muscle, linked with a firm sense of demonstrable continuity between the greatness of the English religious past and the reemerging evangelical presence.

Many outside the movement were alarmed at the reemergence of evangelicalism in an English context, seeing it as unreflective and uncritical. The last truly great evangelical revival had reached its climax in the early 1800s, after which, despite a significant and influential presence on the foreign mission field, it was gradually overshadowed at home by the emergence of the Oxford Movement.[73] Many had thought it had been eradicated totally from the English context, and they were anxious about the consequences of its reappearance. As late as 1955, Canon H. K. Luce, headmaster of Durham School, complained about the fact that Billy Graham was being allowed to lead a mission to the University of Cambridge. Universities, he argued, existed for the advancement of learning; so why was an intellectual lightweight being allowed to speak at such an academically distinguished center as Cambridge? "Is it not time that our religious leaders made it plain that while they respect, or even admire, Dr. Graham's sincerity and personal power, they cannot regard fundamentalism as likely to issue in anything but disillusionment and disaster for educated men and women in this twentieth-century world?"[74]

Luce's haughty and condescending attitude, which treated evangelicalism (here referred to as "fundamentalism") as totally unsuited for "educated men and women," was widely echoed at the time. Evangelicalism was seen as being suited to illiterates, not to the cultured and

sophisticated clergy of the Church of England. This attitude was reinforced by Michael Ramsey, then bishop of Durham, who in 1956
published an article entitled "The Menace of Fundamentalism," accus-
ing Graham of being heretical and sectarian. It proved to be a serious
error of judgment; yet it corresponded well to mainline English Anglican attitudes to the new evangelicalism that was gaining momentum
in the United States.[75] (Happily, Ramsey would later change his mind
on this matter, largely through personal meetings with Graham. As
Ramsey's offical biographer noted, by the mid-1960s he "was still sure
that Graham's methods were not the best, but evidence forced him to
admit that every time Graham came to England on a mission, more
young men had vocations to be priests."[76])

The consolidation of evangelicalism within the English Christian
scene has not been without its painful and controversial moments. One
such moment was the historic 1966 confrontation between John Stott
and Martyn Lloyd-Jones at the Second National Assembly of Evangelicals, which was widely seen to center on the issue of separatism.
Lloyd-Jones, who along with leading Anglican evangelical thinkers
such as Packer had played a major part in renewing interest in Puritanism within English evangelicalism during the 1950s, was a staunch
and influential defender of a separatist approach. The future of evangelicalism in England, he asserted, could be safeguarded only as evangelicals left their apostate churches and formed their own explicitly
evangelical groups. The publication of radical works such as *Honest
to God,* written by John A. T. Robinson, a bishop in the Church of
England, had raised serious questions concerning that church's public
commitment to orthodoxy. How, Lloyd-Jones and his allies demanded, could an evangelical credibly belong to a denomination, such
as the Church of England, which was doctrinally mixed? Withdrawal
was the only acceptable option.

Packer, one of the most theologically sophisticated opponents of
this trend, describes it as follows:

Some have urged evangelicals in "doctrinally mixed" churches to
withdraw into a tighter fellowship where the pre-critical pre-liberal

view of Scripture is rigorously upheld and sceptical revisionism in theology is debarred. It has been said that failure to do so is as unprincipled as it is foolish. It is unprincipled, so the argument runs, because by staying in churches which tolerate heretics you become constructively guilty of their heresies, by your association with them; and it is foolish because you have not the least hope of cleaning up the theological Augean stables while liberals remain there. Withdrawal is the conscientious man's only option.[77]

It was perhaps inevitable that a confrontation would develop within English evangelicalism over the same separatist agenda that had caused such bitterness and division in the United States a generation earlier.

Matters reached a head at the Second National Assembly of Evangelicals on the evening of October 18. Lloyd-Jones issued what was widely understood to be a passionate call for evangelicals within the mainstream churches to "come out" and, in effect, form a denomination of their own. Many of those present at the meeting have spoken of the "electric" atmosphere this address created. Stott, acting as chair of the meeting, intervened to suggest that the rightful and proper place of evangelicals was *within* those mainstream denominations, which they could renew from within.

A leading Christian journal summarized Lloyd-Jones's speech under a banner headline "Evangelicals—Leave Your Denominations," printed above a photograph of the platform party.[78] A week later the same journal published a protest note, complaining that all save one of the platform party were opposed to Lloyd-Jones's policy; the journal's headline, it was alleged, implied that they all supported it. To many observers, Lloyd-Jones became increasingly a voice in the wilderness, as the move to regain the high ground within the mainline denominations gathered momentum. The results of this would be felt most keenly within the Church of England.

Stott's opposition to the strategy commended by Lloyd-Jones was endorsed and consolidated through the National Evangelical Anglican Congress at Keele University shortly afterward (April 4-7, 1967). This congress was addressed by such leading British evangelicals as Michael Green, Philip E. Hughes and James I. Packer and attended by exactly one thousand clergy and laity. Keele marked the beginning of the positive role of evangelicalism within the Church of England and was determinative for evangelicals staying within the national church. It was also important in opening up the social aspects of the gospel, to which English evangelicalism had become blind (despite its heavy commitment to this area in the period 1780-1830). Although lingering bitterness remains over the issue to this day, Keele is widely regarded as marking the end of a numerically significant separatist party within Anglican evangelicalism (although a vociferous and militant campaign to this effect appears to have developed once more since the 1992 decision to ordain women to the priesthood, regarded as unacceptable by some conservative evangelicals).

The full story of this congress has yet to be told, and it promises to be one of the most important tales in recent English church history. At the parish level, the congress drew on the pioneering work for renewal among evangelicals in the north of England, nurtured by people such as Raymond Turvey and given a fresh sense of purpose and direction by Stott. At the intellectual level, the congress benefited enormously from the groundbreaking work being carried out at the recently established evangelical think tank and research center in Oxford, Latimer House. Under the erudite and wise guidance of its warden, James I. Packer, this became the focus of theological and liturgical working parties, bringing together leading evangelical thinkers and representatives from across the nation.[79] A volume of position papers by leading evangelicals of both the older and newer generations, published in advance of the congress, ensured both continuity and consensus within the movement.[80]

Keele was thus no hasty response to the crisis of October 1966; it was a well-prepared attempt to face the challenge of an unknown future, armed with the historic resources of the evangelical tradition fully deployed. In no way, as some recent critics have suggested, was it Stott seeking to impose his will on an English evangelicalism that ought to have supported Lloyd-Jones; it represented a corporate decision by one thousand people, including the most significant evangelical thinkers, leaders and writers within the Church of England. The resulting Keele Statement is widely regarded by nonevangelicals and evangelicals alike as "one of the most important ecclesiastical documents, not only of the sixties but of this century,"[81] in relation to the history of Christianity in England. Evangelicalism could no longer be dismissed as a marginal movement that could be sidelined by the Church of England; it had to be taken seriously—and it was. Some older evangelicals, especially within nonconformist and independent churches, regarded Keele as a sellout and described it as a "tragedy" that could only lead to a weakening of English evangelicalism; this was, however, a minority view.

The growing numerical strength of evangelicalism within the Church of England can be traced back to the new sense of confidence and direction given to the movement at Keele. As Packer commented approvingly, "This pledge of new involvement closed a generation-long chapter of evangelical detachment. . . . Evangelicals today are more deeply involved in the inner life of the Church of England than ever before, and the old days of entrenched 'party' isolationism are gone."[82]

Separatism has continued to have its attractions for a small number of Anglican evangelicals, especially those who feel marginalized from the mainstream of church life or who have only a superficial commitment to the Anglican ethos. As Packer remarks, there are still those in England who claim that "all true evangelicals are committed to Baptist or Congregationalist church principles."[83] But basically separatism is no longer taken seriously as a realistic option, and large numbers of evangelicals are content to worship and minister within the Church of England.

Evangelicalism has continued to increase substantially within Western Christianity, in terms of its numerical strength, its influence at every level of church life and its theological sophistication. Despite rather crude attempts on the part of some church leaders to suppress this influence, it has continued to grow into the 1990s and seems set to exercise still greater influence in the opening of the next millennium. As the reaction against fundamentalism on the one hand and modernism on the other grows in momentum, there is an increasingly clear need for the development of forms of Christianity that avoid both. As Hans Küng pointed out recently, the church "must find a way between a modernism without foundations and a fundamentalism without modernity."[84] Evangelicalism is ideally placed to meet this challenge.

2

EVANGELICAL DISTINCTIVES

I T IS NOTORIOUSLY DIFFICULT TO GIVE A PRECISE DEFINITION of evangelicalism. George Gallup Jr. and other pollsters discovered this years ago. By 1986 Gallup had given up the battle to find a neat set of beliefs typical of evangelicalism and settled for self-identification. "Would you describe yourself as a born-again Christian?" is the key question put to the American people. And about 30 percent—more than sixty million—are happy to accept this form of identification.[1] So significant is evangelicalism to the modern church that claiming affiliation with the movement has become a coveted accolade, where it was once a stigma and term of abuse.

Problems of Definition

Gallup had a point. Those who offer precise definitions of evangelicalism usually have axes to grind—generally the "I'm an evangelical and you're not" kind of ax. On occasion one even encounters what might be called the Elijah syndrome (1 Kings 19:14)—the "I alone am faithful, whereas everyone else has compromised and needs to repent" kind of evangelicals who exclude from their magic circle those who do not conform to their highly specific, and often equally highly dogmatic, definition of evangelicalism. (*Repent* here seems to have been devalued, shedding its true meaning of "turning back to God" and being degraded to "agreeing with a self-appointed magic circle.") This kind of approach has all the tainted odor of the self-righteousness and factionalism censured by Paul (1 Cor 3:1-4), and it can easily lead to evangelical infighting taking precedence over evangelism. It is a simple matter of fact that any theologically rigorous definition of *evangelicalism* tends to end up excluding an embarrassingly large number of people who regard themselves, and are regarded by others, as evangelicals.

The same problem is encountered in a related area of religious terminology—the definition of Calvinism. The term *Calvinism* appears to have been introduced by the German Lutheran polemicist Joachim Westphal (1510-1574) to refer to the theological, and particularly the sacramental, views of the Swiss Reformers in general and John Calvin in particular. Calvin himself was alarmed at the use of the term; by then, however, he had only months to live, and his protest was ineffective.[2] So who is a "Calvinist"? It is possible to lend rigor and precision to the notion by defining it in terms of the religious orthodoxy laid down by the Synod of Dort (1618-1619) or the *Consensus Helveticus* (1675). Such refinements, however desirable from the standpoint of theological meticulousness, would oblige us to limit alarmingly the number of Calvinists, forcing a wedge between an ideal "Calvinist" and many of those who as a matter of history chose to regard themselves as Calvinists. For example, the many French Huguenots who sought refuge in Switzerland after the revocation of the Edict of Nantes (October 1685) had little sympathy with some parts of the *Consensus Helveticus.* Those who did agree with all its statements were unquestionably Calvinists. Yet there were rather a lot of people, also unquestionably Calvinists, who did *not* agree with it. Precise definitions of *evangelicalism* run into the same difficulty.

In part, this problem of definition relates to the origins of evangelicalism. The movement draws on such rich historical resources and has established itself in so many different contexts in global Christianity that a degree of diversity within the movement is inevitable. For example, North American evangelicalism often seems to its Latin American or European critics to have absorbed a number of ideas and values originating from twentieth-century American culture rather than the New Testament. As evangelicalism becomes a more self-consciously *global* movement, opportunities are arising for North American evangelicals to identify which aspects of their evangelical ethos are a direct response to the cultural conditioning of their environment and which are a direct response to the gospel itself. There is a continuing need to ensure that adaptive responses to a culture are themselves authentically evangelical. In much the same way, Asian evangelicals are able to discover which aspects of their ethos represent accommodations to Korean or Cantonese culture and which are integral and proper responses to the gospel itself.

It is both impossible and improper for a work of this kind to lay down what evangelicalism *should* be. That would amount to an improper, presumptuous and dogmatic imposition of one writer's views on the movement. (Evangelicalism recognizes the authority of Scripture, not of self-appointed gurus!) A more helpful and responsible approach is to survey global evangelicalism since the sixteenth century, taking care to include its Latin American, African and Asian forms, and identify the common features that give the movement its shared sense of identity and purpose.[3]

Controlling Convictions

Evangelicalism is grounded on a cluster of six controlling convictions, each of which is regarded as being true, of vital importance and grounded in Scripture. These are not purely "doctrinal," if this term is understood to refer purely to a set of objective truths; they are also "existential," in that they affirm the manner in which the believer is caught up in a redemptive and experiential encounter with the living Christ. These six fundamental convictions can be set out as follows:[4]

1. The supreme authority of Scripture as a source of knowledge of God and a guide to Christian living.

2. The majesty of Jesus Christ, both as incarnate God and Lord and as the Savior of sinful humanity.

3. The lordship of the Holy Spirit.

4. The need for personal conversion.

5. The priority of evangelism for both individual Christians and the church as a whole.

6. The importance of the Christian community for spiritual nourishment, fellowship and growth.

All other matters have tended to be regarded as "matters of indifference," on which a substantial degree of latitude and diversity may be accepted—but a diversity that is itself grounded in the New Testament, in that responsible evangelicalism has refused to legislate where Scripture is silent or where it offers a variety of approaches. This is especially clear in relation to evangelical views on the nature of the church. A recognition of the complexity of the New Testament models of and statements concerning the church has led to a variety of views within evangelicalism regarding both the specifics of church order and the more general issue of doctrinal purity or plurality within denominations.

It should be appreciated that the six positions outlined above in many respects correspond to what C. S. Lewis termed "mere Christianity"—the common faith of the Christian church down the ages. Evangelicals would agree: at its heart, evangelicalism is historic Christian orthodoxy. There is thus a natural affinity between evangelicals and others within Christian churches who are concerned to defend orthodoxy against the various challenges it faces today. It is for this reason that evangelicals are heavily involved in the current attempt to "re-form the center" in mainline denominations.[5]

Yet these six points also represent distinctive *emphases* that are regarded by evangelicals as identity-giving. For example, many outside evangelicalism recognize the need for evangelism yet do not regard it as being particularly significant, let alone of defining importance. Equally, many Christians who would concur with the six points noted above might wish to add additional items of belief or practice that some evangelicals would regard as being of marginal importance, and that other evangelicals might regard as mistaken or unjustifiable.

A Devotional Ethos

I have stressed that although evangelicalism has a solid core of doctrines that are inferred directly from Scripture, it is not characterized *purely* by a set of doctrines. The movement also possesses a distinctive *ethos,* an approach to Christian thinking and living that centers on a number of guiding biblical principles rather than specific doctrinal formulations. It is no dead orthodoxy, but a living faith. Scripture is treated as far more than a theological source; it is the basis of Christian life and devotion, personal and corporate.

Evangelicalism has always refused to treat "knowledge of God" as something abstract; instead, it recognizes it to be strongly experiential and personal, capable of transforming both the heart and the mind. In his masterly survey of the contemporary Reformed ethos, I. John Hesselink comments: "Concern for truth, pure doctrine, and sound theology is important, but should not be an end in itself. If this concern does not result in godliness and the edification of the church it has been perverted."[6]

There is a sense in which evangelicalism is as much a devotional ethos as it is a theological system. There is a creative intermingling here of the Reformed emphasis on right doctrine with the Pietist concern for a "living faith"—that is, a personally appropriated and assimilated faith, expressed in such terms as "a personal relationship with Christ."[7] Evangelicalism is basically Christian orthodoxy, as set out in the ecumenical creeds, with a particular emphasis on the need for the personal assimilation and appropriation of faith and a marked reluctance to allow any matters of lesser importance to get in the way of the proclamation and application of the gospel.

The devotional use of Scripture is thus of central importance to evangelicals. It must be appreciated that this approach involves reading Scripture in a certain manner—not only as the basis of a theological system or for intellectual stimulation but also for the spiritual nourishment of the reader. The "knowledge" of God that evangelicals seek is at least as experiential as it is cognitive, with its concern for a "deeply based consciousness" of the Lord.[8]

Again, evangelicalism is not committed to any one specific theology of conversion (Reformed and Wesleyan perspectives are of particular importance in this context), but rather to a recognition of the *need* for personal conversion.[9] Kern Robert Trembath, in a perceptive analysis of evangelicalism's emphasis on the experiential aspects of faith, says,

> In defining as "evangelical" members of a great range of denominations, evangelicalism discloses a greater implicit emphasis upon the experience of salvation in Jesus than upon cognitive, dogmatic and historical articulations of this experience. Such articulations are not valueless altogether, but are simply of less value than they are to a nonevangelical or "denominational" mindset.[10]

For evangelicals, justification is a conversion experience as well as a doctrine, in much the same way as Jesus Christ is an experienced presence in the life of the believer as well as a historical reality and the central legitimating resource and authority for Christian theology and life.

As noted earlier, some evangelicals are particularly prone to use the term *evangelical* to mean "my kind of evangelicalism" and dismiss as nonevangelical those who happen to differ with them over points that might reasonably be suggested to be of relative rather than ultimate importance. I have no intention of excluding any who might legitimately be considered evangelicals by imposing on them an artificially narrow and restrictive definition of the term. My intention is to *describe* rather than *prescribe,* discussing the characteristic beliefs that give evangelicalism its coherence amidst diversity, rather than lapsing into an unchristian arrogance in laying down what it can and cannot be.

Debate within evangelicalism over its foundational beliefs and their consequences for Christian thought and life is healthy, in that it leads to a greater appreciation of the issues involved. Yet such a debate is short-circuited whenever someone declares that those who, while arguing on biblical principles, reach different conclusions forfeit their right to be called evangelical. Evangelicalism embraces such diverse positions as Reformed and Wesleyan doctrines of grace, "mixed body" and "society of saints" doctrines of the church, and Lutheran and Zwinglian views of the real presence of Christ. Debate over these is helpful and legitimate; they are all, however, biblically based and have a long history within the evangelical tradition. None can be dismissed as "nonevangelical" without doing serious violence to evangelical history and the vital discipline of biblical exposition and interpretation.

Evangelicalism is, as noted earlier, grounded on six central beliefs,[11] each of which is thoroughly rooted in Scripture. I will explore each of these six beliefs with a view to understanding the distinctive ethos of the movement and gaining insight into the controversies that emerge from time to time over major—and, if the truth is to be told, also some rather trivial—issues.

The Supreme Authority of Scripture

To ascribe authority to Scripture is to acknowledge that it is the Word of God. Historically, the authority of Scripture became of central importance during the sixteenth-century Reformation, with its radical and far-reaching reexamination and reappraisal of Christian beliefs and practices in the light of Scripture. The "formal principle of the Reformation," often summarized in the phrase *sola Scriptura* (by Scripture alone), affirmed that only those beliefs and practices that rested firmly on scriptural foundations could be regarded as binding on Christians.[12] This commitment to the priority and authority of Scripture has become an integral element of the evangelical tradition.

For evangelicals, the unique authority of Scripture rests on the activity of the revealing God, both in relation to the biblical material itself and in the subsequent process of interpretation and inward appropriation by the reader.[13] As John Wesley commented, "The Spirit of God not only once *inspired* those who wrote the Bible, but continually *inspires* those who read it with earnest prayer."[14] (Today Wesley's point would be made by distinguishing the original work of the

Spirit in *inspiration* and the Spirit's subsequent work in the *illumination* of the reader.) In neither case does the work of the Holy Spirit negate the work of the human agent.

There is a parallel here with the Incarnation: Christ in his one person was both God and man; so Scripture is both divine and human. Just as Christ's divinity does not abrogate Christ's human nature, so the divine authorship of Scripture does not abolish its human authorship.[15] It is simply not true that evangelicalism denies the presence of a human element in Scripture, as some of its critics persist in maintaining. Evangelicalism rejoices in the presence of a human element in Scripture, as in Christ, and in the fact that God should have revealed himself in and through humanity in both these manners. Inspiration is certainly not dictation.[16] As James I. Packer states this point,

> Because Evangelicals hold that the biblical writers were completely controlled by the Holy Spirit, it is often supposed . . . that they maintain what is called the "dictation" or "typewriter" theory of inspiration—namely, that the mental activity of the writers was simply suspended, apart from what was necessary for the mechanical transcription of words supernaturally introduced into their consciousness. But it is not so. This "dictation" theory is a man of straw. It is safe to say that no Protestant theologian, from the Reformation till now, has ever held it; and certainly modern Evangelicals do not hold it.[17]

As Packer makes clear, where writers such as Calvin discussed the mode in which the Spirit guided the writers of Scripture, they spoke "not of dictation, but of *accommodation,* and rightly maintained that God completely adapted his inspiring activity to the cast of mind, outlook, temperament, interests, literary habits, and stylistic idiosyncrasies of each writer."[18]

An element that must not be overlooked in any account of biblical authority is subjective conviction—an idea expressed in Calvin's doctrine of the "internal testimony of the Holy Spirit."[19] When the Bible is received and taught as the Word of God, it speaks to people's needs and situations with a power and relevance that confirm its inherent God-given authority. The evangelical testimony is that Scripture comes to us as the self-authenticating and convincing Word of God. W. Robertson Smith expressed this with these words:

> If I am asked why I receive Scripture as the Word of God . . . [I answer] . . . because the Bible is the only record of the redeeming love of God, because in the Bible alone I find God drawing near to us in Jesus Christ, and declaring to us in him his will for our salvation. And this record I know to be true by the witness of his Spirit in my heart, whereby I am assured that none other than God himself is able to speak such words to my soul.[20]

In addition to its objective truth, Scripture possesses existential relevance. This is not, it must be stressed, to say that its authority is grounded in such existential relevance. Scripture remains authoritative for evangelicals whether its subjective dimension is appreciated or not. For example, the historical objectivity of the death of Christ (to note one important component of the biblical testimony) is not dependent on its subjective appropriation. To state that Scripture has authority is to acknowledge that such authority potentially has both objective and subjective aspects.

The centrality of Scripture to evangelical theology and spirituality rests on considerations such as these. Yet this is not to say that evangelicalism is narrowly biblicist. Rightly understood, Scripture defines the center of gravity of evangelicalism, not the limits of its reading or knowledge. Scripture is, for evangelicals, the central legitimating resource of Christian faith and theology, the clearest window through which the face of Christ may be seen.

The evangelical insistence on the authority of Scripture reflects a determination not to permit anything from outside the Christian gospel to become the norms for what is truly "Christian." Recent theological history has provided us with examples of what happens when a theology cuts itself loose from the controlling influence of the Christian tradition and seeks norms from outside that tradition—for example, in "German culture," as I will show presently. Evangelicalism is grounded in the belief that Christianity must remain faithful to itself, taking its heritage with the utmost seriousness and refusing to be controlled by anything other than the living Christ as he is made known in Scripture.[21] It is determined to avoid becoming enslaved to what Alasdair MacIntyre has termed the "Self-Images of the Age."[22] To allow one's ideas and values to become controlled by anything or anyone other than the self-revelation of God in Scripture is to adopt an ideology rather than a theology; it is to become controlled by ideas and values whose origins lie outside the Christian tradition—and potentially to become enslaved to them.

Examples of what happens to churches or parachurch organizations that submit to prevailing ideologies are not hard to come by. The rise of Nazism in Germany in the 1930s reflects the willingness of some German Christians to allow Nazi ideology to exert the controlling influence traditionally given to the Scriptures. The collapse of the Student Christian Movement in England reflects its decision in the late 1960s to align itself with left-wing political causes and the morality of progressive humanism and to grant these the authority previously allocated to Scripture.[23] An ideology can easily displace Christian theology, as seen in trends inside some mainline North American denominations, which reflect demands that Christianity submit itself to the latest ideology.

The first casualty in "culture wars" usually seems to be mainline Christianity. The agenda now circulating in North America includes assertions that (1) belief in Christ as Lord should be abandoned, since it implies a religious hegemony in which Christ is sovereign over the world; (2) Christian claims to truth are xenophobic and culturally genocidal; and (3) the cross ought to be eliminated from Christianity, as it entails an atonement in which God abuses his Son, glorifies suffering and encourages victims to be subservient. These are clear examples of the ways in which a culturally accommodated form of Christianity can easily become the prisoner, rather than the liberator, of a culture. It becomes transfixed on the pinion of single-issue politics.

The only way Christianity can free itself from subservience to cultural fashion is to ensure that it is firmly grounded in a resource that is independent of that culture. The traditional evangelical approach is to acknowledge the supreme authority of Scripture as a theological and spiritual resource, and the contemporary task as interpreting and applying this resource to the situation of today. Evangelicalism thus addresses today's culture without needing to become trapped within that culture.[24]

Scripture, then, is of central importance to evangelical theology, ethics and spirituality. Yet it must be appreciated that Scripture sometimes legitimates a diversity of standpoints. On issues of vital importance—such as the need for redemption, the uniqueness of Christ as Redeemer and the "two natures" of Christ—evangelicals, in common with orthodox Christians down the ages, insist that Scripture is clear and perspicuous.[25] At other points it allows a diversity of interpretations. An excellent example is provided by the Reformation controversy over the real presence of Christ at the Lord's Supper.[26] In Matthew 26:26 Jesus said, "This is my body," over the bread at the Last Supper. For Luther this Scripture was unequivocal and required a literal interpretation, and it was therefore necessary to affirm that Christ is really present in the bread of the Lord's Supper. Any other interpretation, he argued, compromises the clarity of Scripture. Ulrich Zwingli was unimpressed. He found the passage open to another interpretation: that the bread *represents* the body of Christ. After all, when Jesus declared himself to be "the bread of life" (Jn 6:35), he was not suggesting that he was a loaf of bread. The issue was representation, not identity. Some passages of Scripture have to be taken literally; other passages require a metaphorical interpretation; in some cases a divergence of approach is possible.

Thus, in the case of the "real presence" question, *three* major views achieved wide influence within the Reformation by 1560: *Luther's* view, that the bread is literally to be identified with the body of Christ; *Calvin's* view, that the bread is an efficacious symbol of the presence of Christ, effecting what it signifies; and *Zwingli's* view, that the bread merely symbolizes Christ in his absence. All of these views can be argued on the basis of Scripture.

Where Scripture is unclear, two leading principles must guide evangelical thinking.

1. Views that attempt to be faithful to Scripture are to be respected and honored as evangelical, even where this necessitates a plurality of possibilities of evangelical doctrines. There is both room and need for debates within evangelicalism over how best to do justice to Scripture and to ensure that its proclamation is most effectively channeled toward and contextualized within the many global situations in which evangelicalism now finds itself expanding. Total fidelity to Scripture must lead to the plurality of possibilities within Scripture on some matters being reflected within evangelicalism. Those who demand total uniformity within evangelicalism impose a straitjacket on Scripture as much as on their fellow evangelicals.

2. If Scripture does not make an issue clear, it is debatable how important the issue actually is. Scripture is unequivocally clear on the central and vital doctrines of the Christian faith. But on others (such as the nature of the real presence, as just noted, or the preferred style of clerical dress) it is open to a range of opinions. The Reformer Philipp Melanchthon described such issues as *adiaphora,* "matters of indifference," on which disagreement can and should be tolerated. This does not amount to the bland assumption that all sincerely held viewpoints are equally valid, but it represents an evangelical insistence that all biblically legitimated viewpoints are to be treated with respect. It is highly undesirable that serious disagreement should arise between evangelicals over such issues; after all, there is an unbelieving world to confront with the truth of the gospel, and time and effort would seem to be better spent pursuing this task! It is all to easy to elevate matters of relative importance so high that they appear to be of absolute importance.

One of the many matters on which evangelicals regard Scripture as unambiguous is the uniqueness of the person and work of Jesus Christ, to which we now turn.

64

The Majesty of Jesus Christ

For evangelicalism, Jesus Christ is of central importance. He is the focal point of Scripture. He alone was raised from the dead. He alone possessed the unique distinction of being at one and the same time "true God and true man." Through his atoning death alone can we have access to God.

Evangelism centers on the proclamation of Jesus Christ, just as Christian worship and adoration focus on his majesty and humility. Any version of Christianity that fails to place Christ at its center has some very awkward questions to face concerning its right to call itself Christian at all. The words of the British evangelical missionary and scholar Stephen C. Neill (1900-1984) are worth weighing carefully: "The old saying 'Christianity is Christ' is almost exactly true. The historical figure of Jesus of Nazareth is the criterion by which every Christian affirmation has to be judged, and in the light of which it stands or falls."[27]

One of the most characteristic features of evangelicalism is that it is radically Christ-centered.[28] This is linked with the high view of Scripture to which evangelicals, as we noted above, are committed. Christology and scriptural authority are inextricably linked, in that it is Scripture, and Scripture alone, that brings us to a true and saving knowledge of Jesus Christ. Calvin correctly defined this as the whole point of Scripture.[29] The New Testament is the only document we possess that the Christian church has recognized as authentically embodying and recollecting its understanding of Jesus and the impact he had on people's lives and thought. The reports we have concerning Jesus from nonbiblical sources are of questionable reliability and strictly limited value.[30]

Four points may be singled out as having special importance to evangelicalism. First, evangelicalism has always maintained that it is impossible to remain faithful to the New Testament witness to Jesus Christ without thinking and speaking of him in terms that transcend all normal human categories. Here is no ordinary historical figure; here is God himself, addressing us in and through his only Son, our

Savior and Lord.[31] Full and true knowledge of God is to be found only in him. The enormously powerful statements of the prologue to John's Gospel make this point with force and precision: "Grace and truth came through Jesus Christ. No one has ever seen God, but God the One and Only, who is at the Father's side, has made him known" (Jn 1:17-18). Karl Barth is but one of the great theologians within the Reformed tradition to affirm this point:

> When Holy Scripture speaks of God, it does not permit us to let our attention or thoughts wander at random. . . . When Holy Scripture speaks of God, it concentrates our attention and thoughts upon one single point and what is to be known at that point. . . . If we ask further concerning the one point upon which, according to Scripture, our attention and thoughts should and must be concentrated, then from first to last the Bible directs us to the name of Jesus Christ.[32]

In terms of the substance of this belief, it corresponds to historic Christian orthodoxy down the ages. If evangelicalism is distinctive at this point, it is on account of the emphasis it has chosen to place on this belief, the inferences that it draws from it, and the consistency with which it has maintained it.

Second, the total evangelical commitment to the divinity of Jesus Christ is seen as vitally important for safeguarding a cluster of theological and spiritual insights. Evangelicals adopt a range of approaches to the *interpretation* of the divinity of Christ.[33] Nevertheless, the fundamental point of reference remains the same: whatever grasp we have on the knowledge of God and whatever hopes of salvation we may possess are totally dependent on the identity of Jesus Christ as our Savior and Lord, the only Son of God, God incarnate.

Third, evangelicalism places a special emphasis on the centrality of the cross of Christ. The cross is the unique and perfect sacrifice that covers and shields us from the righteous anger of God against sin, reconciles us to God and opens the way to the glorious freedom of the children of God. Christ's death on the cross is to be seen as the unique, necessary and sufficient basis of salvation, which both demonstrates the full extent of God's love for us and establishes the centrality of Christ to Christian worship and adoration. It is no accident that many of the greatest hymns within the evangelical tradition focus on the sufferings of Christ on the cross, emphasizing both the costliness and the reality of the redemption that has been won through him and is offered to us and to the world.

Linked with this is an emphasis on the fallen character of the creation and especially of human beings. Here evangelicalism has welcomed the insights of writers such as Karl Barth and Reinhold Niebuhr, who emphasized the reality of sin and its implications for human culture. It is true that some culturally accommodated versions of Christianity still shy away from speaking about sin.[34] Evangelicalism, however, is insistent that it is impossible to appreciate the majesty of God, the wonder of redemption or the hopelessness of the human situation unless we fully acknowledge the devastating and destructive impact of sin. In this respect evangelicalism maintains the radical realism, so characteristic of Reformers such as Luther and Calvin, that emphasizes the gravity of the human predicament and the joy of the gospel proclamation of the grace of God.

Fourth, this emphasis on the majesty of Christ finds its expression in the doctrine of justification by faith.[35] Justification by faith—or more precisely justification *proper Christum per fidem* ("on account of Christ, through faith")—represents an affirmation of the extension of the lordship of Christ to include not merely the grounds but also the means of justification. Whereas Pelagianism asserted that human beings are capable of meriting or achieving their own salvation, the Reformers, especially Martin Luther, affirmed that even the faith by which the "benefits of Christ" are appropriated must be thought of as a work of God in Christ. The doctrine of justification by faith, often referred to as the "material principle of the Reformation," insists that all that need be done for salvation has been done, and done well, in and through Jesus Christ.[36]

Fifth, and finally, this emphasis on the majesty of Christ leads naturally into evangelism. For evangelicals there is an obvious and organic connection between Christology and evangelism. To recognize Jesus Christ as our Savior and Lord is to proclaim him as the Savior and Lord of others. Evangelism is no optional extra, no add-on to the basic gospel package. It is an integral element of the evangelical recognition of the identity and significance of Jesus Christ. With much justification, evangelicals are highly critical of approaches to faith that speak loosely and vaguely about "our search for God." The whole point of the Christian faith is that God has chosen to make himself graciously known in and through Scripture, especially through its focal point, Jesus Christ. Evangelism represents both the proclamation that this revelation has taken place and an invitation to respond to it.

The Lordship of the Holy Spirit

Evangelicals give an important place to the Holy Spirit, seeing the Spirit as the One who brings spiritual understanding and rebirth, who seals our knowledge of our salvation and who works to conform us to Christ. Word and Spirit are joined together in the final stage of conversion, in which the Holy Spirit applies the Word of God to our minds and our lives, causing faith to be born from understanding. This, in the famous words of the Westminster Shorter Catechism, "is the work of God's Spirit whereby, convincing us of our sin and misery, enlightening our minds in the knowledge of Christ, and renewing our wills, he doth persuade and enable us to embrace Jesus Christ freely offered to us in the gospel."[37] This point had also been stressed by Calvin, whose definition of faith has had a significant impact on classical evangelicalism: "Now we shall have a right definition of faith if we say that it is a steady and certain knowledge of the divine benevolence towards us, which is founded upon the truth of the gracious promise of God in Christ, and is both revealed to our minds and sealed in our hearts by the Holy Spirit."[38] The Holy Spirit thus plays an important role, which I have already noted, in the evangelical understanding of biblical authority.

Within evangelicalism, it is the charismatic movement that has given the greatest recognition to the person and work of the Spirit. The movement has brought fresh life to the church through its rediscovery of the role of the Holy Spirit in Christian life and experience. Many of those who had regarded Christianity as simply "right believing" have discovered the power and delight of an immediate and direct experience of God in their lives, often accompanied by such outward manifestations of the presence of the Spirit as speaking in tongues. Yet this new emphasis on the role of the Holy Spirit has also brought with it tensions and controversy, most notably over the issue of the importance of experience of the Spirit in the normal Christian life and the relation between Word and Spirit.

The rediscovery of spiritual gifts is linked with the movement known as Pentecostalism, generally regarded as the first modern movement to demonstrate clearly charismatic inclinations. Although this movement can be argued to have long historical roots, its twentieth-century development is generally traced back to the ministry of Charles Fox Parham (1873-1929) and events at the Azusa Street Mission, Los Angeles, in 1906-1908.[39] The impact of the charismatic movement within evangelicalism, however, dates from the more recent past. The incident that brought it to public attention took place in Van Nuys, California. When the rector of a local Episcopal church, Dennis Bennett, told his congregation that he had been filled with the Holy Spirit and had spoken in tongues, reaction varied from bewilderment to outrage. Bennett's bishop promptly banned speaking in tongues from his churches. However, it soon became clear that others had shared Bennett's experience. Philip E. Hughes, a noted evangelical theologian, witnessed the phenomenon at first hand, and he wrote up his experiences for both the North American *Christianity Today* and the British *Churchman*.[40] Hughes reported that he was convinced that "the Breath of the Living God is stirring among the dry bones of the major, respectable, old-fashioned denominations, and particularly within the Episcopal Church." From that moment, the Holy Spirit was firmly on the agenda of evangelicalism.[41]

But more recent developments have proved even more controversial within evangelicalism. The ministry of John Wimber and the Vineyard Christian Fellowship is a case in point. In his study of the development of charismatic movements in the twentieth century, C. Peter Wagner, professor of church growth at Fuller Seminary, distinguishes three "waves."[42] The first wave was classic Pentecostalism, which arose in the early 1900s and was characterized by an emphasis on speaking in tongues. The second wave was in the 1960s and 1970s, as noted above, and took place mostly within mainline denominations as they appropriated spiritual healing and other charismatic practices. The third wave, exemplified by Wimber, places emphasis on "signs and wonders." Wimber claimed that a new wave of supernatural power has been unleashed on the churches, by which God can use ordinary Christians to do extraordinary things.

Controversy has centered on this "third wave." Wimber and Wagner ran Fuller Seminary's class MC510, known as "Signs and Wonders," from 1982 to 1986, when faculty and trustee controversy closed it down; it was reinstated, with a lower profile, a year later.[43] Some have charged Wimber with presenting the gospel in terms that make no reference to repentance or forgiveness—charges that were pressed particularly forcefully after the 1990 Spiritual Warfare Conference at Sydney.[44] Further controversy centers on the theology of healing itself.[45] Clearly there is an ongoing debate over these new developments within the more charismatic wing of evangelicalism.

The tension between theologies and spiritualities that center on the "Word" and those that focus on the "Spirit" goes back to the first period of the Reformation.[46] Word-centered evangelicals often express a concern that an emphasis on the Holy Spirit might result in Scripture's being bypassed in favor of an immediate personal revelation to an individual. Sadly, there is ample evidence to suggest that this concern is well-founded, as a study of some American televangelists makes clear.[47]

In his article "Take Time to Pray" in the February 1987 issue of *Believer's Voice of Victory,* Kenneth Copeland relates a message he claims to have had from Jesus Christ himself: "Don't be disturbed when people accuse you of thinking you're God. . . . They crucified me for claiming I was God." Here Copeland seems to come very close to placing himself on the same plane as Jesus Christ, claiming the same divine authority for his actions. Copeland relates how in the same vision he heard Christ speak these words to him: "I didn't claim that I was God; I just claimed I walked with him, and that he was in me. Hallelujah! That's what you're doing."[48] The uniqueness of Jesus Christ is thus denied: Christ was just someone who walked closely with God, like others, including Copeland himself. The ontological gap between Christ and Christians, so vital a safeguard against irresponsible leadership and the more vexing theological developments normally linked with the New Age movement, is thus denied. And as Jesus Christ is unable to make personal television appearances, get on the lecture-tour circuit or deliver personalized sermons, those who claim to have authority on the same level as his would seem to have a significant advantage over him in this respect. Indeed, one of the most troublesome features of some sections of modern evangelicalism is irresponsible leaders' willingness to allow a blurring of the vital distinction between the will of God and the will of the charismatic Christian leader.

Word-based evangelicals are rightly alarmed at these developments and see the only solution as being a return to the *corporate* authority of Scripture, which cuts the ground from under the posturings of those who claim to have unique and vital revelations from God. All that God needed to say authoritatively *has* been said authoritatively, and it is entrusted to the church in Scripture.

On the other side of the debate, those with a more Spirit-based theology or spirituality argue that a Word-based approach can easily degenerate into a cerebral approach to Christianity that fails to engage with Christian experience. Christian faith can easily become understood as intellectual assent to revealed knowledge, rather than as being possessed by the Spirit of the living God.[49] The charismatic movement has led to a rediscovery of the New Testament emphasis on the need for spiritual gifts and discernment, which is sometimes linked with matters of church life such as speaking in tongues, and a call for these gifts and practices to find their way back into the church. The church is impoverished without these gifts, advocates say, and it needs them badly if it is to survive and prosper.[50] Yet the new awareness and experience of the presence of the Holy Spirit in the modern church has raised a series of debates over the nature of the baptism of the Spirit and which of the various "spiritual gifts" *(charismata)* are of greatest importance, in relation both to personal faith and to the building up of the church as a whole.[51]

Each side has important contributions to make to this debate; in practice, Word and Spirit are perhaps easier to reconcile than the polarization of the debate might suggest.[52] For example, a Word-based theology can be developed without difficulty to take the experiential side of Christian faith and life into account,[53] just as a Spirit-centered theology can remain firmly anchored to Scripture. Polarization has perhaps led to a distortion of this situation rather than to a constructive attempt to settle it. There are excellent reasons for hoping that the next generation of evangelicalism may see an increasing maturity in both camps.

At present both sides appear to be wiser in their spiritual intuitions than in their theological formulations. But both agree on at least one matter: that a decisive enriching of personal Christian experience is possible through the work of the Spirit. The charismatic movement is to be welcomed as a "God-sent corrective of formalism, institutionalism and intellectualism"[54]—weaknesses to which classic evangelicalism is itself prone. A real encounter with God is and should be something transformative, a notion that is often expressed in the characteristic evangelical emphasis on the need for personal conversion.

The Need for Personal Conversion

At the heart of evangelical spirituality lies the concept of a personally assimilated faith. Christian faith is not, and cannot be allowed to become, passive assent to propositions. It is a living and dynamic personal relationship with the crucified and risen Christ. Evangelical-

ism, it must be emphasized, is more than assent to Christian orthodoxy; it is such an assent coupled with a living personal faith. It is
possible, for example, for someone to offer formal assent to the doctrine of the lordship of Christ without ever having experienced or
personally accepted such lordship. It is, as Martin Luther pointed out,
perfectly possible to discourse eloquently on the nature of salvation
without having recognized oneself as a sinner desperately needing the
salvation that is offered nowhere but in Christ.

The issue in question was recognized and stated poetically by the
Pietist writer Johann Scheffler (1624-1667, writing under the pseudo-
nym Angelus Silesius):

Were Christ a thousand times to Bethlehem come,

And yet not born in thee, 'twould spell thy doom.

Golgotha's cross, it cannot save from sin,

Except for thee that cross be raised within.

I say, it helps thee not that Christ is risen,

If thou thyself art still in death's dark prison.

The issue at stake could be described in terms of *personal appropriation of faith*. Christian faith, in the deepest meaning of the phrase,
is to be thought of in *relational* and *personal,* not simply *proposition-
al,* terms. God is One who is known, not simply known about; he is
One who is encountered personally, not just read about in theology
textbooks. James I. Packer makes this point forcefully in a published
lecture entitled "An Introduction to Systematic Spirituality":

I question the adequacy of conceptualizing the subject-matter of
systematic theology as simply revealed truths about God, and I
challenge the assumption that has usually accompanied this form
of statement, that the material, like other scientific data, is best
studied in cool and clinical detachment. Detachment from what,
you ask? Why, from the relational activity of trusting, loving, wor-
shipping, obeying, serving and glorifying God: the activity that
results from realizing that one is actually in God's presence, actually
being addressed by him, every time one opens the Bible or reflects
on any divine truth whatsoever. This . . . proceeds as if doctrinal

study would only be muddled by introducing devotional concerns; it drives a wedge between . . . knowing true notions about God and knowing the true God himself.[55]

Packer's point is that a genuine experience of God makes the detached study of God an impossibility. It is like asking the lover to be neutral about the beloved. God is personal; so also must be our response to him. As the Danish existentialist philosopher Søren Kierkegaard pointed out in his *Concluding Unscientific Postscript,* to know the truth is to be known by the truth. (Kierkegaard is known to have been deeply influenced by John's Gospel at this point, especially its confident declaration that Jesus Christ is the truth.) "Truth" is something that affects our inner being, as we become involved in "an appropriation process of the most passionate inwardness."[56] The evangelical demand for a personal faith corresponds to—indeed, anticipates—this aspect of Kierkegaard, which is clearly rooted in Scripture.

It is here that the Pietist heritage has had its deepest impact on evangelicalism. Reacting against the aridity of a faith that is doctrinally orthodox yet spiritually dead, evangelicals insist on the need for a personal, living faith. This point is especially important in relation to the theological movement associated with Karl Barth, often known as "neo-orthodoxy," which seems to its critics to have the attraction of doctrinal orthodoxy without the personal warmth and vitality of faith that is one of the foundations of evangelicalism.[57]

This point emerged clearly in the 1950s, during the course of a spirited attack on the theologian Reinhold Niebuhr (1892-1971) by E. G. Homrighausen, dean of Princeton Theological Seminary. Writing in the leading mainline journal *The Christian Century,* Homrighausen, head of the National Council of Churches' Department of Evangelism, accused Niebuhr and his sympathizers of being "hesitant and weak in calling persons to a positive faith." Niebuhr could, he suggested, learn some useful lessons from people like Billy Graham. Why, he asked, was "Niebuhrian neo-orthodoxy" so hesitant to call people to conversion?

I have, frankly, been disappointed in its inability to lead the way in the revival or rebirth or restoration of a relevant Protestantism in the local church. And if men like Graham have arisen, and are being heard by the thousands, it may be that what he is and says in sincerity ought to be said in a better way by the neo-orthodox with all their accumulation of intelligence about the Bible and history and personality in our times.[58]

Doctrinal orthodoxy without a living faith is like an empty treasure chest; it awaits the riches for which it was intended, yet lacks that richness itself.

It is often suggested that evangelicals say all Christians must have had a dramatic conversion experience or be able to point to a definite moment at which they became born-again believers. This is not the case. Evangelicals, as stressed above, emphasize the lordship of the Holy Spirit and avoid the fallacy of subjecting his activity to human limits and norms. It does not matter whether one comes to a living faith through a dramatic and sudden "Damascus Road experience" or through a quiet and growing awareness of a personal trust in Christ. It is present convertedness rather than the memory or experience of past conversion that is of fundamental importance.

The evangelical emphasis on the need for personal conversion, either as a "born-again" experience or as an ongoing process, naturally leads on to a discussion of how that conversion comes about. If, as Paul affirms, "faith comes from hearing the message" (Rom 10:17), it follows that the proclamation of the gospel in all its fullness must be central. Evangelicalism is consistent at this point, as it is elsewhere in its coherent presentation of the gospel. The correlative to an emphasis on the need for personal conversion is an emphasis on the priority of evangelism.

The Priority of Evangelism

The evangelical emphasis on evangelism arises naturally from four considerations. First, the need for a personal faith leads to the question of how that personal faith arises and the responsibility of believers toward that development. Second, the evangelical proclamation of the majesty of Christ as Savior and Lord naturally expresses itself in a concern to extend his kingdom. Third, the concern to remain faithful to Scripture means that the great biblical injunctions to proclaim Christ to the world (such as Mt 28:18-20 and Acts 1:8) are taken with the utmost seriousness. And fourth, the intense joy of knowing Christ makes it natural for evangelicals to wish to share this experience with those whom they love, as an act of generosity and consideration.

The evangelical emphasis on evangelism, once treated with little more than contempt by a complacent mainline Christianity, has now been widely recognized as essential to the future of the church in the world. It is perhaps unrealistic to identify any single incident as marking a turning point in such attitudes. However, I propose to single out one development that illustrates this major change in perception.

In the first quarter of 1954, the evangelist Billy Graham was invited to speak at Union Theological Seminary in New York. By that time Graham had attracted considerable national attention.[59] The success of the 1949 Los Angeles Crusade had been widely reported in the secular press, giving Graham a high profile. Nevertheless, he was regarded with suspicion by leaders in mainline churches, who tended to consider him a closet fundamentalist without significant academic credibility. Union Theological Seminary, a bastion of mainline Protestantism and a leading center for theological scholarship, would hardly be expected to receive him warmly.

In the event, Graham spoke for forty-five minutes to a student audience in the seminary chapel and answered questions afterward for another thirty minutes. When he had finished, he was greeted with one of the longest and most enthusiastic ovations that institution had known.[60] It seemed that evangelism had suddenly become respectable.

Yet not everyone at Union was pleased with this development. Reinhold Niebuhr, who had joined the faculty of Union as professor of Christian ethics in 1927, was distinctly disgruntled about the growing enthusiasm for evangelism. (Above I noted the vulnerability of neo-orthodoxy at this point.) He wrote scathingly of Graham's theological incompetence and naiveté.

Billy Graham is a personable, modest and appealing young man who has wedded considerable dramatic and demagogic gifts with a rather obscurantist version of the Christian faith. His message is not completely irrelevant to the broader social issues of the day—but it approaches irrelevance. For what it may be worth, we can be assured that his approach is free of the vulgarities which characterized the message of Billy Sunday, who intrigued the nation about a quarter century ago. We are grateful for this much "progress."[61]

Niebuhr's lofty dismissal of Graham was seen by many of his readers as little more than sour grapes from an academic theologian fearful of being marginalized by the new enthusiasm for evangelical forms of Christianity.

A particularly devastating critique of Niebuhr was mounted by Edward J. Carnell, then president of the fledgling Fuller Seminary in Pasadena, California. For Carnell, Niebuhr's version of Christianity was unintelligible to ordinary Americans and had nothing to offer them in their hour of need:

This . . . is the grand irony of Christian realism. Reinhold Niebuhr can prove that man is a sinner; but man already knows this. Reinhold Niebuhr can develop the dialectical relationship between time and eternity, but this is beyond the tether of a dime store clerk or a hod carrier. When it comes to the acid test, therefore, realism is not very realistic. A concrete view of sin converts to an abstract view of salvation. . . . Niebuhr does not speak about Christ's literal cross and resurrection at all. He speaks, at most, of the "symbols" of the cross and resurrection. But of what value are these symbols to an anxious New York cabby?[62]

Carnell here identified a crucial weak point of Niebuhr's approach—its failure to offer a vision for sinful humanity in terms that its audience could understand and to which it could relate.

Such critical responses were not limited to evangelicals. Many in the mainline churches were concerned at the tone and content of Niebuhr's criticism. Even the president of Union Theological Seminary,

Henry P. van Dusen, weighed in with a withering response to Niebuhr's dismissal of Billy Graham.

> Dr. Niebuhr prefers Billy Graham to Billy Sunday. There are many,
> of whom I am one, who are not ashamed to testify that they would
> probably have never come within the sound of Dr. Niebuhr's voice
> or the influence of his mind if they had not been *first* touched by
> the message of the earlier Billy. Quite probably five or ten years
> hence there may appear in the classrooms and churches of Billy
> Graham's severest critics not a few who will be glad to give parallel
> testimony to his role in *starting* them in that direction.[63]

The point being made was clear. Evangelicalism was calling people to
faith in a way that nobody else was. The most fundamental criticism
made of Niebuhr in this respect was that he was parasitic, feeding off
the fruits of the work of earlier evangelists without "calling persons
to a positive faith." Niebuhr may have been a great thinker and vision-
ary, especially in exposing the weakness of the American "social gospel" movement. Yet he seemed ill at ease with the new emphasis on
evangelism, which was soon to gain an increased hearing.

The new positive valuation of evangelism within the churches must
not be allowed to obscure the fact that this task must rest on a secure
foundation—a foundation that evangelicalism provides, and that is
consolidated through its emphasis on the community that initially
proclaims the gospel and subsequently nourishes and disciples those
who respond to it. So we now turn to the distinctive evangelical approach to the church as the community of faith.

The Importance of the Christian Community

At its heart, evangelicalism has a deep-seated awareness of the importance of the Christian community to the tasks of evangelism, spiritual
nourishment, teaching and discipling. Evangelicalism rejoices in the
Pauline image of the church as the body of Christ, realizing that this
points to a corporate rather than individualistic conception of the
Christian life. The "community of Christ" is integral to an evangelical
understanding of the Christian life and is of growing importance to

evangelical understandings of the tasks of Christian theology.[64]

Evangelicalism is committed to the church, in the sense of a corporate conception of the Christian life. But this does not mean that it is committed to any one *denominational* understanding of the nature of the church.[65] An example from an earlier period in the history of evangelicalism will make this clear. The ecclesiologies of the Genevan Reformer John Calvin and the English Puritan writer William Ames are both unquestionably evangelical, drawing on well-substantiated New Testament roots. Yet these ecclesiologies are rather different. Calvin is committed to a view of the church as a "mixed body," including both the elect and the nonelect, the righteous and sinners, whereas Ames is committed to a view of the church as a gathered society of saints.[66] Both can be argued from Scripture; both have a long and distinguished history within the evangelical tradition.

A doctrine of the church is not of defining significance for evangelicals, in that evangelicals are at liberty to defend and develop any doctrine of the church that is well-grounded in Scripture and carefully thought through in practice. Variants of Calvin's approach are today found in Presbyterian and Anglican circles, while variants of Ames's are found in Baptist and Congregationalist circles. Evangelicals have a right, indeed a *responsibility,* to disagree over matters of church order, as part of the attempt to remain as faithful to the New Testament as possible; nevertheless, evangelicals are not *defined* by a specific church order. It would be unacceptable, for example, for a Baptist to declare that a Presbyterian cannot be an evangelical on account of an allegedly deficient view of the church. As the great Baptist preacher C. H. Spurgeon once commented, "Insinuate that you are the only ones who are really 'the church of God,' and you have scattered seed which will produce a harvest of strife."

One of the most distinctive features of evangelicalism is thus that it is *nondenominational* (or better, *transdenominational;* see below). Evangelicals are most emphatically not committed to any, including any specifically separatist, doctrine of the church or understanding of the fine details of church order. Evangelicalism is as consistent with a convinced denominationalism as it is with a convinced separatist view of the church, and it is not restricted to any specific scripturally based ecclesiology.

If evangelicalism has been undeveloped in some of its thinking about the fine details of church ordering, this is ultimately a reflection of its distinctive belief that the church is the body that gathers where the gospel is truly preached. Some denominations, such as the Southern Baptist Convention, are explicitly and self-consciously evangelical; others, such as Anglicanism, are doctrinally mixed. The latter therefore function as contexts within which evangelicalism may operate and expand, without any expectation of official sanction or support from denominational authorities. The theme of "evangelical catholicity," originally associated with the Mercersburg theology, has begun to reemerge as significant within the Evangelical Lutheran Church in America, in that it gives expression to a corporate view of the church without losing the evangelical emphases noted in this chapter.[67]

This lack of commitment to any specific denomination has resonated with recent social attitudes in North America. Noting recent trends in American church life, the *Los Angeles Times* reported that in response to marketing research showing that upscale congregants spurn denominational tags, many denominationally affiliated churches are dropping their identifying labels. An example: Van Nuys First Baptist Church in Chatsworth, California, is affiliated to the Southern Baptist Convention. However, after surveying folk in local shopping malls and ballparks, its pastor changed its name to "Shepherd of the Hills Church." It was the gospel people wanted, not some specific denominational affiliation. The same trend is now evident across the United States. People seem to be looking for open commitment to the gospel rather than a particular denominational label.[68]

This development may be regarded as totally consistent with the origins of evangelicalism in the late medieval European church. When Luther suggested that the church of his day had lost touch with the gospel, his justified concern over the doctrine of salvation was countered with the charge that he had a deficient view of the church and thus he should submit himself to the established doctrines and practices of the church. Ecclesiology was here used as an instrument of control and repression, prohibiting, or at least restricting, debate over whether the church had remained faithful to the gospel. As the Reformation made clear, such debate was essential if the church was to remain faithful to its calling. Legitimate calls for reform and renewal were silenced by a theological perspective dominated by a specific doctrine of the church.

Historically, evangelicalism has never been committed to any single model of the church, regarding the New Testament as being open to a number of interpretations in this respect and treating denominational distinctives as secondary to the gospel itself. This most emphatically does not mean that evangelicals lack commitment to the church as the body of Christ; rather, it means that evangelicals are not committed to any one *theory* of the church. Calvin stressed the importance of the church for the Christian life; in following his emphasis on the role of the community of faith, evangelicals have not found it necessary to endorse the specific theory of the church that Calvin himself espoused.

I shall begin then, with the church, into the bosom of which God is pleased to gather his children, not only so that they may be nourished by her assistance and ministry while they are infants and children, but also so that they may be guided by her motherly care until they mature and reach the goal of faith. 'For what God has joined together, no one shall divide' (Mark 10:9). For those to whom God is Father, the church shall also be their mother.[69]

The visible institution of the church is thus treated as a fundamental resource for the life of faith. Here believers may encounter and support one another and find mutual encouragement through praising God and hearing his Word. The image of the church as mother brings out clearly the corporate dimensions of the Christian faith: "Let us learn from this simple word 'mother' how useful (indeed, how necessary) it is to know her. There is no other way to life, unless this mother conceives us in her womb, nourishes us at her breast, and keeps us under her care and guidance."[70]

81

The institution of the church is a necessary, helpful, God-given and God-ordained means of spiritual growth and development. It is meant to be there, and it is meant to be used. The Christian is not intended to be a radical and solitary romantic, wandering in isolated loneliness through the world; rather, the Christian is called to be a member of a community. John Stott makes this point as follows: "The very purpose of [Christ's] self-giving on the cross was not just to save isolated individuals, and thus to perpetuate their loneliness, but to create a new community whose members would belong to him, love one another and eagerly serve the world."[71]

Evangelicals are aware of the importance of a well-informed biblical model of the church; they, in common with many other Christians, remain unpersuaded, however, that the New Testament intended to lay down precise details of church polity. This minimalist attitude to the doctrine of the church does not mean that individual evangelicals do not have well-defined understandings of the nature of the church; rather, it points to no single such doctrine being normative within the movement, since the New Testament itself does not stipulate with precision any single form of church government that can be made binding on all Christians. Those who accuse evangelicals of having "immature" or "underdeveloped" theories of the church might care to ask themselves whether they might not have hopelessly overdeveloped theories. More recently, even Roman Catholic biblical scholarship—traditionally wedded to static and highly authoritarian concepts of the church—has recognized that the New Testament portrays the church in dynamic and evolving terms, using a variety of images to represent it.[72]

The evangelical perception that the New Testament allows a considerable degree of diversity in relation to theories of the church has had several major consequences.

1. Evangelicalism is *transdenominational*. It is not confined to any one denomination, nor is it a denomination in its own right. There is considerable cross-fertilization between leading evangelical institutions worldwide, especially seminaries, graduate schools of theology

and research institutes, publishing houses, journals, television and radio networks, and ministerial conventions. There is no inconsistency involved in speaking of "Anglican evangelicals," "Baptist evangelicals," "Methodist evangelicals," "Presbyterian evangelicals" and even "Roman Catholic evangelicals." (In the United States in particular, evangelicalism is becoming a significant force within the Roman Catholic Church, with local Bible study groups being centers of renewal and growth. A *public* loyalty to the Catholic Church is increasingly becoming compatible with a *private* acceptance of leading evangelical beliefs: see pp. 175-80.)

2. Evangelicalism does not necessarily take the form of a denomination in itself, possessed of a distinctive ecclesiology, but can also be a *trend within the mainstream denominations*. The Southern Baptist Convention is an example of a denomination that is explicitly and self-consciously evangelical in orientation, as are many independent or free churches in Great Britain; the second pattern is that of evangelicalism as a reforming and renewing presence within a denomination, as it is within Anglicanism. Even within Anglicanism, however, there are considerable variations: for historical reasons, for example, the diocese of Sydney is committed to an explicitly evangelical position.[73]

3. Evangelicalism itself represents an *ecumenical* movement. There is a natural affinity among evangelicals, irrespective of their denominational associations, which arises from a common commitment to a set of shared beliefs and outlooks. Evangelicals exist in a fellowship that is grounded in and defined by "gospel truth, rather than formal denominational links."[74] The characteristic evangelical refusal to allow any specific ecclesiology to be seen as normative, while honoring those that are clearly grounded in the New Testament and Christian tradition, means that potentially divisive matters of church ordering and government are treated as of secondary importance. As one perceptive scholar of the theology of evangelicalism has commented, "Considered ecclesiologically, evangelicalism is Protestantism's clearest attempt to recapture the pluralist nature of the early church."[75]

A case in point will illustrate this trend. Carl F. H. Henry is widely regarded as a leading evangelical statesman. As noted earlier, his many books and long ministry through a series of evangelical flagships—such as Fuller Seminary and *Christianity Today*—established his reputation as an astute and thoughtful leader of the evangelical movement in the United States and beyond. The fact that Henry is an active Baptist is a source of surprise or indifference to most evangelicals outside North America.[76] His importance and prominence are not linked to any specific denominational association, but to his writing and speaking ministry, which transcends denominational barriers in the name of the gospel. Similarly, many North American evangelicals are unaware that C. S. Lewis was an Anglican; once more, they perceive him as a reliable and trustworthy exponent of "mere Christianity" whose influence goes beyond the narrow limitations of denominational barriers.

But the evangelical commitment to the community of faith goes further than this. It extends to the interpretation of Scripture and the enmeshing of the gospel with culture. These matters are too important to be left to individuals; they are a matter for the Christian community as it reflects on its reading of Scripture, its experience of the Holy Spirit and its sense of being rooted in a long historical tradition concerned to remain faithful to the gospel. James I. Packer, one of the most influential evangelical writers of recent times, stressed this point:

> The Spirit has been active in the Church from the first, doing the work he was sent to do—guiding God's people into an understanding of revealed truth. The history of the Church's labour to understand the Bible forms a commentary on the Bible which we cannot despise or ignore without dishonouring the Holy Spirit. To treat the principle of biblical authority as a prohibition against reading and learning from the book of church history is not an evangelical, but an anabaptist mistake.[77]

Tradition can thus be understood as a history of discipleship—of allowing oneself to be challenged by Scripture. Tradition is a willingness to read Scripture in a way that takes into account how it has been read in the past. It is an awareness of the communal dimension of Christian faith, which calls the shallow individualism of many evangelicals into question. There is more to the interpretation of Scripture than any one individual can discern. It is a willingness to give full weight to the views of those who have gone before us in the faith.

At first sight this emphasis on the community of faith might seem to be in tension with the belief that it is Scripture alone that is authoritative. But this principle was never intended by Luther or Calvin to mean that Scripture is read *individualistically* or to elevate the private judgment of an individual above the communal judgment of the church (although it was interpreted in this way by certain radical Reformers, referred to above by Packer as "anabaptists," outside the mainstream of the Reformation). Rather, it affirms that every traditional way of reading Scripture must, in principle, be open to challenge. As the study of church history makes clear, the church may sometimes get Scripture wrong: the sixteenth-century Reformers believed that Scripture had been misunderstood at a series of junctures by the medieval church, and they undertook to reform its practices and doctrines at those points. This, however, is a case of a tradition being criticized and renewed from within, in the light of the biblical foundations on which it ultimately rests. The Reformers did not regard themselves as founding a new tradition; their concern was to reform a tradition that already existed but that appeared, at crucial points, to have become detached from its scriptural foundations.

The Origins of Evangelical Diversity

The six beliefs considered above may be regarded as the foundations of evangelicalism in today's world. Variations between evangelicals are to be expected, not least on account of the astonishing variety of contexts in which evangelicalism has become established and the distinctive emphases and approaches characteristic of the various strands (such as Reformed, Wesleyan and Pentecostal) that go to make up evangelicalism today. It is probably true to say that evangelicals differ from one another in three manners:

1. The relative emphasis they place on the six elements. I have set out these elements in what I hope is a helpful and clear ordering, allowing the organic connection of the various elements of evangelical belief to be seen. It is not intended, however, to be an absolute and binding statement of priorities. The placing of the authority of Scripture at the opening of the list would command widespread assent within evangelicalism; the placing of evangelism in the penultimate position might seem unacceptable to others, who would wish to give it a much higher profile. Charismatic evangelicals would wish to place considerable emphasis on the person and work of the Holy Spirit, with younger charismatics arguing that the "signs and wonders" element of that activity should be given a very high profile in today's church. This book cannot adjudicate between such debates; it can, however, indicate that they can and do arise.

2. *The precise interpretation of the six elements.* A biblically grounded diversity within evangelicalism is integral to the movement. For example, all evangelicals are united in affirming the divinity and humanity of Jesus Christ and its vital importance in relation to evangelism and spirituality. But evangelicals, in common with most Christians, are not bound to any one specific christological model—that is to say, any one way of conceptualizing *how* the divinity and humanity of Christ coexist in his person. Both the Alexandrian and Antiochene approaches, to note the two great models of Christian antiquity, find their exponents among evangelicals today.[78] Both are biblically based and consistent with historic Christian orthodoxy. Similarly, all evangelicals are agreed that Scripture is the inspired Word of God; the precise model of inspiration is, however, left unspecified. There are several biblically grounded "models of inspiration," just as there are several "models of incarnation."[79] Again, all evangelicals are committed to the proclamation of the "good news of Jesus Christ" but realize that the contextualization of this "good news" may differ on going from Oxford to Delhi to Singapore to Mombasa. The global expansion of evangelicalism means that a movement that has hitherto focused on the Western world has to come to terms with the issues raised by its encounter with other cultures.

3. Additional elements that they may choose to emphasize. Many evangelicals choose to add items to these elements, which they believe can be justified from Scripture and Christian history. Thus some Anglican evangelicals would follow Packer and suggest that the bishop can be seen as a symbol of Christ's ministry to his church. This belief is not defining for evangelicals in general; it merely distinguishes some Anglican evangelicals from, shall we say, Baptist evangelicals. It is when one type of evangelical seeks to impose his or her distinctive ideas—such as an Anglican, Baptist, Congregationalist or Presbyterian understanding of church government—on others that improper and unnecessary disagreement arises. Additional elements distinguish one kind of evangelical from another; they are not constitutive of evangelicalism itself.

The present chapter has set out the basic features of evangelicalism. On the basis of this exposition, it will be clear that evangelicalism has considerable attractions. The following chapter aims to make these more explicit.

3

THE APPEAL OF EVANGELICALISM

WHY IS EVANGELICALISM SO ATTRACTIVE? SOME WRITERS HAVE a neat answer to this question: evangelicalism is attractive because it evades the real issues and offers cheap and easy fixes to complex problems. John Shelby Spong, one of the most aggressive advocates of this dismissive approach, is a case in point. Spong's caricature of evangelicalism appears to be more than a little ungracious and condescending; it does, however, have the merit of drawing attention to the decline of liberalism, both in what Spong terms "the liberal Protestant mainline churches" and in "the silent liberal Catholic minority":

The only churches that grow today are those that do not, in fact, understand the issues, and can therefore traffic in certainty. They represent both the fundamentalistic Protestant groups and the rigidly controlled conservative Catholic traditions. The churches that do attempt to interact with the emerging world are for the most part the liberal Protestant mainline churches that shrink every day in membership and the silent liberal Catholic minority that attracts very few adherents. Both are, almost by definition, fuzzy, imprecise and relatively unappealing. They might claim to be honest, but for the most part they have no real message. They tinker with words, redefine concepts, and retreat slowly behind the rear guard protection of a few pseudoradical thinkers. I have sought to live in this arena. It shrinks daily.[1]

And is this really surprising? Any church that "has no real message" or that manages to make the gospel "relatively unappealing" deserves to fail. How can anyone make the "pearl of great price" something that has no attraction for people? Spong seems to have managed to achieve the inverse miracle of turning wine into water. The rather smug assumption behind his assertions is that the extent of one's popular appeal is inversely proportional to "understanding the issues." This facile modernism, which dominated academic theological thinking in the 1960s and 1970s, has now widely fallen from favor.

A more serious approach to the question of the growing appeal of evangelicalism would be to consider the factors that appear to motivate people to become and remain evangelicals, whether this process involves coming to faith from a non-Christian context or leaving behind a nonevangelical form of Christianity. The following factors are known to be major considerations for many who make these moves.

The Failure of 1960s Liberalism

One of the most alarming trends in twentieth-century Christianity, which reached its peak in the 1960s and 1970s, was a form of what Gabriel Fackre has termed "Christological heart-failure," grounded in the assumption that Christianity had become an irrelevance to modernity. The only hope, many radical thinkers in the mainline denominations believed, lay in modernizing Christianity.[2] Yet this modernizing does not seem to have taken the form of a considered appraisal of how the central elements of the Christian faith might be related to the needs and aspirations of modern society;[3] rather, it appears to have proceeded on the assumption that there was an urgent need to jettison any aspect of the Christian faith that caused people problems—such as the idea of a transcendent God.

Much radical theological writing of the 1960s seems to have been based on the assumption that the new cultural trends of the period were actually permanent changes in Western culture. Yet, looking back, we can see that this period merely witnessed a temporary change of cultural mood, which some were foolish enough to treat as a fixed and lasting change in the condition of humanity:

> In retrospect the dominant theological mood of that time in its hasty, slack, rather collective sweep reminds one a little painfully of a flight of lemmings. . . . A good deal of the more publicized theological writing in the sixties gives the impression of a sheer surge of feeling that in the modern world God, religion, the transcendent, any reliability in the gospels, anything which had formed part of the old "supernaturalist" system, had suddenly become absurd. There were plenty of fresh insights but too little stringent analysis of the new positions. Everything was to be enthusiastically "demythologized" in a euphoria of secularization which was often fairly soft on scholarly rigour.[4]

The comparison with a "flight of lemmings" is all too accurate. As we look back, the remarkable growth of the New Age movement in areas previously dominated by mainline Christianity can, at least in part, be put down to the headlong rush of radical writers and preachers to totally eliminate the supernatural and transcendent from Christianity.[5] Lots of Americans got bored with the result, and, yearning for precisely those supernatural and transcendent elements, they turned to the mystical religions of the East, to paganism and to astrology.

One of the main problems was that the theology of the 1960s turned out to be little more than a transient agglomerate of ideas and values deriving primarily from the culture in which its writers were based. This culture was increasingly dominated by a secular outlook that theology was expected to share if it was to maintain any academic or cultural credibility. Sixties-style theology slipped fatally easily from being the addresser to being the addressee of a secular culture. If it aimed to transform culture, the reverse was achieved: Christianity became transformed by culture, becoming little more than a pale and vaguely religious reflection of secular cultural trends. Thus, in its social thinking, the National Council of Churches can easily be shown to have done little more than reflect the attitudes of contemporary society.[6]

Furthermore, it soon became clear that culture was changing rapidly, constantly outpacing those who tried to keep up with its whims and fads. Peter L. Berger, one of North America's most distinguished sociologists, comments thus on the enormous difficulties facing this theological enterprise in a modern Western pluralist culture:

> The various efforts by Christians to accommodate to the "wisdom of the world" in this situation becomes a difficult, frantic and more than a little ridiculous affair. Each time that one has, after an enormous effort, managed to adjust the faith to the prevailing culture, that culture turns around and changes. . . . Our pluralistic culture forces those who would "update" Christianity into a state of permanent nervousness. The "wisdom of the world," which is the standard by which they would modify the religious tradition, varies from one social location to another; what is worse, even in the same locale it keeps on changing, often rapidly.[7]

Berger's sociological analysis makes it clear that some views will be "the accepted wisdom in one social milieu and utter foolishness in another." Or, to put it another way, there is no one universal way of thinking or set of values; secular "wisdom" is socially located, in a specific class or social group.

> *The wisdom of the world today always has a sociological address.* In consequence, every accommodation to it on the part of Christians will be "relevant" in one very specific social setting (usually determined by class), and "irrelevant" in another. Christians, then, who set out to accommodate the faith to the modern world should ask themselves which sector of that world they seek to address. Very probably, whatever *aggiornamento* they come up with will include some, exclude others. And if the *aggiornamento* is undertaken with the cultural élite in mind, then it is important to appreciate that the beliefs of this particular group are the most fickle of all.[8]

It is thus virtually meaningless to talk about "making Christianity relevant to the modern world." This implies that there is only one "modern world," whereas it is clear that there are many modern worlds. Every attempt to accommodate Christianity to the beliefs of one social grouping distances it from those of another. The paradox underlying any attempt to *make* the gospel "relevant" is that for everyone to whom the gospel is "made relevant" there are probably dozens for whom it is made irrelevant—needlessly.

The end result of this approach to Christianity is depressingly clear. Where it hoped to make mainline Christianity credible to secularists, it ended up making secularism credible to mainline Christians. In their *American Mainline Religion: Its Changing Shape and Future,* sociologists Wade Clark Roof and William McKinney provide an important study of the steady numerical decline in mainline churches. Their conclusion? In the 1990s, the challenge to mainline Christianity will not be just from "the conservatives it has spurned, but from the secularists it has spawned."[9]

Evangelicalism believes that to be right is to be relevant. It is too easy to produce a spurious relevance in response to secular pressures, often localized and transient in their nature; the task of Christian apologetics is to bring out the inherent attraction of the gospel by its faithful and responsible proclamation and presentation.[10] In other words, the best way of ensuring that Christianity remains relevant to the modern world is to be faithful to Christian orthodoxy and articulate this in terms intelligible to the world. As noted earlier, evangelicalism regards itself under a total obligation to remain faithful to the *evangel,* something that cannot and must not be compromised, and that is known to have an attraction of its own, by its very nature. It thus represents a form of Christianity that is sufficiently resilient to resist pressures to conform to its secular context and yet sufficiently attractive to provide a pressure of its own by which individuals may be drawn out of secular culture to Christian communities.

Given that secularization is likely to continue within Western culture, the future of Christianity may come increasingly to depend on evangelicalism and other versions of Christianity that retain insights that distinguish them from secular culture, while simultaneously providing an attractive alternative to it. The very public failure of the kind of liberalism described by Spong has led many to look around for a version of Christianity that makes sense and stays faithful to the gospel—and so they have turned to evangelicalism.

Evangelicalism Is Orthodox Christianity

Evangelicalism is historic Christianity. Its beliefs correspond to the central doctrines of the Christian churches down the ages, including the two most important doctrines of the patristic period: the doctrine of the "two natures," human and divine, of Jesus Christ, and the doctrine of the Trinity.[11] In its vigorous defense of the biblical foundations, theological legitimacy and spiritual relevance of these doctrines, evangelicalism has shown itself to have every right to claim to be a modern standard-bearer of historic, orthodox Christianity.[12]

As many dedicated Christians inside the mainline denominations in North America are discovering to their outrage, the commitment of those denominations to these historic doctrines is often less than wholehearted. This has led both to an increasing exodus from these churches toward explicitly evangelical denominations and to growth in the evangelical tendencies within the denominations. The continuing growth of the Southern Baptist Convention and of evangelicalism within the Church of England illustrates these trends. Another result is the formation of breakaway evangelical churches from mainline denominations. The formation of the Presbyterian Church in America (PCA) in December 1973 is a case in point. The PCA was formed as a result of disillusionment with the headlong rush toward theological liberalism in the mainline Presbyterian Church; since 1973 its membership has grown from 40,000 to 217,000 members—and is still increasing. People are voting with their feet by walking out of liberalism toward orthodoxy. If they stay inside a mainline denomination, it is usually in the hope of winning it over for the cause of orthodoxy— an approach that was adopted in relation to the Church of England back in the 1960s, with considerable success.

Many leaders within the mainline denominations received their theological education during the 1960s and 1970s, and some appear to have accepted uncritically the dominant liberal theological trends of that period. They seem unaware that such liberalism is now widely regarded as passé in academic circles and is incapable of sustaining churches in a relentlessly secularist society. They seem to be trapped in a liberal time warp where all is sweetness, roses, light and 1960s optimism. Oxford New Testament scholar Robert Morgan is one of many recent writers to point out that "the best insights of liberal theology . . . do not suffice to nourish a minority church in an aggressively secular society."[13] Liberalism may stimulate the mind; it cannot sustain a church.

There are now strong pressures within most mainstream denominations to abandon the failed experiments of the last two or three decades and return to the foundations of orthodox Christianity. Opponents of this trend, unable to comprehend this development, often mock it as a "scared fundamentalism," a "search for security" or a "quest for the certitudes of nostalgia." Whatever it is, it is certainly a reaction against the failures of a past generation and a desire to put the churches back on the road to integrity, growth and relevance.

Yet this road does not entail compromising orthodoxy. Liberalism believed that you had to change Christianity to make it acceptable. Orthodoxy believes that the gospel stays the same; we need rather to find better and more effective ways of presenting it. Christianity does not need to be *made* attractive; it *is* attractive. If there has been a failure in this regard, it is that Christians have failed to appreciate this attraction for themselves and to take the trouble to explain it to others.

The ways in which an uncompromising, orthodox gospel can be made more relevant to modern society are illustrated by a series of experiments in the Western world which have sought to eliminate all alienating factors that are not essential to the gospel itself. For example, many people are initially alienated from Christianity by the *strangeness* of traditional Christian worship—Tudor music, an eighteenth-century liturgy and clergy dressed in the style of sixteenth-century England. For some inside the churches, these are important and precious symbols of historical continuity; for most outside the church, they are evidence of an outdated and irrelevant gospel. And so the gospel is rejected on account of the cultural unacceptability of nonessential, perhaps even marginal, aspects of Christian worship!

Willow Creek Community Church is an excellent example of a church that has pioneered an approach that breaks down these incidental barriers. The church auditorium has none of the traditional ecclesiastical trappings. There are no pulpit, no organ, no hymnals and no traditional clerical vestments. Yet the gospel is proclaimed effectively. The U.S. religious magazine *Guideposts* named Willow Creek "1989 Church of the Year" for "presenting timeless truth in a contemporary way."

This approach has its critics: the Easter 1990 Sunday supplement of *USA Today* described Willow Creek as "McChurch," implying it was the religious equivalent of the fast-food chain McDonald's. But there is no doubt that this church and an increasing number of imitators throughout the Western world are getting a hearing for the gospel among those who would regard a traditional church setting as a no-go zone.

Evangelicalism Makes Sense!
One of the most important developments within evangelicalism since World War II is an outbreak of confidence in its own intellectual credentials. In the old days evangelicalism was widely seen as strictly for the uneducated and illiterate, an impression that was reinforced by the intellectual fallout from the Scopes trial (1925). "No thinking man can take evangelicalism seriously" was the (noninclusive) watchword of much liberal academic theology in the immediate postwar period. Indeed, academic integrity was widely seen as the exclusive prerogative of liberal writers, who encouraged the view that a concern for the contemporary intellectual climate is a unique, or even a *defining,* fea-

ture of liberalism.

Yet Thomas Aquinas took seriously the Aristotelianism of the thirteenth-century University of Paris in writing both his *Summa Contra Gentiles* and *Summa Theologiae*. I have yet to find Aquinas described as a liberal for that reason! A more modern example will make this point unequivocally clear. One of the most significant contributions to the modern philosophy of religion comes from a group of American writers, including Alvin Plantinga and Nicholas Wolterstorff. Their discussion of the theme of "faith and rationality" has become a landmark in recent debates centering on this theme.[14] Yet the group has no inclination whatsoever toward liberalism; instead it represents what one might call the classic Reformed approach, drawing its inspiration from the writings of John Calvin. In short: there is nothing distinctively "liberal" about being academically serious and culturally informed. Through the work of philosophers such as C. Stephen Evans and theologians such as Thomas C. Oden, James I. Packer and David F. Wells, evangelicalism is now well on its way to gaining an academic credibility and respectability that would have been unthinkable a generation ago.

Although the Lutheran and Wesleyan traditions have made important contributions to evangelicalism as a whole, it is generally agreed that the renewed intellectual confidence within evangelicalism owes no small debt to its Reformed heritage. The distinguished German historian Karl Holl once wrote that "one must be clear that a good deal of the penetrating power of Calvinism depends upon its intellectualism. Calvinists know what they believe, and why they believe it."[15] The rediscovery of the contemporary relevance and vitality of the great Puritan writer Jonathan Edwards has been one of the most important landmarks in this rehabilitation of evangelical theology and has given evangelicalism a new confidence in its own heritage.[16] There is new interest in the writings and ideas of the Old Princeton School, which gave nineteenth-century American evangelicalism an intellectual resilience that persisted until the rise of modernism in the 1920s diverted evangelicalism into countercultural measures of an often anti-intellectual nature. The Reformed Theology conferences organized by James M. Boice (Philadelphia) ensure the continuing high profile of this tradition in North America, in a manner that parallels the Puritan conferences of the late 1950s and early 1960s, organized in London by Packer and Lloyd-Jones. The same pattern can be discerned in Australia: under the principalships of T. C. Hammond (1936-1953) and D. B. Knox (1959-1985), Moore College, Sydney, has emerged as a major center for Reformed thought in the region. Moore College places a strong emphasis on the objective aspects of the Christian faith, which represents a much needed corrective to the more experiential orientations of other forms of evangelicalism in the region.[17]

In North America, the foundation of the Evangelical Theological Society has been an important element in this consolidation of academic excellence, as has the growing academic presence and reputation of leading evangelical centers of scholarship and research, such as Fuller Seminary, Reformed Theological Seminary, Regent College (Vancouver), Trinity Evangelical Divinity School and Westminster Seminary. The emergence of these centers is partly a response to the realization that evangelicalism requires excellent academic credentials if it is to consolidate existing advances and prepare for those that lie ahead. In England several major recent academic theological appointments have gone to evangelicals, with a new interest in evangelicalism being evident in the formation of the Oxford Evangelical Theological Society in 1993. While there are reasons for being concerned about the long-term future of this intellectual renaissance,[18] the present turnabout in the academic reputation of evangelicalism seems undeniably hopeful, provided appropriate measures are taken to ensure its continuation.

My own history is a testimony to this development. I was brought up in Northern Ireland in the 1960s and soon developed an intense dislike for Christianity. Like many young people during that decade, I came to believe that the future would be dominated by Marxism, a philosophy of life that I myself adopted with all the enthusiasm of youth. I went up to Oxford University in 1971, having chosen a suitably left-wing college (Wadham) to ensure that I would continue to grow personally in a politically correct environment. However, at this moment in my life things started to work out somewhat differently from what I had planned. Shortly after my arrival, I discovered Christianity through the witness of the Oxford Inter-Collegiate Christian Union, the local arm of the Inter-Varsity Fellowship. Like many others, I discovered the enormous appeal of the gospel and made a decision to become a Christian.

I also decided that I would be a thinking Christian; with this end in view I began the study of theology at Oxford in 1976, after gaining my doctorate in molecular biology. I immediately discovered that evangelicalism was regarded as intellectually challenged. More than one of the people who taught me made it clear that part of their job was to rid me of my evangelical views, for which they had little but contempt. One of them subsequently told me, many years later, that his personal mission in life was "to make conservative evangelicals into liberal Protestants." A climax was reached in 1977, when two books were published that seemed to hammer the last academic nail into evangelicalism's coffin. James Barr's *Fundamentalism* dismissed British evangelicalism as academically worthless; the collection of essays entitled *The Myth of God Incarnate* rejected the doctrine of the Incarnation as an outdated and irrelevant hangover from an earlier age, which could no longer be taken seriously by thinking people.[19] The impression created was unambiguous: evangelicalism was for those of impaired rationality and flawed personality.

In fact, these works are now seen to represent the high tide of liberalism, which has been in irreversible decline ever since. The reaction to *The Myth of God Incarnate* neatly illustrates the dead end into which the prevailing theological trends had led. As the noted historian of modern English Christianity Adrian Hastings observes:

If *The Myth* produced excitement, it was principally the smirking excitement of an agnostic world amused to witness the white flag hoisted so enthusiastically above the long-beleaguered citadel of Christian belief, the stunned excitement of the rank and file of weary defenders on learning that their staff officers had so lightheartedly ratted on them. It was hardly surprising that more than one of the contributors soon after ceased, even in a nominal sense, to be Christian believers, or that Don Cupitt, one of the most forceful and publicity minded of the group, published only two years later his commitment to objective atheism.[20]

The book delighted non-Christians, perplexed an increasingly irritated Christian public and convinced many within the churches that the dominant religious liberalism had nothing to offer the church or the world.

Yet I was deeply influenced by these works—not perhaps so much by their ideas but by their general tenor. The message they projected was crystal-clear: evangelicalism was defunct and could not be taken with any seriousness by the academy. I found my confidence in my own evangelicalism severely eroded, and it was only after a period of reconsideration that I was able to regain my assurance. By 1983 that process was complete, and I returned to Oxford to teach theology.

One of my personal life goals, which results directly from my 1977 experience, is both to consolidate and to demonstrate the academic credibility of evangelicalism. My work as a scholar, speaker and writer has centered on the defense of the intellectual foundations of the gospel. It is a great joy to me to know that the enormous attraction of evangelicalism rests on solid foundations. Having been attracted to evangelicalism in 1971, I can now appreciate its intellectual caliber as well, and I intend to pursue and advocate the intellectual, as well as the spiritual, attraction of evangelicalism in the remainder of my ministry.

Evangelicalism Stresses the Attraction of the Gospel

Evangelicalism is committed to evangelism—that is, the proclamation of the gospel in the full confidence that it contains something God-given that will enable it to find a response in the hearts and minds of men and women. Evangelism is natural to evangelicals. "The church," wrote Emil Brunner, "lives by mission as a fire lives by burning."

Evangelism is something intrinsic to the identity of the church—not an optional extra, but something that is part and parcel of its very being.

To give such an emphasis to evangelism is thus to recognize both the inherent *rightness* of the gospel and its intrinsic attractiveness. That attraction is supremely the person of Jesus Christ. It is a "pearl of great price," something that is recognized to be worth seeking and possessing, and whose possession overshadows everything else. Evangelicalism thus fosters an attitude of expectation—an expectation that the gospel will be a delight and joy to others. This is coupled with a systematic endeavor to uncover the ways in which the inherent appeal of the gospel can be best articulated, in the certainty that this appeal rests on a reliable and responsible historical and theological foundation.

It must be stressed that there is no question of altering the gospel to make it more attractive. For evangelicalism, that is the supreme error of liberalism—doing violence to the gospel itself in an attempt to make it more easily acceptable to modern culture. The issue is ensuring that the gospel is preached faithfully for all it is worth, without the misrepresentations that cause offense to so many. As Kenneth S. Kantzer puts it,

> We are certainly not interested in shaping evangelical Christianity, and certainly not biblical Christianity, into a form that will prove palatable to the sinful hearts and minds of all humans. We are not trying to remove the "offense of the cross." That offense is an inherent part of biblical and evangelical identity. It would be an irresponsible denial of our deepest faith to remove it. Yet we are deeply concerned also to remove false obstacles to the gospel. We do not want anyone to reject a perversion or misunderstanding of the gospel.[21]

Responsible evangelism, by seeking to remain faithful to the gospel, ensures that its proper and inherent attraction—rather than something spurious and fabricated—is presented to the world.

Many secular writers respond to this emphasis on evangelism by reaching for the nearest cliché and writing of "Christian imperialism"; others suggest that the churches have become obsessed with marketing their product, presenting evangelism as some kind of religious public-relations industry.

Both these comments are deeply revealing of the failure of an increasingly secular society to understand the fundamental motivation for evangelism. For there is something intrinsic in the Christian faith that leads to a natural connection between faith and evangelism. The fundamental motivation for evangelism is generosity—the basic human concern to share the good things of life with those we love. It does not reflect a desire to sell or dominate; it arises from love and compassion on the part of those who have found something wonderful and want others to share in its joy. It is, as the old adage has it, like one beggar telling another where to find bread.

A central task of evangelism is to make Christianity credible in the modern world. The area of Christian thought that has dealt with this matter is apologetics—the "defense of the faith," to give a rough translation of the Greek word *apologia,* used in 1 Peter 3:15. A good working definition of *apologetics* would be "the attempt to create an intellectual climate favorable to Christian faith" or "a concern to enhance the public plausibility of the gospel." In the past, apologetics has been a significant aspect of the ongoing mission of the church, to which evangelicals have made a contribution.

Yet the situation in which the Western church finds itself has radically changed, with the dawn of a post-Enlightenment world. The rise of the movement usually called postmodernism, which I shall consider in more detail in a later chapter, is a telling sign of the loss of confidence in reason and "modern" ideas and values in today's culture. The rise of postmodernism reflects the seriously eroded credibility of a universal rationality once regarded as central to "liberal" theological method. As one leading liberal commentator has remarked,

> Liberalism lost its cultural hegemony largely because of the demythologization of its allies, universal rationalism and science. At one time we thought them not only our finest sources of truth but our

surest means to human ennoblement. Today the sophisticated know that they deal only in possible "constructions of reality," and the masses sense that they commend ethical relativism more than necessary values and duties.[22]

Liberalism has thus lost its credibility in the area of apologetics; that mantle has passed to evangelicalism. And evangelicalism is becoming increasingly confident in its presentation of both the truth and the attractiveness of the gospel.

However, for many people, a concern with "truth" has become irrelevant. The first question people tend to ask these days is not "Is this right?" but "What will this do for me?" The rise of what Tom Wolfe called the "Me Generation" has necessarily led to a focusing of apologetics on the relevance of the gospel to the needs of individuals. This person-centered apologetics aims to remain faithful to the gospel while ensuring that it fully addresses the contemporary situation.[23]

But we do not need to throw away Christianity's claims to truth in the light of this cultural development. We just need to realize that it is now bad tactics to major on the truth question. If we are going to get a hearing in today's culture, we need to be able to show that Christianity has something relevant and attractive to offer. The bonus is that this attraction is securely grounded in God's self-revelation, not invented yesterday in an effort to get a hearing in the marketplace. Thus we may commend the attractiveness of Christianity while resting securely in the knowledge of its truth. The attractiveness of a belief is too often inversely proportional to its truth. The Christian, in enthusing about the attractiveness of the gospel and its enormous potential to transform human life, can be certain that the gospel rests on the bedrock of revealed truth and that acceptance of the gospel glorifies God as well as transforming human life.

But we need to take the trouble to relate the message to its audience. The gospel presentation must be receptor-oriented—we need to be sensitive to the hurts, needs and concerns of individuals. That means appreciating the wonder of the gospel and thinking through its potential attraction for others.

Evangelicalism Shuns "Denominational Sovereignty"

As this chapter draws to its close, a final issue must be noted. One of the factors that has crippled attempts at collaboration among mainline denominations has been the issue of "denominational sovereignty." This term was coined by Francis Potter at the 1944 Golden Jubilee of the Foreign Missions Conference of North America to refer to the struggle of various Protestant denominations to dominate any cooperative movements of which they participated. Within both the World Council of Churches and the National Council of Churches (NCC) in the United States, the institutional interests of the denominations are fought over, often with a ferocity that alarms their constituent members. In addition to its commitment to an outdated liberal theology that nobody seems to want anymore, the NCC has to cope with the strident ecclesiological claims of its constituent churches. It is little wonder that the NCC has seemed to lurch from one crisis to another.[24]

In part, the success and attraction of evangelicalism rests on its relative immunity to such petty squabbles. Evangelicalism has been no stranger to controversy; yet the fact that it is not a denomination in itself has allowed evangelicals of all kinds to see themselves as committed to something that transcends denominational divisions and rivalries.[25] An evangelical inside a mainline denomination, for example, will feel a far greater sense of affinity with fellow evangelicals outside that denomination than with fellow members of that denomination who deny or challenge central aspects of the Christian faith.

But the real points at issue run much deeper than this and center on the role of charismatic leaders and the necessity of a specific church structure for ensuring salvation of church members. By playing down the importance of denominational allegiance, evangelicalism is able to maximize the use of charismatic gifts among its leaders—gifts that would probably be suppressed within mainline denominations. The importance of this point may be appreciated if we consider the situation in Latin America, where evangelicalism is making huge advances at the expense of the Roman Catholic Church.[26] One of the reasons for this is the rise of charismatic leaders:

It is in leadership that evangelical churches have their greatest advantage over the Catholic church. The high profile of foreign missionaries and autocratic pastors can obscure an important point about evangelical leadership: the ever-available principle of separation. Those who get fed up with their spiritual mentors start their own churches, which is how the rapidly growing number of Latin American denominations began. This free-enterprise, leveling form of ministry is quite a contrast to the authority structure of the Catholic Church, whose origin in the Roman Empire makes it the oldest bureaucracy in the world. Whereas evangelical structures provide ample room for the power of personal charisma, enabling new leaders to organize their own, equally legitimate churches, the Catholic structure of appointment from above is calculated to keep charisma under strict control, if not stifle it altogether. It is not hard to see which system will prosper at a time in history which ruptures old social bonds and forces personal initiative. Evangelicals can break away and remain evangelical, but Catholics who reject the authority of their clergy may well become evangelicals.[27]

It is at this point that the second factor noted above comes into the equation. Evangelicalism insists that it is not necessary to be a member of a specific denomination in order to be saved; it is necessary only to repent of one's sins and believe the true gospel. The Roman Catholic Church, however, generally remains committed to the more restricted idea that it is necessary to be a member of the "true church"—which, historically, it has identified as itself—in order to be saved. Although the Second Vatican Council softened this position significantly, the maxim "Outside the church there is no salvation" *(extra ecclesiam nulla salus)* continues to have a deep impact on Catholic reflection.

Evangelicalism rejects the idea that "the church" can in any way be equated with one ecclesiastical body. The true church is found wherever the gospel is truly preached and truly received. Denominational allegiance is ultimately of less than ultimate significance; the criterion of being saved has nothing to do with which church or fellowship one attends, but with whether one has heard and responded to the gospel.

In an age in which social mobility has emerged as a major cultural force, evangelical ecclesiology has proved to be a winner.

Let me stress that I am not for one moment suggesting that this evangelical view of the church was formulated in an opportunistic manner, with an eye to benefiting from this development! I am simply pointing out that this long-standing aspect of evangelicalism happens to meet up exactly with a significant current in the global cultural changes of our times.

Consider, then, the position of a Roman Catholic family in Brazil who are fed up with the teachings of their church and decide to leave. So where do they go? By definition, there is no other Roman Catholic church for them to go to. But there are lots of evangelical denominations, all offering scripturally grounded promises of salvation and more attractive styles of worship and prayer. The result? Inevitably there is a natural tendency for disaffected Roman Catholics who wish to retain their Christian faith to become evangelicals.

Now consider an evangelical Brazilian family who are fed up with their denomination's views on some issue and decide to switch denominations. Where do they go? The answer is quite simple: they have a wide range of choices of evangelical churches and communities. They can move around within the vast spread of evangelicalism without having to stop being evangelicals. Diversity within evangelicalism over matters of only relative importance (including the personality of their pastors) allows agreement over essentials.

Conclusion

The present chapter has sketched out some of the features of evangelicalism that are known to contribute to its attraction to many modern Christians. Yet the picture sketched in this chapter runs the risk of being too optimistic, perhaps even unrealistic at points. There are a number of serious matters of a more negative nature that need to be addressed. The remainder of this work will take up these issues and suggest means of dealing with them. The first such issue to be addressed is whether evangelicalism is falling apart.

4

A LOSS OF VISION? EVANGELICAL EXPANSION & A CRISIS OF IDENTITY

S INCE 1950, EVANGELICALISM HAS CONTINUED TO EXPAND AND
consolidate its influence, and at present there are no reasons to
suppose that this expansion is ending. Indeed, a variety of factors, such as the continuing evangelical commitment to evangelism and enhanced approaches to pastoral care, point to its continuing growth. But with that expansion has come a difficulty: numerical
growth has led to a growing fuzziness and the risk of a potentially
disastrous loss of vision.

Diversification Within Evangelicalism

Gabriel Fackre of Andover Newton School of Theology, writing as
both participant in and observer of modern American evangelicalism,
argues that "contemporary evangelicalism is no undivided empire." He
discerns at least six varieties of evangelicals, as follows:

1. Fundamentalists. Here "ultra-inerrancy is the criterion of faithfulness," associated with the "polemical and separatist mentality that
characterizes every religious and secular fundamentalism." The move-

ment is often apolitical but can be associated with right-wing political causes.

2. Old evangelicals. Here the experiential (or "affective") side of faith assumes priority, with the "personal experience of regeneration being of decisive importance, together with its expression in mass evangelism."

3. New evangelicals. Here Fackre refers to "neo-evangelicalism" with its characteristic emphases on "the social import of faith and its apologetic persuasiveness."

4. Justice and peace evangelicals. These "activist evangelicals advocate a political agenda drastically at variance with the Religious Right." In many ways this strand in contemporary evangelicalism consciously picks up a radical political agenda associated with Anabaptist roots in the sixteenth century.

5. Charismatic evangelicals. This section of the movement places emphasis on "glossolalia, healing and celebrative worship," with a strong emphasis on the person and work of the Holy Spirit.

6. Ecumenical evangelicals. This group, "more a tendency than a constituency," is concerned to move evangelicalism "toward relationships with the larger Christian community." Of particular importance are its "alliances with mainline Christians on common social concerns."[1]

I cite this taxonomy not to endorse it but simply to illustrate how the diversity within evangelicalism is perceived by a sympathetic and informed observer.

Diversity, it must be stressed, does not and need not imply that things are falling to pieces. However, there is a real danger that a lack of evangelical focus or shared concerns will lead to factionalism. In particular, there is serious danger that an apparently increasing lack of interest in matters of doctrine may come to erode the core of the movement.

For example, in the United States there is evidence of a severe loss of doctrinal vision within the Southern Baptist Convention. This loss of vision can easily arise through a lack of concern for one's heritage.

In their recent survey of Baptist thought, especially in the United States, Timothy George and David S. Dockery identify the following sentiment as increasingly prevalent among Baptists: "Baptists are not essentially a doctrinal people. We have no creed but the Bible, which everyone should be left to interpret according to his or her personal predilection. The basic criterion of theology is individual experience. . . . Baptist means freedom, freedom to think, believe and preach without constraints."[2] It also, as George and Dockery point out, can easily come to mean "rootless." This "full-blown ideology of indifference" has obvious parallels within many other mainline denominations.

One of the more perceptive observers of the trend away from a concern for matters of doctrine and theology in modern American evangelicalism is David F. Wells, professor of historical and systematic theology at Gordon-Conwell Theological Seminary. As Wells points out, it is easy to understand why this development has taken place. The move from prewar fundamentalism to postwar evangelicalism involved loosening up on the idea of doctrine as a cultural barrier:

> In the 1920s, 1930s and 1940s, Fundamentalists were clearly cognitive aliens within the culture and often used doctrine to define their own cultural boundaries. Doctrine served to seal in believers and seal out unbelievers. . . . They held to an inspired, authoritative Bible and to the centrality and indispensability of Christ's substitutionary death on the cross. These beliefs were then hedged about by supporting doctrines the role of which, it would seem, was quite as much to alienate an unbelieving culture as it was to preserve Christian orthodoxy.[3]

The more world-affirming attitude typical of the "new evangelicalism" of the 1950s inevitably led to an erosion of this social role of doctrine. As Wells puts it, evangelicalism "has reacted against this sense of psychological isolation. It has lowered the barricades. The great sin in fundamentalism is to compromise; the great sin in evangelicalism is to be narrow."[4] The tight sense of definition to which a concern for doctrine gave rise is unquestionably being lost in modern American evangelicalism.

In England, older evangelicals often suggest that there has been a distinct blurring of definition and loss of coherence since the 1930s and 1940s. In those days, they argue, evangelicalism was a well-defined and coherent movement. True, it was a small movement, which more or less deliberately chose to center itself on doctrinal forms of self-definition. The relatively few people who were attracted to this somewhat attenuated version of evangelicalism thus found themselves united by a core of doctrinal conviction. A shared persecution complex is a significant nontheological element in contributing to the sense of corporate identity within a movement.[5]

With the massive growth of the evangelical presence in the English national church, a degree of diversification began to set in as evangelicalism began to address new issues. These ventures into unfamiliar territory caused alarm to many older evangelicals. A nostalgia for the good old days began to develop. Hardly anyone had been an evangelical in those days, admittedly, but at least those who were had known what they meant by the word. Numerical weakness could be seen almost as a positive matter: the fewer we are, the more we can agree with each other. This form of evangelicalism has subsequently shown itself largely incapable of coping with the growth in the movement, and it has reacted by forming small subsets or pressure groups within which a tight doctrinal identity can be maintained. These groups consider themselves to represent a pure form of evangelicalism in the midst of a corrupt and confused movement.

Yet this, it must be stressed, is the inevitable outcome of an expanding movement. An analogy will perhaps bring out the point. In 1968 Leszek Kolakowski was dismissed from his position as professor of history of philosophy at the University of Warsaw, Poland. He had run afoul of the somewhat rigid Marxist orthodoxy then gripping that nation. Settling in Oxford, he took the opportunity of chronicling the development of Marxism from its origins in the 1830s through its "golden age" to its internal confusion and decline in the second half of the twentieth century.[6] There are, it may be noted, strong parallels between Marxism and evangelicalism, not least in the manner in which an international movement fired and sustained by ideas develops, consolidates and adapts to new contexts and situations. Commenting on the expansion of Marxism, Kolakowski remarks: "It is a well-known fact, to which history records no exception, that all important ideas are subject to division and differentiation as their influence continues to spread."[7] The same development may be seen in the early expansion of Christianity itself, especially in the way it adapted as it addressed local situations and opportunities and different cultures and world-views. And precisely the same pattern can be seen in the recent history of evangelicalism.

The price of expansion is an increasing diffuseness and, potentially, a loss of identity and vision. Occasionally one gains the impression that some evangelicals would be happier if the movement continued to be a despised minority presence within the churches, an outlook that could easily become a self-fulfilling prophecy. Yet evangelicalism must plan on the basis of the assumption that it will have to cope with the pressures and challenges of being mainline.

Cohesion and Contextualization

One of the most astute analyses of this issue comes from James I. Packer in a careful and highly influential study of the problems facing a distinctively evangelical ethos within the Church of England:

> Critics sometimes say that today's evangelical Anglicans are utterly different from their fathers, but judging them by those evangelical essentials which we spelt out [earlier] one is struck most forcibly by the depth of continuity. That today's evangelicals understand themselves and their faith in essentially the same terms as did their fathers, and have essentially the same goals in life and ministry, seems too plain to be denied. But, just as a ship can only stay on course as the steering is adjusted to meet wind, tide, currents and other hazards, so Anglican evangelicals can only stay on course— that is, steadily pursue the defined goal of spreading pure Christi-

anity, by God's power and for God's praise—by responding with appropriate adaptations to what goes on in the church and the community around. This is the truth embedded in Newman's dictum (so objectionable, in the form in which he developed it) that to remain the same a thing must change often.[8]

There is a temptation to believe that both unity and an assured common identity can be achieved only by insistence on holding fast to the established evangelical traditions of the past. Yet this threatens to place human tradition above the Word of God. It is an integral part of the evangelical ethos to judge everything in the light of Scripture. The possibility that the evangelicals of yesterday may have got things wrong must be upheld and explored.

The future belongs to those who can relate the heritage of the past to the realities of the present. This cannot be done by a mere repetition of, for example, Calvin's church polity. Calvin's genius lay in his interpretation and application of the gospel to sixteenth-century Geneva. The gospel remains the same; yet modern New York and London bear little relation to Calvin's Geneva. The faithful disciples of Calvin are not those who slavishly repeat his every move, but those who, like him, pasionately and prayerfully seek to relate the gospel to their own situation. Calvin's own followers showed remarkable skill in applying the Calvinist tradition to situations in the Lowlands, England and North America, which were far removed from Calvin's Geneva.[9] Evangelicalism has shown a remarkable ability to embed itself in a wide variety of cultural contexts, precisely because it has taken the trouble to link the gospel with the experiential worlds of those to whom it has proclaimed that gospel.

I have already used Marxism as an example of a movement that has undergone alterations in its developments. One of the questions that troubled many Marxist writers in the early part of the twentieth century was this: Why has Marxism totally failed to gain a following in the United States, when, on the basis of its European experience, it ought to be building up a massive following? A ferocious debate resulted between two leading Marxist theoreticians, Karl Kautsky and

Edward Bernstein.[10] Bernstein's explanation has won wide acceptance: Marxism failed to win a following in the United States because its outlook was too deeply embedded in the social situation of 1830s Germany. It did not relate to the social realities of twentieth-century America, and Marxist theoreticians were making no effort to alter this situation by interpreting Marxism in a North American context. In short, it had become so conditioned by its original context that it failed to relate to dissimilar contexts.

As is well known, one of the reasons Christianity failed to gain a significant foothold in China during the late nineteenth century was that it was perceived as something Western and thus as totally alien to Chinese culture. Especially in Japan, Christianity was stigmatized as a Western phenomenon. The nineteenth-century Japanese colloquial term for Christianity was *bata kusai,* "it tastes of butter," referring to the fact that both butter and Christianity were seen as Western imports to the region! There is a danger that evangelicalism may come to be so wedded to a Western context, especially a North American context, that it cannot relate adequately to others, such as mainland China or even mainland Europe. Indeed, some Europeans today stereotype evangelicalism as "made in America"[11] and hence just as non-European as Disneyland.[12]

The history of evangelicalism suggests that the success of the movement rests on its willingness to be open to the context in which it finds itself, rather than woodenly repeating the solutions of the past. The issue is applying Scripture to new and hitherto unexperienced contexts rather than slavishly repeating interpretations of Scripture for a different cultural context. Wells comments thus on the task of evangelical theology:

> It is the task of theology, then, to discover what God has said in and through Scripture and to clothe that in a conceptuality which is native to our own age. Scripture, at its *terminus a quo,* needs to be de-contextualized in order to grasp its transcultural content, and it needs to be re-contextualized in order that its content may be meshed with the cognitive assumptions and social patterns of our own time.[13]

113

The approach adopted is classic: identify what Scripture is saying and apply it to new contexts. But both interpretation and application have generated differences within evangelicalism. As the context changes, there is a need to ensure that the gospel proclamation is related to that context.

This implies no change in the gospel; it implies only commitment on the part of the evangelist, preacher and theologian to ensure that the gospel is particularized in that context. It is a simple fact of history that yesterday's evangelical particularization is all too often today's evangelical embarrassment. Edward J. Carnell, former president of Fuller Seminary, once commented, "Fundamentalists defend the gospel, to be sure, but they sometimes act as if the gospel read, 'Believe on the Lord Jesus Christ, don't smoke, don't go to movies, and above all don't use the Revised Standard Version—and you will be saved.' "[14] These were all real issues back in the early 1950s. Forty years further down the road of history, they seem to belong to another world.[15] A wooden repetition of yesterday's ideas may alienate today's people from the gospel—not because the *gospel* is alienating, but because *a particular presentation of the gospel* is seen as out of touch, out of date and out of place. Advance involves adaptation—but adaptation need not involve change.

The Search for an Identity

A further issue must also be addressed. Those who argue that evangelicalism has lost its former tightness of definition generally do so on the basis of the assumption that "tight is right." But this assumption is vulnerable. The rigidity of evangelicalism in the past reflects its precarious position within the churches and society. It would be a mistake to assume that the way evangelicalism was in 1900 or even 1950 must define the way it will be in 2000. Those who complain of the diversification of evangelicalism need to ask themselves in all seriousness whether the phenomenon in question reflects the improper present fuzziness of the movement or its improper past rigidity. Their assumption that it is the former is most certainly not the only option.

There is always going to be a temptation for a movement to impose an identity upon itself without taking the trouble to ensure that this general tactic is justified or that the profile adopted is commensurate with its tradition. There is a real danger that evangelicalism, sensing the need for a distinct identity, will define itself overprecisely, negatively or reactively. In an earlier chapter I pointed out that there is a natural affinity among evangelicals, based on six general beliefs. To add to these would run the risk of alienating or disfranchising a substantial number of evangelicals through an unjustifiably attenuated understanding of what evangelicalism actually is. The more rigid the definition of evangelicalism, the greater the number of people who are in fact evangelicals who will be improperly excluded—including Martin Luther, John Calvin and Jonathan Edwards, each of whom could easily be excluded by some of the more experimental definitions of "evangelical" offered by well-meaning yet historically uninformed enthusiasts.

A serious issue of power is at stake as well. For any one evangelical or group of evangelicals to lay down what evangelicals shall and shall not believe is to claim to possess authority to legislate on behalf of evangelicalism as a whole.

The most important strategy for the conservation and nourishment of a sense of evangelical identity is to rediscover the roots of the movement, especially in the New Testament and the sixteenth-century Reformation. The evangelical emphasis on Scripture as the source of theology and the ultimate criterion for Christian living ensures that diversity within evangelicalism can only be a biblically legitimated diversity. In other words, diversity within evangelicalism is to be tolerated where a corresponding diversity can be demonstrated within Scripture. Where Scripture itself contains or legitimates a range of approaches, evangelicalism must expect a comparable range of approaches to be present within its ranks. To suppress this diversity in an attempt to increase cohesion is potentially to distort the biblical foundations of the Christian faith.

The slogan *ecclesia reformata, ecclesia semper reformanda* ("the reformed church is a church that must always be reforming itself") is thus of vital importance to evangelicalism in its continuing quest for identity, for it shows that reformation is a continuous process of correlating Scripture and the issues of today, rather than a slavish repetition of yesterday's solutions. Such solutions may well be right and appropriate—in which case the process of examination will reveal this and legitimate their continuing use. But they might not be. They might rest on errors of judgment, interpretation or translation, or on social or political assumptions that were acceptable in the past but are so no longer.

The Reformation itself also remains an essential element in evangelical self-understanding. Packer has argued that one of the most important ways of preserving or enhancing evangelical cohesiveness is to return to the roots of the movement at the time of the Reformation:

> There is a big risk of fragmentation. Modern evangelicalism is simply too worldly, and the influence of the world is usually always a fragmenting influence. I think perhaps that evangelicalism in America hasn't yet learned the way of unity on anything except the outward trappings of united evangelistic efforts. . . . When it comes to goals and objectives beyond evangelism, then I think that evangelicals are very seriously divided. . . . So I see grave risks of fragmentation down the road. The only thing that can unite us is a bigger, broader, wider and more generally agreed upon theology. And I find that theology only in the Reformation heritage.[16]

Packer here puts his finger on a tried and tested technique: using the evangelical heritage as what the British social psychologist John Bowlby has termed a "secure base," on which we may ground our attempts to ensure that evangelicalism interlocks with contemporary issues and concerns.[17] Evangelicalism thus remains anchored and can maintain a degree of security against the ever-present danger of drifting with the latest cultural current.

An excellent example of an organization concerned to promote this vision is Christians United for Reformation (CURE), based in Anaheim, California. The vision of the organization is to enable modern evangelicalism to rediscover its roots in the writings of the Reformers and to heighten awareness of the ideas and methods developed by those Reformers in addressing the issues of their day. The organization is not sectarian or separatist but is concerned to enable denominations, or groups within denominations, to recover a sense of identity and purpose grounded in this foundational period of evangelical history. The strongly pastoral orientation of the theology of the Reformation, for example, is shown to make it an invaluable resource for the church today.

Other individuals and movements in evangelical history also merit close study, especially the Puritans and the Wesleys. A growing evangelical awareness of family history is an important means of giving the movement a sense of historical location and rootedness, as well as access to theological, pastoral and spiritual resources that can be of continuing relevance to the churches. It cannot be emphasized too much that evangelicalism has a family history of which it is painfully unaware. The rediscovery of that heritage is of major importance to the long-term future of the movement. Now I turn to explore its relevance to the quest for a distinctively evangelical spirituality, unquestionably one of the most important challenges to face modern evangelicalism.

5

THE QUEST
FOR AN EVANGELICAL
SPIRITUALITY

S PIRITUALITY" IS ONE OF THE MOST RAPIDLY DEVELOPING
fields of Christian thought and practice. It has caught hold of
the imaginations of many people, especially in the United
States. The New Age movement is seen by many observers as
a reaction against the spiritual aridity and barrenness of modern culture. There is a real thirst for the "spiritual" element in life. Yet this
has as often led people away from Christianity as it has toward it. In
his celebrated study *Alternative Altars,* Robert S. Ellwood drew attention to the spiraling interest in all forms of spirituality. Many of
them are quite openly and profoundly anti-Christian.[1] This new interest in spirituality has thus brought dangers as well as opportunities for
the Christian churches, and there is a real need to adopt a critical
perspective toward this development.

Evangelicalism has not been immune from this new interest in spirituality. Despite its many strengths, some sense that the movement can
too easily become dry and cerebral, lacking any real spiritual vitality.
Earlier I noted the comment of the German historian Karl Holl, that

"a good deal of the penetrating power of Calvinism depends upon its intellectualism. Calvinists know what they believe, and why they believe it."[2] Yet intellectualism, as the rise of the New Age has made clear, can be spiritually arid. Intellectual resilience must be supplemented by spiritual vitality.

As evangelicalism moves to claim the intellectual high ground in Western Christianity, there is a real danger that it may neglect the needs of the human heart. There is a tension within evangelicalism over this issue, especially between those who define evangelicalism primarily with reference to explicitly theological propositions and those who emphasize the individual experience of faith and personal holiness.[3]

The question whether there are distinctively evangelical approaches to spirituality, which might enable us to consolidate still further the appeal and hold of the gospel proclamation, is thus clearly of considerable importance. For reasons that I will explore presently, there is a real need to develop evangelical forms of spirituality that are faithful to the gospel on the one hand and to the pressures of modern life on the other. The powerful thrust of major evangelistic campaigns runs the risk of being dissipated unless those who come to faith are kept *in* faith by every proper means of spiritual nourishment, encouragement and guidance. Some come to faith because of the power of an evangelistic sermon, delivered by a preacher skilled in the art of delivery and a master of oratory. Yet the content of that sermon may live on only in the presence and personality of the preacher. The sense of immediacy, of personal dynamism and excitement, is lost once the preacher moves on. A new believer is left behind to discover the full implications of that important decision to begin the Christian life and adjust accordingly. It is here that Christian spirituality has a vital role to play.

At the height of the Great Awakening in eighteenth-century Massachusetts, a young woman convert wrote a letter to Jonathan Edwards. She had come to faith; now she needed guidance, as she put it, as to "the best manner of *maintaining* a religious life." In that letter may be seen an anticipation of the modern realization of the need for follow-up in relation to evangelism. One of the most significant aspects of the Springboard initiative within Anglicanism, headed up by Michael Green and Michael Marshall, has been the realization of the vital role of spirituality in a considered and realistic approach to evangelism. Green has stressed the importance of apologetics prior to evangelism and spirituality subsequent to it. Apologetics is seen as leading naturally into evangelism, which in turn naturally leads on to spirituality as a means of keeping converts and enabling them to grow in faith. An earlier emphasis on evangelistic techniques has been supplemented by a recognition of the need for the long-term spiritual care of those who come to faith. Evangelism makes Christians; spirituality keeps them.

On December 11, 1989, James I. Packer was installed as the first Sangwoo Youtong Chee Professor of Theology at Regent College, Vancouver. The title he chose for his inaugural lecture, as much as its content, is telling: "An Introduction to Systematic Spirituality." In that lecture Packer spelled out the importance of spirituality to all concerned with the preaching and ministry of the gospel:

> We cannot function well as counsellors, spiritual directors, and guides to birth, growth and maturity in Christ, unless we are clear as to what constitutes spiritual well-being as opposed to spiritual lassitude or exhaustion, and to stunted and deformed spiritual development. It thus appears that the study of spirituality is just as necessary for us who hope to minister in the gospel as is the study of physiology for the medical trainee. It is something that we cannot really manage without.[4]

My concern is that evangelicals have not paid anything like the necessary attention to this major theme of Christian life and thought. As a result, evangelicalism has become impoverished where it ought to be rich; it has depended on the insights of others, whereas it ought to be contributing to the life of the church. I wish to suggest that the time has come to throw off the cult of dependency and move toward the development and rediscovery of spiritualities that will complement the

great evangelical emphases on the sufficiency of Scripture, the centrality of the death of Christ, the need for personal conversion and the
evangelistic imperative. Evangelism gets us started in the Christian
life, but spirituality keeps us going and refreshes us along the way.

Spirituality, Evangelism and Spiritual Growth

Earlier I pointed out how, virtually alone of all contemporary versions
of Christianity, evangelicalism possesses the ability to bring individuals to faith from a secular culture. But having won people for the
gospel, can evangelicalism keep them? I now wish to address a serious
anxiety that is shared by many within evangelicalism. The perceived
lack of a credible, coherent and distinctive spirituality is one of the
greatest weaknesses facing evangelicalism today. I do not in any way
wish to be alarmist or suggest that we are confronted with a crisis, a
total lack of evangelical interest in spirituality.[5] My concern is simply
to identify what seems to me to be a serious weakness at present—but
a weakness that can, given commitment and concern, become a future
strength.

As we have seen, many people begin their Christian lives as evangelicals. They have been attracted by the power of evangelical testimony and the obvious difference that faith makes to the lives of their
evangelical friends and neighbors. But what happens next? I have seen
the same pattern happen too often for comfort in my own ministry at
Wycliffe Hall. Many students begin their ministries as evangelicals, yet
end up—often after a period of many years—committed to a form of
Catholicism. They seem to gain the impression that evangelicalism is
of relatively little help to those who are trying to deepen their understanding of God and develop approaches to prayer and meditation to
enrich their faith and sustain them in the Christian life. In short,
evangelicalism fails to take the pressures and realities of Christian
living in the modern period seriously enough to devise spiritual strategies to enable new and struggling Christians to cope with them.

A case study from the United States will illustrate the point. It is
generally recognized that the only churches that are growing in the

United States are evangelical in orientation; indeed, for many secular observers, *evangelical* has become synonymous with "active and growing," even if it has also developed negative moral and political associations. But some—admittedly, very few—churches of a much more liberal orientation are also expanding. An example is All Saints Episcopal Church, Pasadena,[6] which has received widespread media attention because it bucks the trend. Its liberalism is not in doubt; it is strongly prochoice in its attitude to abortion, and it made international headlines in November 1990 when its rector announced that he would begin performing blessings in church of "same-sex" couples.

So why is this church growing, when it is not evangelical? Just about every other church with such liberal social commitments is losing members in droves. Because the phenomenon is so unusual, it has been studied with particular care. Donald E. Miller, professor of religion at the University of Southern California's school of religion, puts his finger on the point at issue: although the church is liberal in its politics, "it is also deeply conservative in its recognition of the importance of worship, pastoral care, and personal spiritual disciplines."[7] Attention to the personal spiritual needs and concerns of its individual members seems to have been the key in this situation. People need help with prayer, devotion and personal discipline—and if evangelicalism is not providing it, is it really surprising that they may turn elsewhere?

Evangelicals are often told by their Catholic colleagues that they have no spirituality worth talking about. It is perhaps inevitable that this becomes a self-fulfilling prophecy, in that it brings about a sense of inferiority within evangelical circles. Many evangelicals, convinced that they have nothing to offer in this area, quickly turn to the resources of other traditions. Not surprisingly, many who begin their Christian life as evangelicals end up on the more Catholic wing of the church, on account of the perceived superiority of its spirituality.

I write as one who is deeply appreciative of the Catholic tradition, especially within my own Church of England. I have no hesitation in declaring that I have learned much from my more Catholic colleagues, especially concerning the need for personal discipline and the importance of community for spiritual development. I expect to learn even more in the future, when I finish my study of the great French spiritual writers of the late seventeenth century, such as Bossuet and Fénelon. My concern is not to criticize Catholicism in any of its forms. It is simply to note that for some evangelicals, Catholic forms of spirituality can be the thin end of a wedge. For some, Catholic spirituality leads to Catholic forms of theology. And why? Because there is something wrong with evangelical theology? No. It is, quite simply, that evangelicalism is seen to lack a spirituality to give its theology staying power in the modern period.

Clarifying the Term *Spirituality*

Spirituality has become one of the buzzwords of our time and has been taken up with enthusiasm by many evangelicals. But from an evangelical point of view, the term has highly questionable associations and a dubious historical pedigree. In a careful study, Owen Chadwick, until recently professor of modern history at the University of Cambridge, points out how the origins of *spirituality* and many other related terms (such as "the inner life" or "the interior life") lie in the French spiritual writings of the seventeenth century.[8] From its beginnings, the term has had strong associations with "a striving after the purely spiritual" or "a rejection of anything related to the material world." Seventeenth-century French writers, deploring the development of negative attitudes toward the material order, were prone to lay the blame firmly upon *la nouvelle spiritualité de Madame Guyon.*[9] In particular, there is a danger of lapsing into a purely mystical understanding of the Christian life, not least on account of its implicit neo-Platonic foundations.[10]

The word *spirituality* thus appears to have been associated initially with a radical division between the spiritual and the physical, between the soul and the body, between contemplation and everyday life. It implies that its subject is primarily the interior nurture of the soul, undertaken in withdrawal from the distractions of ordinary life. The older vocabulary of the Protestant tradition, on the other hand, reflects more faithfully a central aspect of its spirituality—the total integration of faith and everyday life.[11]

We can begin to neutralize this difficulty if we are more attentive to the Pauline idea, so faithfully echoed by Luther, of the "spiritual" as life in the world oriented toward God, and if we move away from the unhelpful association of the idea of "life undertaken in withdrawal from the world." In its fundamental sense, spirituality is concerned with the shaping, empowering and maturing of the "spiritual person" (1 Cor 2:14-15)—that is, the person who is alive to and responsive to God in the world, as opposed to the person who merely exists within and responds to the world. As Luther reminded us, the reference is to *totus homo*—the "entire person"—not just the human mind.[12]

Robert Banks expresses this holistic view of spirituality well when he speaks of it as "the character and quality of our life with God, among fellow-Christians and in the world." Banks deliberately avoids two inadequate approaches to spirituality—a purely intellectual or cerebral approach, which engages the mind and nothing else, and a purely interiorized approach, which bears no relation to the realities of everyday life. Spirituality concerns our "spirit," yet as Banks forcefully reminds us, "not only our spirit—also our minds, wills, imaginations, feelings and bodies."[13] There is no difficulty in reclaiming this authentic sense of the term within the evangelical tradition, with its vital concern—shaped and nourished both by Scripture and the Reformers—to map out the contours of responsible Christian living in the world.

An evangelical spirituality will thus be Bible-centered, and it will be concerned more with the facilitation and enhancement of the personal redemptive encounter of the believer with Christ than with precise theological formulation or with the merits of one particular denominational approach. "The test of Christian spirituality is conformity of heart and life to the confession and character of Jesus as Lord."[14] Evangelical approaches to spirituality thus aim to resonate with these central concerns while opening the way to serious engagement with personal discipline, spiritual formation and the various difficulties that those trying to deepen the quality of their spiritual life routinely encounter.

Yet where evangelicalism ought to be devoting its enormous creativity and theological strengths to the forging of patterns of spirituality suited to the evangelical ethos, it appears instead to have been crippled by some form of lethargy. This is a feature of evangelicalism worldwide. Consider the insights of Australian evangelical writer John Waterhouse in his significant article "The Crisis of Evangelicalism" in the April 1992 issue of the leading Australian Christian magazine *On Being:*

> Ten years ago, I felt we were on the edge of an evangelical renaissance in Australia, a flowering of biblical scholarship that would touch secular society at its point of need and lead Australians to a new awareness of their creator. It even had a name: "a theology of everyday life" or "incarnational theology." We got out some books that seemed to do the job . . . but then they stopped.[15]

Waterhouse, the founder and publishing director of the New South Wales publishing house Albatross Books, did much to encourage this new spirituality.[16] But it dried up. For Waterhouse, part of the "crisis" is that evangelicalism has suffered "a loss of spiritual energy, originality and creativity." In short, evangelicalism has become spiritually derivative. Instead of falling back on its own distinctive approach to spirituality, evangelicalism has become lazy: it has borrowed other people's.

In failing to give full attention to this network of issues centering on spirituality, evangelicals fail the modern church. Evangelicalism owes that church the duty of ensuring that its distinctive approaches to spirituality remain alive, credible and available. It is shocking that evangelicalism should be so parasitic in this manner, exploiting the spiritual riches of other traditions yet failing to make its own distinctive contributions available to the church at large. Evangelicalism has too often become blind to its own heritage, unable to discern this heritage itself, let alone share it with others. As a result, the modern church is being denied access to a resource that ought to be there—

a spirituality that is radically and consistently grounded in Scripture and oriented toward the cross. Modern evangelicalism has a duty to ensure that this kind of spirituality remains a viable option in today's church.

The Evangelical Heritage

In the past, evangelicalism has been associated with certain specific approaches to the spiritual life, especially the private "quiet time." However, these approaches to spirituality, which have worked well before and have a distinguished history of use behind them, do not seem to work as well as we might like today. Why not? I would like to suggest several reasons that allow us to understand the problem we face and to be realistic in planning for the future.

Evangelicals are often inattentive to or confused about their own spiritual heritage. In part, this difficulty arises from the circumstances of their conversion. Many evangelicals are "born-again" Christians who have come to faith from a secular context, sometimes at later stages in their lives. They have not been nurtured in the evangelical tradition from birth. It is something that they have to discover in later life, as part of the total package of reorientation that accompanies their conversion. Few have the time to become acquainted with the evangelical spiritual heritage of the past, when they have other matters that require higher priority.

In his recent survey of the outlooks of younger American evangelicals,[17] James Davison Hunter pointed out that they had no real idea of the spiritual relevance of work. It had become something ordinary and humdrum. Something has been lost here. Yet I cite this case not because it is of vital importance in itself, but because it points to a seriously worrying trend: evangelicals are unaware of their own roots and the riches that these have to offer the modern church.[18]

One of the reasons for the considerable success of evangelicalism in recent years has been its willingness to relate to the issues of the day rather than indulge in the luxury of nostalgia for the past. This has, however, often led to a devaluation of our heritage. The publication of the Library of the Fathers and the Library of Anglo-Catholic Theology gave the nineteenth-century Catholic wing of the Church of England a solid intellectual and spiritual foundation on which it could build. We can learn from that example.

Some are learning already. Many younger evangelicals, especially in the United States, are rediscovering classic evangelical spiritualities and are working toward refashioning them to meet the needs of our own day.[19] James I. Packer's *Quest for Godliness* is an excellent example of a work by an older evangelical leader that conveys the relevance of this tradition to the needs of the modern church;[20] others can be instanced without difficulty. The Puritans emerge as individuals with real insights for the spiritual difficulties and dilemmas that confront Christians today. We need, as a matter of some urgency, to make past forms of spirituality—such as those linked with the Puritans— intelligible and accessible, as a duty both to evangelicalism and to the wider church at large. Just as the woman rejoiced at finding her missing coin (Lk 15:8-9), so we can share the joy of rediscovering spiritualities that our forebears knew.

Yet there are surely other Christ-centered and Scripture-nourished ways of living the Christian life waiting to be uncovered and developed! Our task is not simply to rediscover the past; it is also to construct the future.

The Changing Patterns of Life

Many of the classic evangelical approaches to the spiritual life were developed in the seventeenth and eighteenth centuries. They reflect the periods of their origin. Often they require a degree of leisure and an absence of personal pressure that are totally unrealistic in the midst of the stresses and tensions of modern Western life. Whatever their past greatness, they have often proved unworkable in the modern era.

For example, the classic quiet time is a virtual impossibility for many of my colleagues in the highly stressed worlds of business and medicine, where personal space is a rare and cherished luxury. Echoing the received wisdom of the past, Billy Graham counseled new

Christians to read their Bibles daily; without this "daily spiritual nourishment" they could expect to starve and lose their spiritual vitality.[21] That advice, given forty years ago, has become increasingly problematic with changes in the pace of living. This means that many new Christians find themselves being presented with demands that prove to be quite unrealistic. Their faith comes to be made dependent on something that cannot be sustained in the long term.

Yet evangelicalism has traditionally—and, it must be said, with considerable wisdom—reacted against any tendencies that could lead to the reification or the objectification of spiritual practices, so that these are seen as ends in themselves rather than as means to a greater end. Thus evangelicals prefer to speak of "praying to the Lord" rather than "saying prayers"; the former focuses on the end of prayer, which is an enhanced communion with the Lord, whereas the latter focuses on a human activity. Indeed, one of the major evangelical concerns relating to "spirituality" is that the emphasis often seems to fall on human activities and practices as ends in themselves, rather than as means to deepen a relationship with God. The evangelical will insist that the emphasis fall on the relationship between the believer and God, rather than on spiritual disciplines in themselves.

The traditional quiet time must therefore not be allowed to become an end in itself. It is our responsibility to try to develop ways of reading Scripture or praying that are realistic in the modern period, are tailored to the rhythms of the individual and yet retain a thorough grounding and immersion in Scripture. A respect for the past does not mean that we are wedded to that past; we owe it to our evangelical forebears to embody their vision in practices that are more suited to our changed situation. Above all, we need to take the sheer humanity of those to whom we minister much more seriously.

The Human Factor

Many start the life of faith with great enthusiasm, only to discover themselves in difficulty shortly afterward. Their high hopes and good intentions seem to fade away. The spirit may be willing, but the flesh proves weak. Fallen human nature all too often proves incapable of sustaining the high levels of enthusiasm and commitment that characterize the early days of faith. People need support to keep them going when enthusiasm fades.

Catholic spirituality—as evidenced in the writings of Teresa of Ávila, Brother Lawrence and Thomas à Kempis—has provided just such a support system for many in the past, precisely because it pays attention to the human side of the religious life without neglecting the Godward side of things. It is all very well to stress the total sufficiency of the gospel and to focus on God as he has made himself known and available in Jesus Christ. But that gospel is addressed to sinful human beings, who need all the help they can get to live by its precepts and harness its power in their lives. Evangelicalism, whenever it has stressed merely the Godward side of the Christian life, has been guilty of neglecting the human side of things.

Evangelicalism rightly insists that the quest for human identity, authenticity and fulfillment cannot be undertaken in isolation from God. But that is only half the story. What about ourselves? What about the needs and weaknesses of those to whom the gospel is addressed? Calvin states this principle with characteristic lucidity in the opening sentence of the 1559 edition of his *Institutes of the Christian Religion:* "Nearly all the wisdom we possess, that is to say, true and sound wisdom, consists of two parts: the knowledge of God and of ourselves. And although they are closely connected, it is difficult to say which comes first."[22] Precisely the same point is made in Jacques Bénigne Bossuet's *Traité de la connaissance de Dieu et de soi-même* (published posthumously in 1722) and is a leading theme of that major Catholic writer's spirituality.

There are thus two aspects to the Christian life—knowing God and knowing ourselves. (*Knowing* here designates "knowing *and experiencing,*" as one "knows" a person.) These cannot be separated, according to Calvin.[23] Thus any notion of spirituality as a quest for heightened religious experience as an end in itself is totally alien to the outlook of classic evangelicalism. "Feel-good" spiritualities are unacceptable unless they are firmly grounded in Scriptural passages that give us *reasons* to "feel good." The extensive appeal made to secular psychological and psychoanalytical disciplines in recent "inner life" spirituality—such as Morton Kelsey's *Christo-Psychology* (New York: Crossroad, 1982) and much New Age material—needs to be criticized.[24] To draw solely on insights concerning the human condition is only half of the story that Christian spirituality is concerned to tell; indeed, if only half of that story is told, it has not been properly and authentically told at all.

But perhaps evangelicalism in its turn has only told half the story. It has neglected to give weight to the human weaknesses and needs that make certain forms of spirituality so attractive an option for many people. David Powlinson of Westminster Seminary, Philadelphia, explains the attraction of psychology to many evangelical pastors along the following lines:

> The church has become weak in the domain of personal and interpersonal problems. Evangelical churches and theologians have typically not grappled with the problems in living that Christian people have. The church has either misconstrued, oversimplified, or avoided facing the existential and situational realities of human experience in the trenches of life.[25]

Powlinson's analysis is highly suggestive. It points to a failure to address the realities of the human situation—the "existential and situational realities of human experience in the trenches of life" which make spiritualities which center upon human needs so attractive to many Christians who feel that their spiritual lives are impoverished and find evangelicalism unable or unwilling to offer them guidance.

Evangelicalism has neglected its own heritage here. Through not knowing its own history, it has failed to realize how such issues were addressed in the past. Calvin spoke of God "accommodating himself to our abilities"—in other words God, knowing our needs and abilities, revealed himself in a form suited and adapted to us.[26] Powlinson points out how the Puritans knew this and developed pastoral strategies and approaches to spirituality to cope with it. But now others outside evangelicalism have addressed this issue better than we have; the result is that, in the long term, we are losing people to other Christian traditions or to secular psychotherapies in which the "human factor" is given pride of place. If we cannot change human nature, then we must ensure that forms of spirituality that are authentically *evangelical* are on offer in the religious marketplace.

It was concern over such issues that led my wife and me to write a book relating to a major area of modern anxiety—self-esteem. It is widely thought that a number of influential North American works such as Robert Schuller's *Self-Esteem*[27] are too reliant on purely secular understandings of the nature of self-esteem and ways in which it may be enhanced. We therefore decided to develop an approach to the issues surrounding self-esteem which was thoroughly grounded in Scripture and the Reformation yet also responsive to helpful insights from modern psychology.[28] As psychologist and theologian respectively, we aimed to use both the evangelical heritage and the best psychological insights to address these pressing modern needs.

Spirituality and Evangelical Theological Education
There are indications that spirituality still has a low profile in many evangelical theological centers of education. Where are the evangelical institutions dedicated to promoting evangelical spirituality? Regent College, Vancouver, currently has two chairs of "spiritual theology," occupied by the distinguished writers and speakers James M. Houston and Eugene H. Peterson. This development offers exciting possibilities for the development and consolidation of evangelical spiritualities; yet, sadly, it is an exception rather than the rule. All too often there is a massive blind spot here in evangelical institutions, which serves only to perpetuate the neglect and devaluing of evangelical spirituality.

Equally, where are the journals of evangelical spirituality? There are now many specialist journals devoted to evangelical theology. Yet evangelicalism has always had its greatest strengths in the pulpit, on the mission field and on its knees. As I stressed earlier, its distinctive feature is not so much a theology as a devotional ethos. There is an obvious need for a journal devoted to this theme. Evangelicalism can draw on a variety of resources within its own family history—the Reformation, the Puritans, the evangelical revivals of the eighteenth century, the holiness movement and the charismatic movement—in seeking to confront and transform the future, aided and challenged by the resources of the past.

Role Models for Evangelical Spirituality

Many people feel the need for a "spiritual director," someone who will offer them spiritual guidance, discipline and support over a long period. There has, however, been a long tradition of suspicion concerning this idea within both classic Protestantism and contemporary evangelicalism.[29] So, sensing that this is not a real option within evangelicalism, seekers will look for this kind of direction outside. The result? Some evangelicals end up adopting both the theology and the spirituality of their more Catholic colleagues. I have seen many of my students in Oxford gradually lose sight of their evangelical roots in just this way.

Yet in the past, evangelicals were aware of the vital role that experienced Christians could play in the spiritual formation of their younger colleagues. The "letters of spiritual counsel" of great Christian pastors and leaders are a powerful reminder of the importance of this kind of nurturing and guidance in the history of evangelicalism. Somehow we seem to have lost sight of our heritage here.

I suspect that this situation will change as the years pass. However, at the moment there are not enough active and credible practitioners of the craft of evangelical spiritual direction. One of the reasons many seem to have lost confidence in evangelical spirituality is that relatively few individuals are publicly available to embody that spirituality. We need national conferences to identify resource people, books, approaches, methods and possibilities. We need international summer schools to allow us to see what is happening at the global level in this field, in the hope that we may learn from what is going on elsewhere. We need local workshops to allow all concerned with strategies for the deepening of faith to come together and share their experiences, hopes and frustrations. In short, we need to get spirituality on the evangelical agenda and make sure it stays there until we get this one sorted out.

The situation is made worse by the dominance, both in Western universities and in seminaries, of styles of teaching and learning that rely solely on books and lectures. The older approach, which lingers on in the Oxford and Cambridge tutorial systems, is for the teacher to serve as a nurturing companion, a living role model that the student may imitate, rather than a mechanical dispenser of facts and information. (A recent study of C. S. Lewis as a spiritual mentor has noted how Lewis's Oxford tutorials provided the arena for much of his counseling.[30]) Spiritual direction is to be *done* rather than *lectured about*.

This is not to say that there are none concerned to foster evangelical approaches to the Christian life; it is to say there are not enough. So who are the potential role models? Let me identify some landmarks, positions of importance to travelers who wish to move on beyond the regions that have thus been marked. I must stress that the writings of many other individuals could be added to those I list.

In the first place, such an evangelical spirituality will be Scripture-centered. However, this is a necessary yet not a sufficient condition. It is not simply that Scripture must be at the heart of evangelical spirituality; it must be approached and read in a certain manner. It *can* be read with the cool, critical detachment of the scholar, who treats it "as if it were any other book" (Benjamin Jowett). The distinction between a critical and a devotional commentary is well founded. Scripture *ought to be* approached and read in the sure and confident expectation that God will speak to the reader. By meditating on the scriptural text, the reader can deepen his or her relationship with God, forging a deeper bond of commitment, adoration, fellowship and love.

The importance of Scripture is easily stated. What is considerably more difficult, and arguably more important, is to develop methods of enabling readers to engage in a more satisfactory and fulfilling manner with the biblical text. One of the best ways of doing this, in my view, is that developed by Eugene Peterson. Peterson's technique, developed in works such as *A Long Obedience in the Same Direction*—reflections on the "Songs of Ascents" (Psalms 120—134)—is to engage the reader's attention as he reflects on the meaning of biblical texts and relates them to the situations of everyday life. He offers an extended meditation on the text and makes a judicious appeal to the imagination—that vital human resource which has been so badly neglected by a generation of evangelicals who have soaked up the rationalistic spirit of the Enlightenment.[31]

Here Peterson takes up a point made by writers such as Cheryl Forbes and others. We cannot pray effectively unless we can "see" or "envision" the One to whom we are praying.[32] There is a real need to allow our imaginations to supply such images, always ensuring that they remain controlled by the scriptural text on which we are meditating. Our encounter with the Lord will be given new depth and wonder if we allow ourselves to imagine what the Lord might look like and how we might respond to the "beauty of the LORD" (Ps 27:4). Peterson's *Reversed Thunder* makes excellent use of this technique, allowing his readers to gain a sense of the wonder of the Lord by responsible use of the prayerful imagination as it feeds on the rich imagery of Revelation, the fascinating final book of the New Testament.[33]

In the second place, an evangelical spirituality will place considerable emphasis on the transforming character of the knowledge of God. Calvin stressed that "knowledge of God" is no indifferent matter but results in obedience on the one hand and adoration on the other. This is a natural consequence of "devotional" Bible study. However, people need help and guidance as to how such study can transform their relationship with God or their feelings and emotions.

James Houston has offered us invaluable guidance on how to address these issues in two recent works, *The Transforming Friendship* (1990) and *The Heart's Desire* (1992).[34] In both books Houston explores the way meditation and prayer can change our perception of God, our relationship with him and our experience of him. Each work is richly illustrated with helpful quotations from the great writers of the past and brief case studies of individuals to whom readers can relate. Throughout the works there is a persistent and persuasive affirmation of the way knowing God changes things. "When the death and resurrection of Jesus Christ have affected our lives in such a way, our transformed desires will immediately witness to the change within us."[35] Houston is perhaps one of the most lucid exponents of the dangers of allowing head and heart to go their separate and unrelated ways. Thus he writes of those whose experience of Christ is restricted to "the top of their heads, with no substance to it at the bottom of their hearts."[36]

In the third place, evangelicalism—here drawing especially on its Reformed roots—insists that spirituality must rest on a solid and reliable foundation in the self-revelation of God. There is thus the closest of connections between spirituality and theology. This organic relationship prevents spirituality from degenerating into a human-centered quest for heightened religiosity, for it insists that our spiritual lives rest securely on the foundation of God's self-revelation. It also keeps a check on theology, preventing it from becoming abstract speculation about God without any appreciation of the importance of "knowing God" for devotion and fulfillment.

One of the finest exponents of this point is Packer, whose *Knowing God* is a masterpiece of its kind.[37] I wish, however, to consider here his seminal 1989 lecture "An Introduction to Systematic Spirituality," noted earlier, in which he points out the utter impossibility of separating theology and spirituality. In particular, Packer draws attention to the need for "more biblical and theological control" of spirituality, regretting the "egocentric perspective" of many spiritual writers who use radically subjective criteria in developing and commending spiritual practices. "As I want to see theological study done as an aspect and means of our relating to God, so I want to see spirituality studied within an evaluative theological framework; that is why I want to arrange a marriage, with explicit exchange of vows and mutual commitments, between spirituality and theology."[38] There is much wisdom to be gleaned from this great contemporary expositor of the Puritan ideal, just as there is much to be gained from the heritage that he so capably expounds.

Finally, evangelicalism will rediscover the importance of spiritual discipline—a discipline that has too easily been stigmatized as "legalism." The easy accommodation on the part of many evangelicals to the laid-back attitude of Western culture has led to a serious erosion of Christian effectiveness and maturity. Rediscovering our own heritage, in both the New Testament and the older evangelical tradition, could be the first step toward re-creating a disciplined and effective evangelicalism, prepared for the battles that await it at every juncture in the church and world. Our role models here are pastors and writers such as Richard Baxter, John Owen and Matthew Henry, whose insights we cannot afford to neglect, yet whose writings are virtually unknown to the younger generation of evangelicals.[39]

If there is any long-term threat to the future of evangelicalism, it may well be its lack of attention to spirituality. Unless we can develop or rediscover forms of spirituality that are thoroughly evangelical in their roots and outlook, today's evangelicals may be tomorrow's ex-evangelicals. This is one of the most urgent tasks we face. Unless something is done to promote evangelical spirituality, the present growth of the movement may not be sustained in the longer term.

Yet I end on a note of justified optimism. In the past, evangelicalism has shown itself capable of rising to great challenges and turning perceived weaknesses into opportunities to develop, grow and expand. I have every reason to suppose that the present weakness in spirituality will lead to a dedicated and sustained quest within evangelicalism to meet this deficiency. Evangelicalism is the slumbering giant of the world of spirituality. It needs to wake up. If it does, the new millennium could see some very exciting developments.

6

THE DARK SIDE
OF EVANGELICALISM

E VANGELICALISM OFTEN HAS A NEGATIVE PUBLIC IMAGE. IN
the United States this often rests on its associations with right-
wing politics; in Britain it more commonly rests on the past
isolationism and intellectual mediocrity of the movement, especially its "spiritual conceit, ecclesiastical isolationism, social uncon-
cern, pessimism about both the world and the church, and a cultural
philistinism."[1] In part, that negative image is caused by the perpetu-
ation of stereotypes by those concerned to discredit evangelicalism.
But only in part. Evangelicalism continues to have its darker side.

Thus far I have considered issues relating to the identity and attraction of evangelicalism and addressed some of the challenges it faces
as it confronts the future. I have made clear my confidence in the
movement while expressing reservations concerning some of its aspects. I now wish to address the negative side of the movement in more
detail.

Some, I fear, will accuse me of betraying evangelicalism in offering
the criticisms that follow. I fear this accusation, not because there is
any truth in it, but on account of its confirming the siege mentality
that persists within some corners of the movement. For these threat-

ened individuals, any criticism, however true and however lovingly made, stinks of betrayal. This emotive reaction points to the deeply isolationist outlook of certain forms of evangelicalism, which take delight in numerical weakness, apparently believing it to be directly correlated with doctrinal purity.

But my point is simple. The criticisms that follow are not simply made by those outside evangelicalism. They are made from *within* evangelicalism, by evangelicals who believe that the movement needs to remain faithful to its biblical mandate to continue evaluating every aspect of its life and thought and rejecting those aspects that need purging or reforming. I make these criticisms in the firm belief that they command widespread assent within evangelicalism and that they are capable of being remedied.

Guilt Trips and Burnout

One of the more worrying aspects of some evangelical preaching and counseling is the creation of a sense of guilt, paralysis and self-doubt that results from a deficient understanding of the Reformation doctrine of "knowledge of sin." Writers such as Calvin have emphasized that the full benefits of the gospel can be known only if the full seriousness of sin is first appreciated. With this insight there can be no arguing. Luther said that no one has the right to be called a theologian unless he has first experienced the wrath of God. With such insights in mind, many evangelicals develop preaching and counseling styles that aim to destroy any human self-confidence and any sense of personal worth. Only when these are destroyed can God's grace be appreciated for what it really is!

Yet the strategy too often fails. It is just about as effective and as Christian as that of Job's comforters. All that happens is that such styles create Christians whose self-confidence is shattered and who believe that they are of no value whatsoever. As a result they are of no use to the kingdom of God. They feel unable to do anything for God, for others or for themselves. The counseling rooms of secular psychologists are full of Christians who have been destroyed by this kind of evangelical preaching. What is perhaps most disturbing of all is that it rests on a biblically and theologically shallow understanding of the issues, an understanding that offers a one-way ticket on a guilt trip without the concomitant assurance of God's acceptance and valuing of the sinner.

There is a real need to develop authentically Christian understandings of self-esteem that challenge the secular view of self-sufficiency and affirm our dependence on God—*without* destroying a person's sense of self-worth in the presence of God. Christ died to save sinners; that means sinners matter to God, even if some evangelical preachers, through deficient understandings of the Reformation doctrines of justification by faith, fail to see this point and destroy their congregations through their failure.[2]

God values us! That is one of the central themes of the doctrine of grace. Too often we hear only the negative side of the gospel of grace—that we, as unworthy sinners, can do nothing worthwhile in the sight of God. We cannot achieve our own salvation. Yet the doctrine of grace is not intended to humiliate us. It is meant to bring us to our senses. It is meant to deflate any ideas we might have of our ability to earn our salvation. It is only by bringing home to us the grim hopelessness of our situation that God can persuade us to turn to him.

It is almost as if there is some kind of pretension of adequacy or delusion of sufficiency built into fallen human nature. It is natural for us to suppose that we are in full possession of the resources we need for our own redemption. It seems obvious. As Luther pointed out, it is natural to assume that God will not give us something as wonderful as the redeeming presence of Christ unless we do him a favor first.

Yet this attitude cuts us off from salvation. It is only when we realize that we cannot save ourselves that we begin to look outside our situation for salvation. God is therefore obliged to break down our resistance to the idea that we need his help. He has to expose the falsity of our delusions of self-sufficiency for salvation. Telling the truth can often be painful, as it can expose a tissue of lies that we have spun around ourselves, like a protective cocoon, to shield ourselves from the unbearable reality of truth.

It hurts to be told the truth in a situation like this. It is painful to face up to the way things really are, instead of relaxing in the belief that we can redeem ourselves. But we need that shock to our system if we are to discover our need to turn to God and his willingness to supply what we so sorely lack. God challenges our own ideas of our personal value, in order to allow us to see us as he values us.

This, then, is the negative aspect of the grace of God. It declares our powerlessness and spiritual poverty. And that may hurt our self-esteem. But it only hurts a *spurious* self-esteem, in order to put a genuine God-grounded self-esteem in its place. For the positive side of the grace of God allows us to see ourselves in a new and significant light: *God regards us as worth saving.* He makes his riches available to us beggars. More than that: he who was rich beyond all splendor became poor for our sake. God set aside his majesty in order to enter into our world of darkness and sin and redeem us. We can thus set to one side bogus notions of self-esteem, grounded on illusions about ourselves, and instead learn to ground our self-esteem in the value that God places on us—a value that is shown in his sending Christ to die for us.

The Son of God died in order that we might live. That is the full extent of the love of God for us. That is how much God values us. And that is how we ought to esteem ourselves. We must learn to see ourselves as God sees us; the cross of Christ is the window that allows us access to that perception. The gospel declares that God is determined to save us, and that he is prepared to pay the price this salvation entails. Evangelicals need to appreciate that the costliness of redemption is directly correlated to the value God places upon us. Christ himself declared that he came "to give his life as a ransom for many" (Mk 10:45). Paul reminded his Corinthian readers that they had been bought at the price of the death of the Son of God (1 Cor 6:20; 7:23). Some evangelicals seem to think that God does not love sinners very much. Perhaps they ought to reread Luther and Calvin; they certainly ought to reread Scripture.

Our sense of self-esteem and personal worth ought to be grounded in the cross of Christ. It is here that we discover the full extent to which God loves us, cares for us and values us. The death of Christ marks his total self-giving. That is how much he values us. He gives everything he has, and everything he is, for us. That thought must allow us to walk tall. Even though we are sinners, God loves us. There is no contradiction here, no delusion or deception. Paul Tillich helpfully declared that the doctrine of justification by faith means "accepting that you are accepted, despite being unacceptable."

Informed criticisms of evangelicalism often focus on the burnout it causes to both its pastors and its people. The very high levels of commitment to the movement often cause casualties. Evangelicalism has had its great successes; it also seems to produce more than its fair share of walking wounded. In part, as I noted in an earlier chapter, this reflects its failure to address adequately issues of spirituality and the need to pay considerably more attention to the "human factor" than has hitherto been the case. It also needs to pay more attention to the gospel itself, ensuring that the whole gospel—not just the "consciousness of sin"—is faithfully preached.

Evangelical Dogmatism

It is no secret that many people are alienated from some forms of evangelicalism by what they regard as their intensely dogmatic attitudes. University and college students in particular are known to be suspicious of the intellectual narrow-mindedness of some of their evangelical peers. *Dogmatism* is probably best defined as "a refusal to allow disagreement or doubt." The problem has two aspects: the emphasis it places on certainty, which causes difficulties for those experiencing doubt; and the kinds of things that some evangelicals choose to be dogmatic about. Let's explore both of these difficulties.

First, evangelicals, drawing on the Reformation heritage,[3] generally place considerable emphasis on assurance. This has the pastoral consequence of making doubt a serious problem for evangelicals—not so much on account of the intellectual issues involved but on account of the pressure people are made to feel, often at an early stage in their Christian life, to suppress their doubts. Admission of doubt is often seen as a sin, perhaps insulting to God. Os Guinness points to this difficulty:

> On the one hand, those who are theologically liberal tend to be too soft on doubt, lionizing such notions as *ambiguity* and *uncertainty*. This spiritual permissiveness becomes a slipway to unbelief. On the other hand, those who are theologically conservative tend to be too hard on doubt, demonizing the dire consequences of unresolved doubt and verging on a spiritual perfectionism that leaves doubters in such a state of guilt or despair they dare not acknowledge their doubts to others or even to themselves.[4]

Yet the evangelical emphasis on assurance is generally not accompanied by the pastoral concern and theological framework erected by Reformers such as Luther and Calvin to safeguard doubters against precisely this "spiritual perfectionism." For example, Calvin defines faith in terms that might at first sight allow no room for doubt: "a steady and certain knowledge of the divine benevolence towards us, which is founded upon the truth of the gracious promise of God in Christ."[5] Yet Calvin goes on to point out that

> when we stress that faith ought to be certain and secure, we do not have in mind a certainty without doubt, or a security without any anxiety. Rather, we affirm that believers have a perpetual struggle with their own lack of faith, and are far from possessing a peaceful conscience, never interrupted by any disturbance. On the other hand, we want to deny that they may fall out of, or depart from, their confidence in the divine mercy, no matter how much they may be troubled.[6]

Evangelicals need to rediscover the pastoral consequences of an excessive emphasis on certainty, make the vital distinction between *intellectual* and *existential* certitude clearer[7] and realize that people have different outlooks on life that can affect them in different ways.

The second aspect of the issue is perhaps more serious. All Christians can agree on the need to defend what is of vital importance to the Christian faith. Yet often issues of relative importance are blown up beyond any sense of proportion, forcing evangelicals to defend themselves to each other when they ought to be proclaiming the gospel to the world. The demand to "defend the gospel" too often turns out to be "defend my rather rigid version of the gospel." Billy Graham and Francis Schaeffer are among those who have noted the movement's perennial tendency to become dogmatic over issues of relative rather than absolute importance. The former was convinced that the fundamentalist obsession with a series of ultimately minor issues got in the way of the much greater work of evangelism; the latter believed that dogmatism destroyed evangelical unity and created a climate of suspicion and hostility within the movement.

Let me make it clear immediately that evangelicalism is not the only version of Christianity to show signs of degenerating into dogmatism. One of the greatest tragedies of our times is that in recent years liberalism has, in the view of many observers, degenerated from a commitment to openness and toleration into an intolerant and dogmatic worldview that refuses to recognize the validity of any views save its own. Let me quote from my distinguished Oxford colleague John Macquarrie, unquestionably one of the world's greatest living mainline theologians, as he notes this problem:

> What is meant by "liberal" theology? If it means only that the theologian to whom the adjective is applied has an openness to other points of view, then liberal theologians are found in all schools of thought. But if "liberal" becomes itself a party label, then it usually turns out to be extremely illiberal.[8]

The deeply disturbing paradox of much modern theology is that some of the most dogmatic of its representatives lay claim to be liberals. Liberalism, in the traditional and honorable sense of the word, carries with it an inalienable respect for and openness to the views of others. The new dogmatism within liberalism is itself a sure indication of a deep sense of unease and insecurity and an awareness of its growing isolation and marginalization within mainline Christianity, not least on account of the rise of evangelicalism.

But the problem is not confined to liberalism. Evangelicalism is just as vulnerable. The issues over which dogmatism is encountered include the following.

1. Whether evangelicals ought to be members of mainline denominations, aiming to reform them from within, or whether they ought to form doctrinally pure denominations. This debate became viciously polarized in the United States during the 1920s and 1930s, and it came close to destroying evangelicalism at the time. This same viciousness and lack of Christian love threaten to reemerge today, even in traditionally tolerant contexts such as England.

2. The precise way the authority of Scripture is to be stated and defended. The celebrated "Battle for the Bible,"[9] which erupted in 1976, centered on a debate within evangelicalism over distinctions between "inerrancy" and "infallibility" which some regarded as pointless and unbiblical and others as absolutely essential to the future of evangelicalism.[10] The issues at stake are vitally important, and the debates were unquestionably necessary. It is, however, the manner in which the debate was conducted that caused concern to leading evangelicals such as Carl Henry. Although he classed himself as an "inerrantist" and shared many of Harold Lindsell's anxieties concerning the directions some evangelicals were taking, Henry complained that Lindsell was "relying on theological atom bombing" in which "as many evangelical friends as foes end up as casualties."[11] Evangelicalism as a whole, he argued, was being forced to comply with the particular perspectives of one of its component parts. It seemed to him that there was a need for greater tolerance and understanding if the emerging evangelical coalition was to survive.

3. The place of the Holy Spirit in the Christian life. The rise of the charismatic movement has placed the issue of the experience and gifts of the Spirit firmly on the Christian agenda. It has also caused some serious divisions, with some charismatics suggesting that those devoid of spiritual gifts such as "speaking in tongues" are second-class Christians.

4. The role of women in the church. The biblical understanding of

the role of women in Christian ministry is complex and the subject of some debate. Alongside texts suggesting that women have a limited role in ministry are others suggesting that gender is no longer of decisive importance for Christians.[12] The result has been a debate that has at times become intensely polarized, with those who argue, for example, for the ordination of women being classed as "dangerous liberals" and those who oppose it being described as "reactionaries."

Other instances could be given. While there are issues on which evangelicalism rightly chooses to be dogmatic (such as the divinity of Christ), there are others for which a variety of evangelical options are available. At times the assumption underlying the polarization has been that Scripture can only legitimate one position, so that no divergence can be tolerated over anything. At other times the governing anxiety is clearly the "slippery slope" model, which fears a lapse into a liberalism that tolerates more or less anything. Yet the painful reality is that at some points Scripture authorizes and itself models a diversity of possibilities. Where such diversity is clearly biblically grounded, evangelicals will have to learn to live with their disagreements.

One of the most intelligent and insightful voices within the Southern Baptist Convention is Timothy George, dean of Beeson Divinity School at Samford University. Noting the issues that divide this evangelical denomination—such as the role of women in ministry and charismatic renewal in the life of the church—George pleads for toleration in relation to marginalia, with a focus on agreement on the central issues. "If in this age of pluralism and every-tub-sitting-on-its-own-bottom individualism, we cannot achieve consensus theology, perhaps we can at least learn to respect the integrity of individuals who in conscience do not agree with us."[13] As he observes, "A church which has become obsessed with the marginalia of the faith will soon find itself shipwrecked on the shoals of a fractured fellowship."

Evangelicalism faces so many challenges and external pressures that the last thing it needs is a protracted civil war, which can only lead to fragmentation, bitterness and a negative public witness. "See how these Christians love one another!" was the public reaction to faith recorded by Tertullian in the second century. Is it too much to hope that a similar response might be evoked by evangelicals today?

The alternative to such a scripturally grounded tolerance and forbearance is ultimately schism, personal vilification and the emergence of a self-righteousness that refuses to acknowledge as "evangelical" any save those who conform totally to the views of what C. S. Lewis called "the magic circle."

The Reformation itself illustrates both the issue in question and the consequences of a failure to respect evangelical integrity. In the 1520s, Luther and Zwingli found themselves disagreeing forcefully over the nature of the real presence (see chapter two, under "The Supreme Authority of Scripture"). For Luther, the words "This is my body" (Mt 26:26) could only mean "This [bread] *is* my [Christ's] body." To deny this was to compromise the clear meaning of Scripture. For Zwingli, it was clear that the words meant "This *signifies* my body." A failure to resolve and respect the issues involved led to a serious polarization between Luther and Zwingli at precisely the moment when unity was desperately needed. The opening up of this division made it a relatively easy matter for the antievangelical emperor Charles V to exploit differences within the movement, which would eventually lead to the military and political defeat of Lutheranism in the 1540s.

Evangelicalism continues to have its opponents, and they do not hesitate to exploit weaknesses and disagreements within the movement with the ultimate aim of weakening or destroying it. Individual evangelicals owe the movement as a whole the responsibility of taking each other seriously, wherever Scripture permits more than one reading, just as they are obliged to defend evangelical truth wherever this seems to be under threat. But it needs to be realized that evangelicals are free to differ on matters of secondary importance. The escalation of such disputes serves no useful purpose, and it ultimately marks a serious lack of evangelical maturity and judgment.

The Curse of the Evangelical Personality Cult
"Evangelicalism is great," a friend of mine remarked. "A pity about

the evangelicals." His point was simple. It is all very well to talk about evangelicalism as if it were a set of ideas or attitudes. But what about the kind of people who seem to end up as its leaders? There is, at least in his view, a genuine cause for concern about the all-too-human face of evangelicalism, especially in its North American forms.

Evangelicals, like everyone else, are human. They want to know things for certain. And if someone tells it to them straight, they will listen. Now there is nothing wrong with that. The problem concerns the personality cults that grow up around leading figures in the evangelical world. Trust in God can easily become muddled with trusting someone who claims to speak, with authority, on his behalf. There seems to be something in fallen and sinful human nature that wants to make us trust people who speak with confidence and boldness. The firm, disciplined and confident voice comes to matter more than the credibility of what is being said. It is the preacher as much as, if not more than, the message that is being trusted.

This attitude was subjected to withering satire in Sinclair Lewis's *Elmer Gantry*.[14] Gantry is a fictional evangelical preacher whose high-profile public posture of self-righteousness and virtue masks an inner life of deception and fraud. *Elmer Gantry* is a caricature of both the dangers of a personality cult and the gullibility of ordinary people who are prepared to trust their fellow men and women, whether politicians or preachers. Lewis's novel spawned the popular image of TV evangelists that has become a cultural cliché of our time.

Yet Lewis was, in a sickening way, right in some of his criticisms of evangelical preachers. The 1987 saga of televangelists Jim and Tammy Faye Bakker illustrates both the dangers of evangelical personality cults and the enormous media interest in the sexual and financial weaknesses of high-profile evangelical preachers. Jim Bakker's sexual exploits and Tammy's attempts to break free from addiction at the Betty Ford Center for drug rehabilitation scandalized a nation. Yet in a series of pitiful episodes, events showed that some people kept on trusting them despite the growing body of evidence of corruption and misdemeanor. One such scene, described by *The Washington Post,* took place outside the Heritage Grand Hotel in South Carolina:

> As hundreds of largely adoring devotees sang hymns, shouted ad-
> oration and thrust gifts, a black 450 Mercedes sedan eased to a stop
> at the luxury Heritage Grand Hotel here today. One smoke-tinted
> window rolled down. A man's gold Rolex popped into view. Down
> came the other window. Long red fingernails appeared. Jim and
> Tammy Faye Bakker were back.[15]

Not only did the Bakkers cause grief to many ordinary American
Christians, who believed that "being a preacher" ensured someone's
intellectual and moral honesty; they also achieved a public relations
disaster for evangelicalism which came close to paralleling that
achieved for Islam by the Ayatollah Khomeini. Other related episodes
could be detailed of preachers who failed those who placed their trust
in them.

Many uneducated Americans are naive and trusting, willing to put
their faith in someone who claims to speak on God's behalf. There are
many such preachers who claim to speak for God and are accorded
honor by trusting devotees. Scripture, they assert, is difficult to interpret. God has generously given them spiritual talents to "explain" the
Word. Yet on closer examination, they seem to add on some unusual
ideas to Scripture and deny some that are clearly present. This is
especially the case within the movement that is coming to be known
as "power evangelicalism," both on account of the emphasis it places
on power in the Christian life (whether this is understood in charismatic or political terms) and because of the considerable power it has
come to wield, especially in right-wing U.S. politics. There is a real
danger of scandal and disillusionment here.

It is well known that some people lose their faith not on account
of any difficulties with belief in God but on account of their utter
disillusionment with those who claim to speak in his name. Many
former evangelicals have had their faith shattered by discovering that
a religious leader or teacher whom they greatly admired had a less
winsome side. Trapped in a personality cult, they found that their faith
in God had become inextricably linked with their faith in a person who

for them *was* God. It is arguable that this is a relatively recent phenomenon, brought into existence by the financial pressures of religious television and the relentless search for sensational stories on the part of secular media, anxious to score highly in the ratings. But the danger has always been there. Now it has become a major threat to the public credibility of evangelicalism in the West.

In practice, however, the danger of this has been diminished in recent years, for two reasons. First, the TV evangelists are putting their house in order. Aware of the relentless public interest in their bank accounts and nesting habits, they have now come under increasing pressure from an irate constituency determined to ensure that the highest standards are set and maintained. Second, people outside the United States tend to regard TV evangelists as an American, rather than a specifically evangelical, phenomenon. "That's just the way Americans behave" is a typical European comment on the televangelist phenomenon.

Yet it is not enough for evangelicalism to react to such scandals after the events and to expose the danger of personality cults after the damage has been done. Shutting the stable door after the horse has bolted has limited potential as a means of curbing and discouraging these failures. A more radical reappraisal is required at the level of expectations and attitudes among ordinary evangelicals and those whose calling it is to pastor them. Evangelicalism must become more proactive by encouraging evangelicals to develop and nourish respectfully critical attitudes toward those who adopt high profiles on their behalf. Underlying all this is the vitally important need for evangelicals to rediscover the Reformation doctrine of the "priesthood of all believers."

The temptation to rely on others to tell us what God is like reflects both laziness and lack of confidence. Many evangelicals want to be *told* what is right rather than taking the trouble to check it out for themselves. As a result they are often unknowingly influenced by highly contentious or misleading expositions of Scripture or a fatally flawed reading of church history. And they often lack the confidence to read Scripture for themselves.

The Reformation marked a decisive turning point in the history of the church, when Reformers such as Luther and Calvin blew the whistle on bad theology and called on ordinary Christian believers to discover how far the church had wandered from its biblical foundations. We need our own reformation, for the cult of the personality discourages ordinary Christians from thinking about their own faith, thus denying them the personal enrichment and effective evangelistic potential that a study of their faith can bring.

Whenever traditional power structures seem to be in decline or confusion, people are disposed to seek out authority elsewhere. When society seems confused concerning its moral values and traditional academic institutions seem muddled over questions of truth, people will look for—and find—those who speak with a powerful and clear voice, offering them crisp, neat and authoritative solutions. This is precisely the point made by Max Weber in his famous essay "The Sociology of Charismatic Authority"; it is also a point that has been appreciated and is now being exploited by the "power religion" movement within modern evangelicalism.[16]

For in response to the longing for certainty and authority within the Christian life, a form of evangelicalism has arisen that places an emphasis on *power*. Just as much of contemporary American culture is obsessed with a quest for power, so evangelicalism has come to mirror this quest. The preoccupation with individual and corporate power has passed over into evangelicalism, which advocates "power ministries," "power evangelism" and "power healing." The term "power evangelicalism" has been used to draw attention to this new preoccupation with power, which can be seen in the interest in church growth, political activism and the "signs and wonders" movement.

If people want powerful, neat and authoritative answers to hard questions, they will get them. The contemporary demand for "powerful preaching" is usually understood as referring not to the preaching of powerful *doctrines* but to powerful and authoritative *styles* of preaching. Power evangelicalism owes a substantial part of its appeal to its force of conviction: perhaps not so much the *views* that are held, or the *doctrines* that are preached, but the *conviction and authority* with which they are held and preached. And within power evangelicalism, this conviction is increasingly coming to be based on subjective criteria, such as "The Lord told me to say this."

There is a vital lesson here for the denominations of mainline Protestantism, which are losing members in droves on account of their failure to give a clear moral lead or preach with conviction anything that even vaguely resembles the gospel. But there is also a vital lesson for evangelicalism itself. It needs to realize that at least some of its power and appeal may come to rest on human qualities rather than on the gospel itself. Force of conviction is not an adequate criterion of truth. One can be forcefully wrong, just as one can be sincerely erroneous. "Authority" can very easily become "authoritarian." The appeal to subjective experiences of God, personal visions of Christ or esoteric and unverifiable words of knowledge is as powerful as it is dangerous. Power evangelicalism deemphasizes the objective means by which these revelations and visions, this knowledge, may be checked out against some publicly available and objective deposit of truth—that is, Scripture. The virtual marginalization of Scripture within power evangelicalism is one of the greatest scandals of our age.

The rise of televangelism and television preaching ministries has led to a growing cult of personality within power evangelicalism. It is not what Scripture says that matters; it is what this preacher or that TV evangelist says that Scripture says. Often Scripture is ignored altogether: it is what God is saying directly and personally to this preacher that counts. But how can we know what God said to this preacher? How can we check out his message? How can we be sure that he is indeed speaking in the name of the Lord and not simply claiming a spurious divine authority for his own ideas? Let us remember that the original sin is to wish to be like God.

I am not suggesting that each and every preacher within the tradition of power evangelicalism is deluded or is indulging in some kind of ego trip. Rather, I am suggesting that the emphasis laid on individual preaching and prophetic ministry is very vulnerable to sinful human exploitation. Deep within us, our old sinful nature remains, still not totally conquered by the grace of God. There are still traces of the Old Adam—who seeks to be like God—within all of us. Power evangelicalism, for all its virtues, is fatally vulnerable at this point. Why? Because it encourages both preachers and their congregations to expect some individuals to be able to declare, with a degree of infallibility that would be the envy of any modern pope, exactly what the will of God for his people is.

But how can this difficulty be removed? How can we acknowledge the reality of human sin, with all its attending dangers and temptations, while at the same time maintaining that it is possible to know what God wants us to do? How can we uphold the idea of prophetic ministry and preaching while safeguarding our people from being misled or exploited? In short, how can we recover a *responsible* attitude to ministry?

Happily, an answer lies to hand in the writings of the sixteenth-century Reformers. There are remarkable, and disturbing, parallels between the distorted idea of priesthood in the medieval Catholic Church and the notion of ministry found within modern power evangelicalism. Both are intensely authoritarian. Both rest on an ideology of power, which places the right to speak for God in the hands of a small and unaccountable elite. Both studiously ignore the possibility that they might get God wrong and the deeply threatening and humiliating possibility that God might choose to challenge and correct them through ordinary layfolk within their undervalued congregations.

At the dawn of the Reformation, the Reformers posed a powerful biblical challenge to this distorted and disturbing idea of priesthood. The name given to their challenge has passed into history—the doctrine of the "priesthood of all believers." We badly need to recover this doctrine and explore its consequences. For the simple fact of the matter is that modern evangelicalism needs the same kind of clean-up that the Reformers brought to the late medieval church. Astonishing though it may seem, the bad old ways of the pre-Reformation church have surfaced again, even among those who claim to be evangelical. Those who speak of the "new Reformation" often turn out to be perpetuating the delusions and distortions of unreformed Christendom.

And if evangelicalism has lapsed into pre-Reformation ways of thinking, it needs to be confronted once more with the ideas of the Reformers. Why? Because in the first place, we need to see how far modern evangelicalism has wandered from the paths laid down for it by the Reformers. And in the second, we need to learn all over again their solutions to the ills of the late medieval church. If those problems have returned, we need to rediscover their cure. So let us listen to Luther as he deals with attitudes to ministry that he associated with a corrupt and fallen church. What would he say if he knew they had resurfaced in Christian communities that claim to be evangelical?

Luther's doctrine of the priesthood of all believers served as the foundation for his criticism of distorted concepts of priesthood. Every Christian is a priest on account of his or her baptism. There is no fundamental difference in status between the ministers of the gospel, by whatever name they might choose to be known, and the ordinary believer.

All Christians are truly of the spiritual estate, and there is no difference among them except that of function. Paul says in 1 Corinthians 12:12-13 that we are all one body, with every member having its own function by which it serves the others. This is because we have one baptism, one gospel and one faith, and are all Christians, just the same as each other; for baptism, gospel and faith alone make us spiritual and a Christian people. . . . And so it follows that there is no true fundamental difference between lay persons and priests, between princes and bishops, between those living in monasteries and those living in the world. The only difference has nothing to do with status, but with the function and work which they perform.[17]

There is no place in Christianity, Luther says, for any notion of a professional class within the church whose members enjoy a closer spiritual relationship to God than their fellows.

In his treatise *Concerning the Ministry* (1523), Luther argued that all believers share in the priesthood of Christ as high priest, on account of being united to him through faith. But this does not, he insisted, imply that all believers are called to be priests. He suggested that the selection of ministers should take place in the following way. Members of the church should meet together and pray for the guidance of the Holy Spirit among them individually and as a community. Having done this, they should make their choice of minister. This person is then presented and commended to the community of faith as one who has been called to the office and work of a minister of the gospel. This would not amount to a permanent change in the status of the person thus selected; the community could subsequently choose additional or alternative persons to act in this way. Equally, they could "deselect" an existing minister on account of failings in public ministry. All Christians are given the status of priests; the exercise of that function is nevertheless conditional on the approval of the people of God.

And this insight seems to have been lost within power evangelicalism. The idea of the conditionality of priesthood—not to mention prophetic ministry and preaching—seems to have been swallowed up in the personality cult surrounding the leaders of this movement. The approval of the people of God is assumed to be at best automatic, at worst an irrelevance. The prophetic power evangelicals can set their views to one side, claiming that God has given them a personal word of knowledge, and there is no resource by which they can be corrected.

It is here that the Reformation doctrine of the priesthood of all believers is seen to be closely linked with its sister doctrine of the material sufficiency of Scripture. God reveals himself publicly through the life, death and resurrection of Jesus Christ and through Scripture. It is there for all to read. It is not the exclusive knowledge of some elite. It is not the restricted privilege of a self-selected group. It is common to all the people of God. It is available to all—and it is *meant* to be available to all. The marginalization of the publicly available revelation of God in Scripture in favor of unverifiable and exclusive revelation to individuals is the first step toward religious totalitarianism.

The accountability of ministers to their people, a central feature of the Reformation concept of the priesthood of all believers, rests on the existence of means by which their preaching, ministry and teaching may be checked out. Scripture is the sole God-given and God-authorized means by which the people of God can check out those who claim to speak in the name of their God. We must "test the spirits to see whether they are from God, because many false prophets have gone out into the world" (1 Jn 4:1). We must "test everything" and "hold on to the good" (1 Thess 5:21). If we lose sight of the objective and public character of Scripture, we are defenseless against the power evangelical who declares, "God told me to say this" or "I had a personal revelation from God authorizing me to behave in this way." The Reformation provides us with vital safeguards against such developments, enabling ordinary Christians to blow the whistle on their leaders. And as recent history has made impressively clear, Christian leaders are often just as prone to sin, failure and pride as those whom they believe they are called to lead.

The Reformation doctrine of the priesthood of all believers thus gives every Christian believer, male and female, both the *right* and the *means* to ensure that his or her church and pastors remain faithful to their gospel calling. We need to be critical of those who claim to have unverifiable personal messages from God and who make the denial or challenge of these messages tantamount to mortal sin. The Reformation principle is public accountability of preachers to the Word of God and the right of all believers to read and interpret Scripture and challenge their pastors where they appear to deny it, depart from it or subtract from it.

They say that power corrupts, and power evangelicalism too easily becomes a corrupt evangelicalism. The Reformers, our forebears in the faith, had the wisdom to restrain the potential of sin, in the light of the scriptural declaration that we are indeed a royal priesthood in the sight of God (1 Pet 2:9). We would do well to follow their wisdom in a day when corruption is so newsworthy and power so easily gained—and so easily retained. Evangelicalism needs to set its house in order here.

If in the years ahead evangelicalism gains still more spiritual and political power, it must demonstrate that it possesses the maturity and wisdom to handle that power in a responsible and authentically Christian manner. Only then will it be seen to merit its increasingly powerful position within global Christianity.

7

EVANGELICALISM & THE FUTURE OF CHRISTIANITY

T HUS FAR, MY CONCERN HAS BEEN PRIMARILY WITH EVANGEL-
icalism. I have explored its strengths and weaknesses, with a
view to understanding the threats and opportunities that lie
ahead of it. But another issue has remained unexplored, an
issue that has relevance far beyond the growing evangelical constituency. What bearing has the growth of evangelicalism on the future of
Christianity itself? A growing tendency within evangelicalism—often
described as "ecumenical evangelicalism"—is concerned to address
this issue. As this study draws to a close, it is appropriate to explore
some of the wider implications of the evangelical renaissance for the
Christian church as a whole.

The New Emphasis on Evangelism
It is being increasingly recognized that the future of Christianity depends on evangelism. Traditionally, Western understandings of the
nature of the church have been grounded on the assumption that the
church is situated within a largely settled Christian context, as in

England or Pennsylvania, and is thus primarily concerned with pastoral care and teaching. The dominance of this model within the Western tradition can be seen in the written form of the Japanese term for "church," *kyōkai,* where the two characters *(kanji)* have the natural meaning of "a teaching organization," representing the dominant ecclesiology of the nineteenth-century Western missionaries. Similarly, the written form of the term for "preach" has a strongly didactic and pastoral orientation, with the natural sense of "an explanation of the teaching." There is no sense of proclamation, for example, in this understanding of preaching, which corresponds well to the dominant Western model of "church as carer and teacher." Likewise, the Korean characters for "church" would have the natural sense of "a teaching community," just as those for "preaching" would bear the meaning "a teaching discourse." The prevalence of this model of the church is due to the historical predominance of the Western churches at a time when their social bases were at least nominally Christian.

But that period is over. One of the major developments in Western culture within the last thirty years has been massive immigration into Western cities, especially from Asia. Whether one looks at London, Toronto, Vancouver, Los Angeles, San Diego, Sydney or Melbourne, the same pattern emerges. There is a growing presence of non-Christian religions in regions that hitherto might have regarded themselves as nominally Christian.

The result has been far-reaching. The mainline Western churches, which up to this point could, with varying degrees of credibility, regard their societies as nominally Christian and thus requiring a ministry of teaching, pastoral care and social justice, are now having to adjust to the emergence of a missionary situation directly paralleling those faced by Christians elsewhere in the world. The need for evangelism has come to the fore.

This can be seen in the dramatic turnaround in thinking within mainline denominations in the West since the mid-1980s. Anglicanism will serve as a case in point.[1] Every ten years the bishops of the Anglican churches gather in England to discuss matters of mutual interest and concern. The 1988 Lambeth Conference called unequivocally for a renewed commitment to evangelism and a recognition that "evangelism is the primary task given to the church."[2] Traditionally, Anglican understandings of the nature of the church have been based on the presumption that the church is grounded in a largely settled Christian context and is thus primarily concerned with pastoral care and teaching. This assumption is not peculiarly Anglican; it is fairly typical of mainline Western Christian thinking, especially during the late nineteenth and early twentieth centuries.

But all that has changed. The primary task of the church is now to be seen as *evangelism*—that is, "a dynamic missionary emphasis going beyond care and nurture to proclamation and service."[3] In an increasingly secular age, evangelism is coming to be seen as being of decisive importance in reaching out beyond the bounds of the church. "The pressing needs of today's world demand that there be a massive shift to a 'mission' orientation."[4]

That "mission orientation" now includes a much greater awareness of the social context in which evangelism takes place. It is increasingly being realized that the proclamation of the good news cannot be restricted to individuals but must include the transformation of the context in which individuals live. A recovery of the biblical notion of the corporate and social aspects of both sin and redemption has led many younger evangelicals to be concerned about the transformation of society as well as of individual lives.[5]

There is now a growing realization, even within the depths of a frequently rather complacent Western church establishment, that the future existence and well-being of the churches depend on a determined and principled effort to proclaim the gospel. There are those who resist this development and equate evangelism with "Christian imperialism." These attitudes, which have, in the recent past, been chiefly associated with the World Council of Churches (WCC), are totally unfounded and rest on dangerously superficial understandings of the nature of the gospel in general and evangelism in particular. As Yale theologian Kathryn Tanner has pointed out, it is actually the kind of religious pluralism associated with writers such as John Hick that is guilty of "colonialist" attitudes toward other religions, on account of its endemic patronizing assumption that "all religions are saying the same thing."[6] Tanner points out that "respect for other religions" is totally consistent with the recognition that they are *not* all "saying the same thing." As the English liberal writer David L. Edwards remarks, to pretend that "religions 'teach the same thing' is to insult them profoundly by claiming that all they really teach is a view of life so vague that practically any interpretation of it by creed, code or cult is equally valid."[7]

The rise of pluralism poses no fundamental objection to the theory or practice of evangelism; indeed, if anything, it brings us closer to the world of the New Testament itself. Commenting on the situation confronted by the early church, as described in the Acts of the Apostles, the leading Anglo-Canadian evangelist Michael Green remarks,

> I find it ironic that people object to the proclamation of the Christian gospel these days because so many other faiths jostle on the doorstep of our global village. What's new? The variety of faiths in antiquity was even greater than it is today. And the early Christians, making as they did ultimate claims for Jesus, met the problem of other faiths head-on from the very outset. Their approach was interesting. They did not sit down and dialogue with other faiths very much, as far as we know. They did not denounce other faiths. They simply proclaimed Jesus with all the power and persuasiveness at their disposal.[8]

The Christian proclamation has *always* taken place in a pluralistic world, in competition with rival religious and intellectual convictions. The emergence of the gospel within the matrix of Judaism, the expansion of the gospel in a Hellenistic milieu, the early Christian expansion in pagan Rome, the establishment of the Mar Thoma church in southeastern India—in all these situations Christian apologists and theologians, not to mention ordinary Christian believers, have been aware that there are alternatives to Christianity on offer. And that has not stopped them from preaching the good news!

Evangelism, then, is not based on an imperialist craving to dominate the world, but on a longing to *share* the good news of God with a world that sorely needs hope and forgiveness, and on a fundamental conviction of the *truth* of the gospel. Evangelism is "the steel hand of truth encased in the velvet glove of love" (James S. Dennis).[9] Here is something that is true and relevant, which no caring person could fail to wish to share with others. Evangelism springs from deep feelings of love and a heartfelt desire to share something wonderful and trustworthy, something that it would be selfish and irresponsible to keep to oneself.

The WCC, apparently blinded by an inclination to see things only in terms of "power" and "domination," has lost sight of a central theme of the Christian gospel. Its agenda seems to be so out of line with "mere Christianity" that it is little wonder it is treated with such disregard by many Christians.

The WCC has often been criticized for its uncritical use of the language and categories of Marxism, where those of Christianity might seem more appropriate. The language of "imperialism" is a case in point. The term first passed into general use through the writings of Lenin, especially his 1916 pamphlet *Imperialism: The Highest Stage of Capitalism*.[10] Lenin tended to think of imperialism primarily in economic terms. But Karl Kautsky (1854-1938), the leading Marxist thinker of the Second International, defined imperialism more generally, in terms of the relationship between the advanced and underdeveloped nations, such as the political domination of underdeveloped countries by developed nations. The uncritical posturing reflected in the use of the term *imperialism* to refer to evangelization appears to be grounded in the belief that Christian mission is merely the religious component of a general program of domination by the West.[11] If there is any element of Western culture that can be described as "imperialist," it is not Christianity but a cluster of reductionist attitudes and values that in the eyes of many are ultimately anti-Christian. The WCC, which faithfully reflects these tendencies, especially in its attitude toward other religions, is far more vulnerable to the charge of "colonial" or "imperialist" styles of thinking than evangelicalism.

However, such attitudes are now seen to belong firmly to the past. Those who publicly defend them today are often aware of being viewed as "old-fashioned" or "out of touch" by their increasingly unsympathetic audiences. There is a growing realization throughout the Christian world that the threat of secularization must be met. The churches cannot rely on a legacy of cultural religiosity to ensure their continuing presence in the world. They must proclaim the profound attractiveness of faith to the world, in the full and confident expectation that the gospel is inherently attractive and relevant. As the distinguished Jesuit theologian Karl Rahner put it, "The possibility of winning new Christians from a milieu that has become unchristian is the sole living and convincing evidence that Christianity still has a real chance for the future."[12] The embargo placed by the mainline churches on evangelism is finally over.

The new realization of the importance of evangelism throughout global Christianity means that there is clearly a special place for those forms of Christianity that recognize the evangelistic imperative, that have developed resources and techniques to ensure that the gospel is faithfully and effectively proclaimed, and that have adopted a "discovery perspective" on the gospel that *expects* to find that gospel attractive. These insights, which Christianity as a whole needs to rediscover, are distinctives of evangelicalism.

But those evangelistic insights can be sustained only if they are firmly grounded in an evangelical context. Evangelism makes little sense unless there is a real and passionate conviction concerning the uniqueness of Christ, his atoning work on the cross and the need for a personal response of faith from those who hear the gospel message. A high Christology will naturally lead to evangelism, just as a low Christology (such as "Jesus as one among many religious teachers") will remove any such motivation. Evangelicalism insists that a high Christology is the inevitable and proper outcome of the New Testament witness to Christ, and thus it provides a solid christological foundation for evangelism. If this is not done, the foundational motivation for evangelism will be removed and we will return to the situation of mainline American denominations in the 1960s, when the growing influence of modernism and liberalism eroded both missionary and evangelistic efforts.[13] Evangelicalism thus provides global Christianity with a firm theological foundation and motivation for evangelism. It is no exaggeration to suggest that the future of Christianity will depend on this continuing motivation.

Yet evangelicalism has something to learn about evangelism as well. The gospel is good news for society as well as for individuals. Some evangelicals continue to argue that evangelism means nothing less and nothing more than demands for personal conversion. The concerns lying behind this position must be noted and honored. Any account of evangelism that fails to do justice to the wonder of the "good news" for individuals is to be censured as deficient. Yet in faithfulness to Scripture itself, it must be pointed out that the gospel is also "good news" for society. It is virtually impossible to read the Old Testament without being aware of the social dimensions of faith. The Old Testament prophets in particular stress that the privilege of being the people of God carries with it social responsibilities—such as demands for social justice. The Hebrew term $ṣ^e dāqâh$, which can be translated as either "righteousness" or "justice," conveys the notion that every aspect of life, personal and corporate, must be brought into line with the will of God.[14]

In England, especially during the late eighteenth and early nineteenth centuries, the social dimensions of the gospel were very much appreciated, with evangelicals such as Lord Shaftesbury taking a leading role in demands for social change.[15] But in the twentieth century some evangelicals have tended to suppress or ignore these demands, perhaps fearing a reversion to the "social gospel" that achieved such influence in the United States during the 1920s.[16] This movement, whose origins are especially associated with Walter Rauschenbusch (1861-1918), eliminated the specifically *evangelical* elements of the gospel in favor of its social implications.[17] Horrified at this development, evangelicals reacted against the "social gospel" in its entirety, fearing that any acknowledgment that the gospel does include social elements might legitimate the movement's reductionist program. This trend is especially evident in the Sydney region of Australia, where a vigorous "social gospel" movement emerged during the 1930s and seemed to many to undermine the evangelistic thrust of the gospel.[18]

Yet it needs to be understood that the "social gospel" movement is now a thing of the past. Its threat has receded to the point of insignificance. While there will always be a need for caution and concern to ensure that socially reductionist tendencies are countered, there is no longer any serious threat that a recognition of the social dimension of the gospel will lead to an abandonment of its evangelistic dimensions. Evangelicals must ensure that the social aspects of the evangel are faithfully and responsibly articulated as integral and essential elements of the evangelical affirmation of the centrality of Scripture. The proclamation of the gospel is addressed to a society, not simply a collection of individuals. And that means taking society, as well as its constituent individual members, seriously.

This vision was set out with clarity and confidence at the 1989 trend-setting Evangelical Affirmations consultation in the United States, at which six hundred leading evangelicals affirmed the need to engage with issues of human rights and social justice:

> We affirm that God commands us to seek justice in human affairs whether in the church or in society. In accord with the biblical call for righteousness, God's people should model justice in social relationships and should protest, confront and strive to alleviate injustice. . . . We affirm that evangelicals living in democratic societies should be active in public affairs. We advocate a public philosophy that advances just government and protects the rights of all.[19]

The commitment to issues of social justice is placed after the laying of a solid theological foundation for such action, thus ensuring that social action is seen as the *consequence* of a theology, rather than something that is independent of theology or takes priority over theology. A fundamental Pauline principle is thus maintained: *Theological affirmation precedes and informs moral reflection.*[20]

Evangelicalism here signaled its intention to advance into the sphere of public affairs, which it vacated for understandable, yet ultimately counterproductive, reasons in the 1920s. But this time it will engage with society from a position of theological resilience, numerical strength and a growing conviction that biblical Christianity has much to say to today's social ills. This brings us to the issue of evangelicalism's growing realization of the need to engage with public polity.

Evangelicalism and Public Polity
As evangelicalism continues its expansion, the issue of power is becoming of greater significance. In the United States and elsewhere, evangelicals are beginning to flex their political muscles, and they are taking an increasing interest in influencing local and national social agendas.

Evangelicalism has only recently come to realize the enormous importance of the formulation of a philosophy of the public square—in other words, of a public polity, by which evangelicalism can engage with the political views of America as a whole, as an insider rather than a curious and slightly perplexed outsider. The reasons for this are not difficult to discern. The public emergence of evangelicalism as a force to be reckoned with is a comparatively recent development. In its early stages, especially in the period between the two world wars, evangelicalism was dominated by fundamentalist attitudes toward the world. As Carl Henry pointed out in his prophetic work *The Uneasy Conscience of Fundamentalism* (1947),[21] this inevitably led to the privatization of faith and impoverishment of the Christian vision. "The lordship of Christ" expressed itself in individual piety and in the life of the Christian community—but did not have an impact on the world. This approach to Christian political activity resulted in the withdrawal of evangelicals from the public arena.

Now, with the benefit of hindsight, we can see that there may well have been some wisdom in this strategy. Evangelicalism needed to garner its resources and build its strength and self-confidence, rather than engaging in a potentially pointless struggle with better-organized, politically sophisticated and more numerous opponents. But that has changed. In 1976 America found itself living in *Newsweek*'s "Year of the Evangelical," with Jimmy Carter, a born-again evangelical Christian, in the White House. Yet the unprecedented media interest in evangelicalism that resulted highlighted the movement's lack of political sophistication. An evangelical president was in the White House, but evangelicalism as a whole was widely regarded as handicapped by the lack of a credible and Christian public polity. As Os Guinness comments, "Failure to articulate and abide by a vision for the common good has been the Achilles Heel of public involvement by evangelicals."[22] In part this is a direct consequence of the privatization of Christian faith by evangelicals in the earlier part of the twentieth century.

Many evangelicals have now realized that they must enter the public arena. Jerry Falwell is an example of an evangelical (one whom many would in fact regard as a fundamentalist) who has appreciated the importance of public engagement:

> Back in the sixties I was criticizing pastors who were taking time out of their pulpit to involve themselves in the civil rights movement or any other political venture. I said you're wasting your time from what you're called to do. Now I find myself doing the same thing and for the same reasons they did.[23]

Falwell is an important witness to the evangelical need to get involved in the affairs of the world. He reminds us that "we are not to be only the light of the world but also the salt of the earth."[24] But that also means understanding the world we are proposing to engage with—and especially the public life of the United States of America.

The political life of the United States is dominated by a form of liberal pluralism that seeks to allow all social groupings the maximum liberty possible. The present dominance of liberal public polities in the American political context is a factor that evangelicals must wrestle with as they seek to bring the gospel to bear on society. It must be appreciated that this liberal polity *wants* Christianity to become a private matter, without any public impact. Why? Because it can then be mastered more effectively and accommodated more easily within a pluralist culture. Guinness puts this point neatly:

> To many Americans, especially among the thought leaders, the question of religion in public life has become unimportant. It is viewed as a non-issue or a nuisance factor—something which should be a purely private issue, which inevitably becomes messy and controversial when it does not stay so, and which should therefore revert to being private as quickly as possible.[25]

A form of Christianity that vigorously asserts that by its very inalienable nature it has social implications will cause difficulties for a liberal social polity. Why? Because that polity will be obliged to admit that it tolerates actions and doctrines only to the extent that they do not undermine liberal values. This point is clearly recognized and stated by liberal political theorist William A. Galston:

> The moral commitments of liberalism influence—and in some cases circumscribe—the ability of individuals within a liberal society to engage fully in particular ways of life. If, to be wholly effective, a religious doctrine requires control over the totality of individual life, including the formative social and political environment, then the classic liberal demand that religion be practiced privately amounts to a substantive restriction on the free exercise of that religion. The manifold blessings of liberal social orders come with a price, and we should not be surprised when those who are asked to pay grow restive.[26]

One of the tasks of evangelical writers, speakers and lobbyists is to bring home the point that the alleged neutrality of juridical liberalism conceals a definite bias against any version of Christianity that extends its interests and concerns into the public domain—and that it thus encourages precisely the kind of quietism and individualism that allowed Hitler to come to power in 1930s Germany. It forces Christians to retreat from the public square, precisely because they cannot give full expression to their faith in this area. As Guinness wrote, "To demand 'neutral discourse' in public life, as some still do, should now be recognized as a way of coercing people to speak publicly in someone else's language and thus never to be true to their own."[27]

But how then is evangelicals' advance into the public square to be achieved? In practice, the answer that has been given is quite simple: through gaining power. Evangelicals can achieve their social vision only through domination of the political system and agenda. And this is what causes the problems. For the real issue is domination in a fallen world. Evangelicals, like everyone else in this sinful world, can fall victim to what Walter Wink has termed the "Domination System."[28] Evangelical preachers and pastors have been deeply influenced by a Machiavellian obsession with power. Power is what is seen to matter, in the church and in the world. Evangelicals need to gain power, it is thought, if they are to influence people and their society.

It is my conviction, instead, that evangelicalism needs to rediscover the cross of Christ and its fundamental challenge to the world. God chose to redeem the world through an act that in the eyes of that world was weakness and foolishness. At no point in the narrative of redemption that centers on Jesus Christ is secular power endorsed. Indeed, Jesus took every opportunity to distance himself from possible political or secularizing interpretations of his ministry as Messiah.

There is a real need for evangelicals to consider carefully whether they are in danger of being overwhelmed by the world, precisely because they have chosen to imitate its methods and norms as they attempt to confront it. Joseph Goebbels, the skilled propaganda minister of the Third Reich, is reported to have said, "Even if we lose, we shall win, for our ideals will have penetrated the hearts of our enemies."[29] Evangelicals may be able to defeat the threat to faith posed by a secular world; but by using its methods they will have allowed it to gain its greatest victory. The evangelicalism that thus overwhelms the world has itself been overwhelmed and taken captive by the one it sought to defeat. As Wink puts it,

> One does not become free from the Powers by defeating them in a frontal attack. Rather, one dies to their control. Here also the cross is the model: we are liberated, not by striking back at what enslaves us—for even striking back reveals that we are still deter-

mined by its violent ethos—but by dying out from under its juris-
diction and command.[30]

Getting involved with the world runs the risk of falling into the world.
However, so long as those risks are identified, strategies may be devised to minimize their impact.

Since about 1920, evangelicals have neglected to pay attention to
social and political thought; yet the family history of the movement
bears witness that its earlier generations showed a passionate concern
for public issues. Inevitably, many evangelicals today feel overwhelmed by the task confronting them. But a proper theological and
historical perspective is in order. As Guinness has said, "Revival and
reformation in America in the late twentieth century have about as
much chance as the likelihood of an obscure provincial sect overturn-
ing Imperial Rome."[31] There are encouraging developments within
English evangelicalism, where there are signs of the emergence of a
concerted and considered evangelical approach to issues of public
ethics.[32]

This development breaks down one of the major barriers to further
evangelical expansion in many Third World regions, where issues of
social justice are of major importance and the social implications of
the "good news" are seen as an integral aspect—but by no means the
only aspect—of evangelism. Evangelicalism is now well on the way to
becoming a full partner in addressing issues of global social justice,
without suppressing or reducing the gospel itself.

Third World evangelicals were deeply disturbed by the overtly political stance of the 1968 World Council of Churches meeting at Upp-
sala, widely regarded as a travesty of the gospel. Yet they were equally
alarmed at the individualism of some Western evangelicals, who
seemed to suppress the social implications of the gospel by focusing
solely on its personal benefits to individuals. A "middle way," it
seemed to them, needed to be found. That development is now fully
under way, both in the Third World and in the West.

It is clear that much more needs to be done; yet it is also clear that
there is a growing sense of confidence and purpose within evangeli-

calism and that it now feels sufficiently stable to be able to address the issues troubling the world. This involves developing strategies to allow evangelicals to work alongside others on shared concerns.

Collaboration on Issues of Orthodoxy and Ethics

As evangelicalism gains in self-confidence, it has begun to form alliances with other Christian groupings in an effort to further its goals and objectives. Of particular importance here is the evangelical emphasis on the importance of doctrinal orthodoxy and ethical standards. Evangelicals have increasingly shown themselves willing to collaborate with nonevangelicals who are concerned with such issues.

The origins of this trend can be traced to the mid-1950s, when Billy Graham began to lead crusades involving coalitions that included some churches with no formal evangelical commitment. The goal of preaching the gospel to as many people as possible, in Graham's view, took priority over lesser issues. This did not entail formal approval of the doctrinal positions of such churches; rather, it represented a willingness to regard these as subsidiary to the more important goal of evangelism. Since then, the approach adopted by Graham has been developed and consolidated.

The basic tactic involved, developed by Francis Schaeffer and elaborated by James I. Packer and others, is generally known as "cobelligerence." Its basic principle can be stated as follows. There is no inconsistency in evangelicals' forming alliances or coalitions with others to address issues on which they can agree. Such a coalition would be temporary in nature and limited in its objectives. It would not commit evangelicals to collaboration on any other issue, nor to any acknowledgment or admission of the correctness or incorrectness of the outlooks of such other groups.

Cobelligerence is a strategy that acknowledges differences between Christians while allowing them to collaborate on limited and well-defined goals. Recognizing that the church may find itself unable to command universal assent throughout society, Schaeffer argued for the need to form coalitions with other groups on issues upon which agreement could be reached. This approach rested on both pragmatic and theological considerations. Pragmatically, there was the realization of the need to work together with others for the common good and that aspects of the Christian vision for the common good were shared by others outside the church. To run with them on some issues was not to run with them on others.

But there is also a theological dimension to this approach. It is the notion of common grace, by which God is able to allow at least traces of his righteousness to be picked up outside the Christian faith. We should aim to look for these resonances between the gospel and the world, and we should exploit them where we find them. The point at issue is well made by Harry Blamires:

> Desperate as we Christians are to stem the tide of immorality and degeneracy, we must not pretend that it is simply *qua* Christians that we man the barricades. . . . It is not just St. Paul, St. Augustine, John Bunyan, or John Wesley who would be horrified at what we have come to acquiesce in the way of legalized embryonicide and pornography. Surely Virgil and Seneca, Plato and Plotinus would be horrified too.[33]

Yet an obvious danger lurks here. The Christian churches can easily be seen simply as a sectarian power group or lobby.[34] Charles Colson, writing from the context of an experience of the corrupting effects of power that few of us hope to share, stresses the perils of allowing the church to be seen as just another special interest group. He points to the case of Ronald Reagan's 1980 campaign. When Reagan met up with some Religious Right activists, he was challenged for mixing politics and religion; his response was to the effect that the church is just like any other special interest group, such as a union.[35] Colson takes a certain delight in relating how he himself had been able to set traps for religious leaders to ensure that they gave President Richard Nixon maximum exposure and credibility when he needed it.

Any permanent alliance between the church and a political party or tendency will result in the church's losing its public credibility. Citing his own experience in prison ministries, Colson has stressed, rightly, that the moral witness of the church must be grounded in its pastoral care and compassion for people. If it is to gain respect and credibility, the church needs to be seen to be above politics.

So what sort of objectives are suited to this approach? Evangelism is one goal that has caused the emergence of alliances between evangelicals and nonevangelicals; at present, however, it seems that issues of doctrinal orthodoxy and ethics, public and private, appear to be of major importance. An example of both will illustrate the scope of this development and its potential implications.

During the late 1960s a scheme of union was proposed between the Church of England and the Methodist Church. This proposal was backed with some enthusiasm by those committed to ecumenism. It was regarded with some alarm, however, by many Anglicans, who were convinced that the outcome of such a merger would be the formation of a liberal Protestant denomination with little serious commitment to doctrinal orthodoxy. So a temporary alliance was formed between Anglo-Catholics and evangelicals within the Church of England, with the limited and specific objective of blocking the proposal. The leading lights of this effort were Eric L. Mascall and Graham Leonard in the Anglo-Catholic wing of the church and James I. Packer and Colin Buchanan in the evangelical wing. The tactic succeeded. The irritated critics of this coalition dubbed it "an unholy alliance"; it was, however, a simple and effective instance of cobelligerence.

In the United States in more recent times, growing anxiety concerning a number of ethical issues, including abortion on demand, has led to the formation of alliances between evangelicals and Roman Catholics. Despite substantial doctrinal differences between the two groups, there is an increasing recognition of convergence in relation to a series of major moral issues. The considerable numerical strength of both groups has led to the emergence of a pressure group with considerable political influence, which seems set to exercise growing leverage over public polity in this area. The general program outlined by Os Guinness, and embodied in the Williamsburg Declaration, may also be seen as an aspect of this trend, with particular reference to the concern to reinstate religion in the public life of the United States.[36]

The long-term implications of this growing trend are considerable. At one level it represents the formation of a strategic alliance of doctrinally and ethically conservative Christians against aggressively liberal trends in church and society; at another it represents evangelicals' deliberate decision to break free from the final remaining aspect of the legacy of fundamentalism—the demand for total doctrinal agreement before collaboration of any kind is permissible. The growing willingness of an increasingly powerful and articulate evangelicalism to collaborate on issues of shared concern is an important indication of future trends in global Christianity. It also raises the issue of the relationship between evangelicalism and Roman Catholicism.

Evangelicalism and Roman Catholicism
The relationship between "evangelicalism" and "Protestantism" requires careful thought. A Protestant is not necessarily an evangelical, for it is quite possible to give formal assent to a Protestant confession of faith (such as the Westminster Confession or the Formula of Concord) without personally assimilating the faith to which it points. The need for a living personal faith in Christ, as opposed to mere doctrinal alignment with a Protestant denomination, is of major importance. So not all Protestants are evangelicals. *But are all evangelicals Protestant?*

In the past this question would have been answered unequivocally in the affirmative. Not all Protestants are evangelicals; but all evangelicals are Protestants. Indeed, older forms of evangelicalism, such as those prevailing in Britain in the nineteenth century, often consciously regarded themselves as anti-Roman Catholic. Yet in the last decade there has been a perceptible shift within Roman Catholicism, especially in North America, which will be of major importance to the future relationship between evangelicalism and Roman Catholicism. I have already noted the growing trend toward collaboration between evangelicals and Roman Catholics on moral issues. But what is happening on the ground is now going beyond this.

Let me make it clear that the development in question is taking place primarily among individual Roman Catholics. At the official level, the Roman Catholic Church remains critical of many aspects of the Reformation agenda, and this agenda continues to be of central importance to most evangelicals. Indeed, I have stressed throughout this work that the Reformation is rightly regarded as a major point of reference for evangelicalism and is honored as an epochal moment in the family history of the movement. As an institution, then, Roman Catholicism remains hostile to evangelicalism.

Ecumenism has gone some way toward reducing this tension. We must acknowledge that there is a real danger of an evangelical misunderstanding and misrepresentation of Roman Catholicism; talking with others is one way of ensuring that we do others the justice that we would like them to do us. It helps clear up misunderstandings and allows us to see how different terminologies can sometimes conceal some degree of agreement. In the past, evangelicals have misrepresented Roman Catholicism (not, I think maliciously, but more out of confusion over the terminology used by the Council of Trent); ecumenism has helped us see Catholics in their true light. We owe it to Roman Catholics to take the trouble to get them right, instead of perpetuating, whether by accident or design, inaccurate stereotypes of their beliefs. For example, some evangelicals continue to insist that the Roman Catholic church officially teaches justification by works,[37] yet this is simply not true.

The same issue arises in other contexts. I recently heard a sermon at a large evangelical church in Oxford which was severely critical of the Roman Catholic practice of using crucifixes as an aid to devotion. "They worship a dead Jesus!" was the charge laid against those who indulged in this practice. "We worship a risen Christ!" Now there is doubtless some truth in that criticism, in that a portrayal of Christ dying on the cross might encourage some people to think of Jesus as a religious hero or martyr rather than the Son of God and our Savior. But it was quite clear that the young preacher was convinced that

Roman Catholics *do* worship a dead man rather than a risen Lord.

Although I have, I think, read just about every major work of Roman Catholic spirituality written from around 1550 to today, I must admit that I have never encountered this view in print nor met a Roman Catholic who accepts it. All of the works I have read make more or less the same point: a crucifix is helpful to prayer because it brings to mind the sufferings of Jesus Christ and hence reminds us of the enormous cost of our redemption. Martin Luther makes much the same point in his "theology of the cross." We may not agree with the practice—but we should take the trouble to understand what is going on! It is too easy to misunderstand and misrepresent.

Yet when all is said and done, there are limits to how far this is going to get us. For there comes a point at which misunderstandings are removed and a hard core of real disagreements over issues of major substance still remains unresolved. The agenda of the Reformation obstinately refuses to go away, and it cannot be ignored by any who hope to bring Protestants and Roman Catholics closer together.

This point is stressed in an important recent essay by Donald A. Carson of Trinity Evangelical Divinity School.[38] While noting substantial points of agreement between evangelicalism and Roman Catholicism, he rightly points out that issues of major importance remain to be addressed and resolved—issues such as the locus of revelation, the means of grace, the nature of the church and the significance of Mary. The agenda of the Reformation remains on the ecumenical table today. Although there are theoretical models available to allow Roman Catholicism to take on board the Reformation agenda without significant loss of face,[39] I do not expect these to be taken up in the near future. The official dialogue between Protestant and Roman Catholicism has probably gotten as far as it can go, and it would be unrealistic to look to it for further progress. At the institutional level, Roman Catholicism remains hostile to evangelicalism, although I gladly note that the level of hostility appears to be dramatically lower than it was fifty years ago. But the real movement is at ground level, among ordinary Roman Catholic believers.

Many evangelicals react with surprise, or even outrage, to the suggestion that evangelicalism is becoming increasingly important within Roman Catholicism. How can a Roman Catholic, who believes in such nonevangelical beliefs as praying for the dead, the Immaculate Conception or Mary's being a coredeemer alongside Christ, be an evangelical? This reaction, though entirely understandable, rests on the assumption that individual Roman Catholics accept the authority of all the official teachings of their church. The empirical evidence available suggests that large numbers of them simply do not. The widespread refusal to obey the Vatican's explicit teachings on artificial methods of birth control is simply one symptom of something much deeper—a tendency to value the Roman Catholic ethos while being selective concerning those aspects of its teaching which are appropriated.[40]

The result is that many Roman Catholics, especially in the United States, remain outwardly and publicly loyal to their church, while inwardly and privately they embrace the leading ideas of evangelicalism. (This contrasts sharply with the situation in Latin America, where a growing sympathy with evangelicalism has led to a public rejection of Roman Catholicism and an equally public embrace of the theological ideas and styles of worship of various forms of evangelicalism.[41])

An unofficial ecumenism is thus growing in both extent and influence. It has two aspects: on the one hand, some individual evangelicals are exploring the attractions of Roman Catholicism; on the other, increasing numbers of individual Roman Catholics are being drawn to evangelicalism while generally remaining publicly loyal to their church.[42] In the short term, this will probably lead to a growing warmth between individual evangelicals and Roman Catholics, despite the substantial official doctrinal divide between them. I would expect this to be catalyzed by a growing sense that Christianity as a whole needs to stand up at every level against an increasingly militant secular culture, with local collaboration being seen as a legitimate way for Christians to come together and fight for their mutual rights. It is not my intention to defend or criticize this trend; I am simply reporting it and assessing its basis and potential impact for the future of both evangelicalism and global Christianity. It is certainly something that evangelicals need to be aware of.

So why are so many Roman Catholics attracted to evangelicalism? From my own conversations, the following issue emerges as being of major importance. It is not the only such issue; but it is a theme that recurs in such discussions. Many Roman Catholics believe that a concern for the gospel itself must overshadow the lesser issue of church order. A disinclination to blindly obey each and every aspect of their church's official teaching allows them to embrace privately many of the ideas and values of evangelicalism while retaining at least the vestiges of an outward loyalty to their church. Often that loyalty is based on a sense of national loyalty (especially in Italy and Spain) or communal identity (especially in Irish and Hispanic communities in the United States). We have been here before; the term Nicodemism was used in the sixteenth century to refer to Roman Catholics, especially in France, who were outwardly loyal to their church while privately admiring and responding to the writings of John Calvin.[43]

If this analysis is correct, it follows that evangelicalism can expect to gain a growing hearing within Roman Catholicism in the next decade. It will do so not primarily on account of any official institutional sympathy for the movement, but because of a growing interest in and admiration for the movement among individual Roman Catholics.

This clearly raises the question of how evangelicalism should respond to this movement. Two broad options are available.

1. Demand that such people leave the Roman Catholic Church and join an explicitly evangelical church, because of the failure of the former to adopt the Reformation agenda and bring its life and doctrine fully into line with Scripture. This is happening on a substantial scale in Latin America; there is little indication that it is happening, or is about to happen, in Western Europe or the United States, where social conditions are significantly different.

2. Encourage the growth of evangelicalism within the Roman Cath-

olic Church, in the hope that this will lead to growing pressure for reform and renewal from within and the return of the church to a more evangelical ethos.

It is beyond the scope of this work to assess the merits of these two approaches. However, the tension between the public and private aspects of this matter suggests that at least in the short term, evangelicalism would be well advised to encourage Roman Catholics to discover the vitality of evangelicalism without pressing them to leave their church. The growing threat of evangelicalism to the Roman Catholic Church in South America may well lead to an increasing toleration of evangelicalism within American Roman Catholicism, as Catholic leaders seek to avoid a repetition of the situation on the Southern continent. For the moment, it would seem unwise for evangelicals to do anything other than encourage what already seems to be happening and ensure that evangelicalism continues to be a real option for Roman Catholics.

In many ways what is now happening seems to be a replay of the situation in the early 1500s, when many individual Roman Catholics, including several cardinals, found no difficulty in adopting evangelical beliefs and attitudes while remaining loyal to their church, which they hoped to reform and renew from within. This phenomenon is especially well documented from the Italian context,[44] but it is also known to have been important in both France and Italy. Had this process been allowed to continue, the history of the Reformation might have taken a very different course.

That history seems to be repeating itself before our eyes. Its eventual outcome will be of major importance to the theme of this book. But the very fact that it is happening is an important affirmation of the growing importance of evangelicalism in global Christianity.

Yet this process should not be seen as a one-way street. It is a simple fact of life that some evangelicals find themselves drawn to Roman Catholicism, and it is important to take the trouble to find out what attracts them to it. The following factors seem to be especially significant.

First, Roman Catholicism has a strong emphasis on the corporate aspects of the Christian life, which is often missing from evangelicalism.

Second, its fixed liturgy gives an element of stability to public worship. Evangelicalism is prone to individualism in both these respects. Its public worship is often dependent on the whims of its pastors, who determine the forms of worship and prayer used on any given occasion. This can—but need not—lead to disconcertingly wild and unpredictable variations in the form of worship, forcing people to concentrate on the worship itself rather than its ultimate object. (This is also known to be an important consideration for many evangelicals who move across into more liturgical churches, such as the Lutheran or Episcopalian church.)

Third, Roman Catholicism is often perceived to be strongly committed at the institutional level to the leading doctrines of Christian orthodoxy, including the divinity and resurrection of Christ. Many evangelicals within mainline Protestant denominations sense that their denomination as a whole is less than fully committed to these doctrines and find themselves attracted to Roman Catholicism in consequence. They regard their new church's commitment to doctrines they regard as at best questionable (such as the assumption of Mary) as a price worth paying in order to guarantee commitment to orthodoxy at other points.

Fourth, Roman Catholicism makes relatively few demands of its laity, so that there is a very low degree of burnout within its congregations, in contrast to the alarmingly high degrees of burnout often seen within activist evangelical congregations. Roman Catholicism provides an atmosphere in which those who have been burnt out by a negative church experience are given time to lick their wounds and recover.

And finally, many within evangelicalism are alarmed at its failure to deal with issues of social justice and believe that the social aspects of the good news are addressed more effectively by Roman Catholicism.

181

Yet each of these issues can be addressed, at least to some extent, within evangelicalism itself. The known appeal of Roman Catholicism to some evangelicals can and should be a stimulus to evangelicalism to check itself out. One of the greatest threats to the future of evangelicalism within the world Christian community would be the emergence of complacency and a smug sense of self-satisfaction within its ranks. This need not happen; being aware of both the attraction of other forms of Christianity to evangelicals and the grounds of that attraction will ensure that evangelicalism is an *ecclesia semper refor-manda,* "a church that is always reforming itself," rather than a body that stagnates while luxuriating in a premature self-congratulation.

Evangelicalism and the Collapse of the Enlightenment

At some point around 1750, a major shift began to take place in Western Europe and North America as a new period in cultural history opened up. The period in question, known as the Enlightenment, would have a major impact on Christianity in those regions.[45] The movement asserted the omnicompetence of human reason. Reason, it was argued, is capable of telling us everything we need to know about God and morality. Some welcomed this development, regarding it as a permanent change in human culture.

The contributors to *The Myth of God Incarnate* (1977), an influential work of English radical theology, seem to have regarded the Enlightenment as something that was given and fixed for all time. It was here and it was right. For example, Leslie Houlden argued that we have no option but to accept the rationalist outlook of the Enlightenment and restructure our Christian thinking accordingly. "We must accept our lot, bequeathed to us by the Enlightenment, and make the most of it."[46] Yet even as Houlden was writing, the Enlightenment worldview was dying. What was once thought to be a universal worldview was increasingly recognized to be a purely Western phenomenon that Western academics and politicians sought to impose on others.

The rise of the movement that is now generally known as postmodernism is a direct result of both the collapse of this confidence in reason and a more general disillusionment with the so-called modern world.[47] Postmodernism is the intellectual movement proclaiming that, in the first place, the Enlightenment rested on fraudulent intellectual foundations (such as the belief in the omnicompetence of human reason), and in the second, it ushered in some of the most horrific events in human history—such as the Stalinist purges and the Nazi extermination camps.[48] The new cultural mood that developed in the 1980s rebelled against the Enlightenment. Who wanted anything to do with an intellectually dubious movement that had given rise to the Nazi Holocaust and the Stalinist purges?

There has thus been a widespread collapse of confidence in the Enlightenment trust in the power of reason to provide foundations for a universally valid knowledge of the world, including God. Reason fails to deliver a morality suited to the real world. And with this collapse of confidence in universal and necessary criteria of truth, relativism and pluralism have flourished. In the 1880s Nietzsche declared, somewhat prematurely as it turned out, "God is dead!" More recently it is the death of the Enlightenment that is being proclaimed. It remains far from clear what will replace it. But what is clear is that the claustrophobic and restrictive straitjacket placed on Western Christianity by rationalism has gone.

The relevance of these comments for evangelicalism will be clear. Its Western critics have often accused it of being "premodern," adopting attitudes, beliefs and outlooks that were incompatible with those of the modern period. For example, its vigorous defense of the resurrection was regarded as totally out of touch with the modern worldview. With the collapse of confidence in the Enlightenment, evangelicalism has suddenly found itself with an unexpected advantage over its rivals, whose bureaucracies are generally still dominated by older people who have yet to learn of the demise of the Enlightenment.

It is important in this context to appreciate that it is younger people, especially those who are currently engaged in academic studies, who are most acutely aware of the death of the Enlightenment and the rise of postmodernism. This has merely reinforced the attraction of evangelicalism to this age group and highlighted how out of touch some of the leaders of the mainline denominations seem to be. Evangelicalism represents a form of Christianity ideally adapted both to the intellectual climate that results from the death of modernity in the West and to that of the developing world, in which the Enlightenment never had much influence anyway. As global Christianity enters an era in which the impact of the Enlightenment is a thing of the past, evangelicalism together with forms of Christianity that have evolved in parts of the world unaffected by the Enlightenment are poised to increase their influence still further.

Evangelicalism as a Threat to Mainline Christianity?
As study after study demonstrates, evangelicalism is drawing people—especially young people—away from mainline churches. Only churches that are themselves evangelical in orientation (such as the Southern Baptist Convention) or that have a significant evangelical presence within their ranks (such as the Church of England) are seen to be benefiting from the growth in evangelicalism worldwide.

What are the implications of these well-documented developments? There are certainly indications that evangelicalism is displacing other forms of Christianity in some regions, such as Latin America. Evangelicalism is also becoming an increasingly powerful presence in many parts of Eastern Europe, such as Russia and the Ukraine. Evangelicalism is clearly destined to be an increasingly significant element in global Christianity, and it is going to pose a significant threat to rival versions of Christianity. There is every indication that it will soon become—if it is not already—the dominant form of Protestant Christianity in North America.

But it would be simplistic to suggest that evangelicalism will merely displace other forms of Christianity in the West, for there are other possibilities. One major possibility is that mainline churches will take the trouble to find out why evangelicalism is proving so attractive and adapt themselves accordingly. Evangelicalism owes its successes partly to the failures and irresponsibility of the dominant liberal trends in

Western Christianity since World War II. By a series of historical accidents and calculated developments, liberalism managed to gain control of most of the seminaries and bureaucracies of the mainline Protestant churches in North America.[49] Many of those now in positions of leadership in such denominations gained their theological education during the 1960s and 1970s, when theological liberalism was at its zenith. Through subsequent isolation and insulation from theological developments, however, they have failed to realize that liberalism is losing its academic appeal; because they have been involved with the bureaucracy rather than pastoral work, they seem to have been shielded from the realization that liberalism has depressingly little to say that can console the world in its grief or challenge it in its apathy. The result is simply that these denominations are being directed in a manner that can only lead them to further numerical decline, as their members desert them for explicitly evangelical denominations. So evangelical success is partly a response to mainline irresponsibility.

If these Protestant denominations were to ask themselves why so many of their members are attracted to evangelicalism, the situation might be rather different. On the basis of the analysis of the attraction of evangelicalism presented earlier, the two following strategies could be expected to go some way toward checking the advance of evangelicalism at the expense of the mainline denominations.

1. Restore Christian orthodoxy to the churches. This need be little more than the basic, consensual "mere Christianity" advocated by C. S. Lewis. One of the attractions of evangelicalism is that it represents a Christian orthodoxy that is all too often conspicuously absent from the public pronouncements of the mainline Protestant churches.

2. Place evangelism at the top of the church's agenda. The failure of many mainline churches to show a public commitment to the gospel is known to be a major contributing factor to the success of evangelicalism. Many mainline churches have appreciated this and laid stress on the need to "lead people to Christ" and to "help others to come to faith."[50] Other strategies could easily be devised on the basis of the

analysis presented in this study. As will be clear, the growth of evangelicalism is partly a result of failure on the part of its rivals.

However, I must point out that merely tinkering with things will not, in the end, remedy the situation. For example, I noted earlier that evangelism can be sustained only on the basis of a theology that legitimates the proclamation of Christ—a theology that is all too often absent from the official pronouncements of some denominations. There is a real need for a radical reappraisal on the part of mainline churches, with a view to rediscovering truths that were abandoned in the headlong rush to modernize in the twentieth century. The rise of liberalism was not an organic grassroots phenomenon; it was imposed upon the churches by an academic and social elite. Evangelicalism, in contrast, is a popular phenomenon, as its rapid development in Latin America in particular makes clear. The rise of evangelicalism may be a judgment on churches that have lost their way, inviting them to rediscover and reappropriate the gospel before they are decimated by the continuing rise of a movement that has retained what they discarded.

Perhaps the most significant contribution that evangelicalism can make to the future of Christianity is to force others to realize that the liberal experiment has failed and the future of Christianity lies in returning to the New Testament and rediscovering the appeal of biblical Christianity. The Enlightenment insisted that this was naive and impossible; the Enlightenment, however, is dead, and with it must also die the petty restrictions it sought to impose on all Western culture. Christianity is free to be itself once more.

And that brings us to our concluding consideration—the major impact that evangelicalism is having on the move to "re-form" the center of mainline denominations.

Evangelicalism and the "Re-forming of the Center"

One of the most significant developments in mainline Protestant denominations since the late 1980s has been a concerted move by a hitherto silent majority to protest against the increasingly ideological stance of their bureaucracies, administrators and senior leaders and return to "mere Christianity"—that is, a consensual Christian orthodoxy. There is widespread disillusionment with the ecumenical agenda and its institutions. The World Council of Churches assembly at Canberra seemed to many ordinary Christian believers to come dangerously close to lapsing into some kind of pagan nature religion. There is every indication of a widespread yearning to return to Christian basics. In no way can this be stigmatized as "fundamentalism." It is just a longing to get back to the basic ideas of the Christian faith and move away from the politically and culturally conditioned versions of Christianity that have recently gained the ascendancy in church hierarchies—but most emphatically *not* among ordinary believers.

Movements to "re-form the center" have sprung up in virtually every denomination. Such movements transcend denominational lines, and they are at their heart concerned with the restoration of orthodoxy after a long period of radical experiments that are now widely acknowledged to have failed. And as I have stressed in this work, evangelicalism is at its heart nothing less than basic Christian orthodoxy. It is therefore to be expected that evangelicals are heavily involved in such movements, with the concept of "cobelligerence" allowing them to overlook the points of difference with collaborators who share their concern to restore orthodox belief to their wayward churches.

Examples of such developments are now obvious everywhere. In the United Church of Christ, evangelicals such as Gabriel Fackre (Andover Newton School of Theology) are heavily involved in the move to steer the denomination away from its recent liberal leanings. In the Episcopal Church in the United States, the Anglican Institute has brought together evangelicals and Anglo-Catholics in a common concern to steer that church away from its obsession with single-issue agendas and restore a vision of the gospel. In Canada, evangelicals are heavily involved in the Essentials '94 movement, designed to re-form the center in a church that has clearly lost its way over the last generation.

As impatience with the radical experiments of the postwar generation grows apace within the Western churches, evangelicalism is in a position to increase both numerically (through its appeal to those who yearn for Christian basics) and in its influence within the mainline churches (through supporting those working for the restoration of orthodoxy). The significance of this development in the longer term is impossible to predict. What can be said, however, is that evangelicalism is now widely seen as both a renewing and a reforming movement by churches whose members are increasingly calling out for renewal and reformation.

The Future of Evangelicalism

It will be clear from the present study that evangelicalism is likely to be of considerable significance to global Christianity as it prepares to enter the next millennium. Evangelicalism is expanding outside its English-speaking context and gaining new ground in Europe, Asia, Africa and Latin America. And what of its future in the West, its traditional heartland? All the signs there too seem to be encouraging.

But we have been down this road of apparent success before. The expansion of Calvinism in late sixteenth-century Europe is a case in point. By 1591 Calvinism seemed to have made irreversible gains throughout Europe. The German Calvinist Abraham Scultetus (1566-1624) wrote of the sense of optimism that pervaded the movement at this time.

> I cannot fail to recall the optimistic mood which I and many others felt when we considered the condition of the Reformed churches in 1591. In France there ruled the valiant King Henri IV, in England the mighty Queen Elizabeth, in Scotland the learned King James, in the Palatinate the bold hero John Casimir, in Saxony the courageous and powerful Elector Christian I, in Hesse the clever and prudent Landgrave William, who were all inclined to the Reformed religion. In the Netherlands everything went as Prince Maurice of Orange wished, when he took Breda, Zutphen, Hulst and Nijmegen. . . . We imagined that a golden age had dawned.[51]

But within decades the vision had perished. Squabbling within the movement became serious long-term division. The political stability of those regions of Europe sympathetic to Calvinism was undermined. Calvinism survived largely through emigration to North America, where it was able to reestablish itself in New England. Yet in the longer term, rationalism crept in where Calvinism had once reigned, both in Europe and in America.[52] Will today's evangelicalism go the same way?

The question cannot be answered. But like a sword of Damocles, it hangs over the movement. Evangelicals are sinful human beings like everyone else. And the sheer humanity of the movement may easily eclipse whatever within it is of God. The movement needs to learn from its own history, which alerts it to the errors of the past. Without this perspective, it may do little more than repeat yesterday's mistakes, resulting in tomorrow's decline. Above all, there is a danger that evangelicalism may break up into mutually suspicious splinter groups, each claiming to be the only representatives of a "true evangelicalism" that others have "sold out" or "betrayed."

The rise of a future "evangelical rationalism" is a real threat, made more serious by further expansion of evangelicalism in academic circles. Yet the emergence of a purely cerebral evangelicalism can be countered by a continuing emphasis on evangelism, an insistence that theology be grounded in and related to pastoral practice and a continuing appreciation of the experiential aspects of faith. If "evangelical rationalism" represents one unwelcome potential development, the other is an unthinking emotionalism that spurns the objective, cognitive dimension of faith in favor of its subjective, experiential aspects. Evangelicalism offers us a vision in which theologians are evangelists and evangelists theologians.

In short, the threats to evangelicalism are real—but so are its opportunities and its resources. This work has attempted to explore the contours of a very complex movement, noting both its strengths and its weaknesses. If I were rash enough to predict the future, that prediction would take the following form. The movement will continue to grow numerically in the next generation and will achieve a still greater academic, social and political significance. Yet with this growth and increasing acceptance will come the risk of becoming another form of the liberal Protestantism that dominated the European and American churches of the late nineteenth century. This need never happen; it remains, nonetheless, a real possibility.

The challenge to evangelicalism is this: can it cope with sustained growth, increasing intellectual sophistication and growing acceptance within the churches? Or will it lose sight of its distinctive ideas and emphases? If this work helps evangelicals to appreciate the genuine attraction and distinctiveness of their beliefs, it may go some way toward ensuring the future well-being of the movement in particular, and of the Christian faith in general.

Notes

Introduction
[1] William Wordsworth, "French Revolution, As It Appeared to Enthusiasts at Its Commencement," lines 4-5.
[2] See Leslie R. Keylock, "Evangelical Protestants Take Over Center Stage," *Publishers Weekly,* March 9, 1984, pp. 32-34.
[3] John N. Vaughan, "North America's Fastest Growing Churches," *Church Growth Today* 5, no. 1 (1990): 1.
[4] See David Martin, *Tongues of Fire: The Explosion of Protestantism in Latin America* (Oxford: Blackwell, 1990); David Stoll, *Is Latin America Turning Protestant?* (Berkeley: University of California Press, 1991). For an excellent assessment of still more recent developments, see Karl-Wilhelm Westmeier, "Themes of Pentecostal Expansion in Latin America," *International Bulletin of Missionary Research* 17 (1993): 72-78.
[5] See R. T. France and Alister E. McGrath, eds., *Evangelical Anglicans* (London: SPCK, 1993).
[6] For evidence of the need for maturity among younger evangelicals, see John G. Stackhouse Jr., "Perpetual Adolescence: The Emerging Culture of North American Evangelicalism," *Crux* 29, no. 3 (1993): 32-37.
[7] Although Francis Schaeffer perhaps overstates such anxieties, his *The Great Evangelical Disaster* (Westchester, Ill.: Crossway, 1984) sounds some important notes of warning.
[8] See Alister McGrath, "Why Doctrine? The Confession of a Disillusioned Liberal," in *Doctrine Matters,* ed. G. Kuhrt (London: Hodder & Stoughton, 1993), pp. 1-18.

Chapter 1: The Evangelical Renaissance
[1] See Wade Clark Roof and William McKinney, *American Mainline Religion: Its Changing Shape and Future* (Princeton, N.J.: Rutgers University Press, 1987). Some useful material may also be found in Robert Wuthnow, *The Restructuring of American Religion: Society and Faith Since World War II* (Princeton, N.J.: Princeton University Press, 1988).
[2] Barry Collett, *Italian Benedictine Scholars and the Reformation* (Oxford: Clarendon Press, 1985).
[3] E. M. Jung, "On the Nature of Evangelism in Sixteenth-Century Italy," *Journal of the History of Ideas* 14 (1953): 511-27.

⁴For the emergence of Reformation spirituality, see Alister E. McGrath, *Spirituality in an Age of Change: Rediscovering the Spirit of the Reformers* (Grand Rapids, Mich.: Zondervan, 1994).

⁵Basil Hall, "The Early Rise and Gradual Decline of Lutheranism in England (1520-1600)," in *Humanists and Protestants* (Edinburgh: T & T Clark, 1990), pp. 208-36.

⁶John Owen, *Works,* 16 vols. (Edinburgh: Johnson & Hunter, 1850-1853), 6:551; 5:14.

⁷See, for example, the titles of the organization *Gemeinschaft europäischer evangelikaler Theologen,* and the journal *Jahrbüch für evangelikale Theologie,* which began to appear in 1987. Older German works of evangelical theology retain the traditional term: see Helmut Thielicke, *Der evangelische Glaube,* 3 vols. (Tübingen: Mohr, 1973-1978). For the origins of the term and its implications, see Ulrich Betz, "Evangelikale in Deutschland: Skizze einer neuen geistlichen Bewegung im deutschen Protestantismus," *Ökumenische Rundschau,* 1973, pp. 309-19. This article illuminates the distinction between the three related adjectives *evangelikal, evangelisch* and *protestantisch.* I owe this reference to Rolf Hille of the Albrecht-Bengel-Haus, Tübingen.

⁸I owe these reflections to Henri Blocher of the Faculté Libre de Théologie Evangélique, Vaux sur Seine. For further reflections, see Neal Blough, "Evangélisme et fondamentalisme au course du XXe siècle," *Fac-Réflexion* 24 (1993): 4-15.

⁹On this, see Alister E. McGrath, *Reformation Thought: An Introduction,* rev. ed. (Oxford: Blackwell, 1993).

¹⁰See Alister E. McGrath, *A Life of John Calvin* (Oxford: Blackwell, 1990), pp. 175-88.

¹¹See the outstanding doctoral thesis of Peter J. Wilcox, "Restoration, Reformation and the Progress of the Kingdom of Christ: Evangelization in the Thought and Practice of John Calvin, 1555-1564," University of Oxford, 1993.

¹²This series of works began to appear in 1749. For details of Wesley's appreciative use of Puritan writings, see John A. Newton, *Methodism and the Puritans* (London: Dr. William's Trust, 1964).

¹³See Dewey D. Wallace, *The Spirituality of the Later English Puritans* (Macon, Ga.: Mercer University Press, 1987), p. xii.

¹⁴See Horton Davis, *Worship and Theology in England from Andrewes to Baxter and Fox* (Princeton, N.J.: Princeton University Press, 1970); Charles Hambrick-Stowe, The Practice of Piety: Puritan Devotional Disciplines in Seventeenth-Century New England (Chapel Hill: University of North Carolina Press, 1982); F. Ernest Stoeffler, *God's Caress: The Psychology of Puritan Religious Experience* (Oxford: Oxford University Press, 1986); Gordon Wakefield, *Puritan Devotion: Its Place in the Development of Christian Piety* (London: Epworth Press, 1957).

¹⁵See the survey in W. R. Ward, "German Pietism, 1670-1750," *Journal of Ecclesiastical History* 44 (1993): 476-504.

¹⁶F. Ernest Stoeffler, *The Rise of Evangelical Pietism* (Leiden, Netherlands: Brill, 1965), pp. 13-15.

¹⁷Gary R. Sattler, *God's Glory, Neighbor's Good: A Brief Introduction to the Life and Writings of August Hermann Francke* (Chicago: Covenant Press, 1982).

¹⁸This does not mean that the evangelical outlook is restricted to such contexts; on the growing influence of evangelicalism in German theology, for example, see Robert W. Yarbrough, "Evangelical Theology in Germany," *Evangelical Quarterly* 65 (1993): 329-53.

¹⁹See the points made by William H. Bentley and Ruth Lewis Bentley, "The Scope and Function of a Black Evangelical Theology," in *Evangelical Affirmations,* ed. K. S. Kantzer and C. F. H. Henry (Grand Rapids, Mich.: Zondervan, 1990), pp. 299-333.

[20] *The Fundamentals: A Testimony of the Truth*, 12 vols. (Chicago: Testimony, 1910-1915). Reprinted in four volumes by Baker Book House, 1993.

[21] The definitive study remains George Marsden, *Fundamentalism and American Culture: The Shaping of Twentieth Century Evangelicalism, 1870-1925* (New York: Oxford University Press, 1980).

[22] For these and other citations see Nigel M. de S. Cameron, "The Logic of Biblical Authority," in *The Challenge of Evangelical Theology*, ed. Nigel M. de S. Cameron (Edinburgh: Rutherford House, 1987), pp. 1-16.

[23] James Davison Hunter, "Fundamentalism in Its Global Contours," in *The Fundamentalist Phenomenon*, ed. N. J. Cohen (Grand Rapids, Mich.: Eerdmans, 1990), pp. 56-72; quote at p. 57 (emphasis in original).

[24] Martin E. Marty, "What Is Fundamentalism? Theological Perspectives," in *Fundamentalism as an Ecumenical Challenge*, ed. Hans Küng and Jürgen Moltmann, Concilium 1992/1993 (London: SCM Press, 1992), pp. 3-13; quote at p. 3.

[25] See George M. Marsden, *The Evangelical Mind and the New School Presbyterian Experience* (New Haven, Conn.: Yale University Press, 1970).

[26] Nancy Ammerman, *Bible Believers: Fundamentalists in the Modern World* (New Brunswick, N.J.: Rutgers University Press, 1987).

[27] A point stressed by Edward J. Carnell during his 1955 campaign to have Fuller Seminary drop its foundational commitment to premillennialism; see George M. Marsden, *Reforming Fundamentalism: Fuller Seminary and the New Evangelicalism* (Grand Rapids, Mich.: Eerdmans, 1987), pp. 150-51.

[28] Martin E. Marty, "Fundamentalism as a Social Phenomenon," in *Evangelicalism and Modern America*, ed. George Marsden (Grand Rapids, Mich.: Eerdmans, 1984), pp. 56-70.

[29] For what follows, see the masterful survey, richly furnished with primary source references, in Bradley J. Longfield, *The Presbyterian Controversy: Fundamentalists, Modernists and Moderates* (New York: Oxford University Press, 1991).

[30] See Martin E. Marty, *Anticipating Pluralism: The Founders' Vision* (Providence, R.I.: Associates of the John Carter Brown Library, 1986).

[31] Marsden, *Reforming Fundamentalism*, p. 7.

[32] Francis Schaeffer, *The Great Evangelical Disaster* (Westchester, Ill.: Crossway, 1984), p. 75.

[33] For the details, see Longfield, *Presbyterian Controversy*, pp. 28-53, 162-80.

[34] Quoted in Ned B. Stonehouse, *J. Gresham Machen: A Biographical Memoir* (Grand Rapids, Mich.: Eerdmans, 1954), p. 440. See further J. Gresham Machen, *Christianity and Liberalism* (New York: Macmillan, 1923).

[35] Details in Longfield, *Presbyterian Controversy*, pp. 181-208. A related controversy broke out in England in 1922, with the formation of the breakaway Bible Churchmen's Missionary Society from the allegedly liberal Church Missionary Society.

[36] George M. Marsden, "Perspective on the Division of 1937," in *Pressing Toward the Mark: Essays Commemorating Fifty Years of the Orthodox Presbyterian Church*, ed. C. G. Dennison and R. G. Gamble (Philadelphia: Orthodox Presbyterian Church, 1986), pp. 295-328.

[37] Most historians of the Federal Council of Churches regard it as reflecting the predominant liberalism of its cultural environment; see John A. Hutchinson, *We Are Not Divided: A Critical and Historical Study of the Federal Council of Churches of Christ in America* (New York: Round Table Press, 1941); Henry J. Pratt, *The Liberalization of American Protestantism: A Case Study in Complex Organization* (Detroit: Wayne State University Press, 1972).

[38]David Bebbington, *Evangelicalism in Modern Britain: A History from the 1730s to the 1980s* (London: Hyman, 1989), p. 227.

[39]See G. A. Rawlyk, *Champions of the Truth: Fundamentalism, Modernism and the Maritime Baptists* (Montreal: McGill-Queens University Press, 1990); John G. Stackhouse Jr., *Canadian Evangelicalism in the Twentieth Century: An Introduction to Its Character* (Toronto: University of Toronto Press, 1993), pp. 177-204.

[40]Stuart Piggin, "Towards a Bicentennial History of Australian Evangelicalism," *Journal of Religious History* 15 (1988): 20-36.

[41]See Ray Ginger, *Six Days or Forever? Tennessee Versus John Thomas Scopes* (Boston: Beacon, 1958).

[42]On Bryan, see Paolo Coletta, *William Jennings Bryan,* 3 vols. (Lincoln: University of Nebraska Press, 1969); Lawrence Lervine, *Defender of the Faith: William Jennings Bryan, the Last Decade, 1915-1925* (New York; Oxford University Press, 1965). Bryan died five days after the close of the trial.

[43]Donald Bloesch, *The Evangelical Renaissance* (Grand Rapids, Mich.: Eerdmans, 1973).

[44]Weimarer Ausgabe 2.72.32-37. See further Scott H. Hendrix, *Luther and the Papacy: Stages in a Reformation Conflict* (Philadelphia: Fortress, 1981).

[45]Heinrich Bornkamm, *The Heart of Reformation Faith* (New York: Harper & Row, 1965), pp. 85-86.

[46]By the time of Martin Bucer, separation seemed inevitable; it was therefore necessary for Bucer to begin to develop a specifically evangelical ecclesiology that made allowance for this development. See Jacques Courvoisier, *La notion d'église chez Bucer dans son développement historique* (Paris: Félix Alcan, 1933).

[47]See Claus-Peter Clasen, *Anabaptism: A Social History, 1525-1618* (Ithaca, N.Y.: Cornell University Press, 1972), and especially G. H. Williams, *The Radical Reformation,* 3rd rev. ed. (Kirksville, Miss.: Sixteenth Century Journal, 1992).

[48]H. Richard Niebuhr, *Christ and Culture* (New York: Harper, 1951).

[49]For responses to Niebuhr from Anabaptist writers, see Charles Scriven, *The Transformation of Culture* (Scottdale, Penn.: Herald, 1988); John Howard Yoder, *The Priestly Kingdom* (Notre Dame, Ind.: University of Notre Dame Press, 1988).

[50]See Marcus J. Borg, *Conflict, Holiness and Politics in the Teachings of Jesus* (New York: Edwin Mellen, 1984).

[51]Carl F. H. Henry, *The Uneasy Conscience of Modern Fundamentalism* (Grand Rapids, Mich.: Eerdmans, 1947). Henry clearly regards evangelicalism and fundamentalism as synonymous at this stage. In his later work *Evangelical Responsibility in Contemporary Theology* (Grand Rapids, Mich.: Eerdmans, 1957), fundamentalism is clearly distinguished from evangelicalism, and it is criticized on account of its narrow-minded polemicism.

[52]Millard J. Erickson, *The New Evangelical Theology* (Westwood, N.J.: Revell, 1968), pp. 22-30.

[53]Harold J. Ockenga, "From Fundamentalism, Through New Evangelicalism, to Evangelicalism," in *Evangelical Roots,* ed. K. S. Kantzer (Nashville: Nelson, 1978), pp. 35-48. The term *new evangelicalism* seems to have its origins in Ockenga's 1947 convocation address to Fuller Seminary. It was popularized by Carl Henry early in 1948, especially in a series of articles in the influential journal *Christian Life and Times.* See Carl F. H. Henry, "The Vigor of the New Evangelicalism," *Christian Life and Times,* January 1948, pp. 30-32; March 1948, pp. 35-38, 85; April 1948, pp. 32-35, 65-69.

[54]Schaeffer, *Great Evangelical Disaster,* p. 97.

[55]There is much useful information in Ronald W. Ruegsegger, ed., *Reflections on Fran-*

194

cis Schaeffer (Grand Rapids, Mich.: Zondervan, 1986).

56See R. Albert Mohler Jr., "Carl F. H. Henry," in *Baptist Theologians,* ed. T. George and D. S. Dockery (Nashville: Broadman, 1990), pp. 518-38; Bob E. Patterson, *Carl F. H. Henry* (Waco, Tex.: Word, 1983). Henry's own reflections on this period may be found in his autobiography *Confessions of a Theologian* (Waco, Tex.: Word, 1987).

57For details of the development of this major institution, see George M. Marsden, *Reforming Fundamentalism: Fuller Seminary and the New Evangelicalism* (Grand Rapids, Mich.: Eerdmans, 1987).

58For useful assessment and reflection, see D. A. Carson and J. D. Woodbridge, eds., *God and Culture: Essays in Honor of Carl F. H. Henry* (Grand Rapids, Mich.: Eerdmans, 1993).

59"Is Evangelical Theology Changing?" *Christian Life,* March 1956, pp. 16-19.

60Billy Graham, "What's the Next Step?" *Christian Life,* June 1956, pp. 20-23.

61Leonard E. Sweet, "The 1960s: The Crises of Liberal Christianity and the Public Emergence of Evangelicalism," in Marsden, *Evangelicalism and Modern America,* pp. 29-45.

62There is a massive literature: see, for example, Robert C. Liebman and Robert Wuthnow, *The New Christian Right: Mobilization and Legitimation* (New York: Aldine, 1983); Richard Quebedeaux, *The Young Evangelicals: Revolution in Orthodoxy* (New York: Harper & Row, 1974); Edith Blumhofer and Joel A. Carpenter, *Twentieth Century Evangelicalism: A Guide to the Sources* (New York: Garland, 1990). On Canadian evangelicalism, often overlooked, see the richly documented study of John G. Stackhouse Jr., *Canadian Evangelicalism in the Twentieth Century: An Introduction to Its Character* (Toronto: University of Toronto Press, 1993), which dispels many of the misunderstandings and misrepresentations of earlier studies of this field.

63James Barr, *Fundamentalism* (London: SCM Press, 1977).

64Clark Pinnock, "Defining American Fundamentalism: A Response," in *The Fundamentalist Phenomenon,* ed. N. J. Cohen (Grand Rapids, Mich.: Eerdmans, 1990), pp. 38-55; quotes at pp. 40-41.

65Quebedeaux, *Young Evangelicals,* p. 19.

66Carl F. H. Henry, "Those Incomprehensible British Fundamentalists," *Christianity Today,* June 2, 1978.

67David Tracy, "On Naming the Present," in *On the Threshold of the Third Millennium,* ed. P. Hillyer, Concilium 1990/1991 (London: SCM Press, 1990), pp. 66-85; quotes at p. 75.

68Details in Randle Manwaring, *From Controversy to Co-existence: Evangelicals in the Church of England, 1914-1980* (Cambridge: Cambridge University Press, 1985). Useful information may also be found in Kenneth Hylson-Smith, *Evangelicals in the Church of England, 1734-1984* (Edinburgh: T & T Clark, 1988); Michael Saward, *Evangelicals on the Move* (London: Mowbrays, 1987).

69Manwaring, *From Controversy to Co-existence,* p. 55.

70For an appraisal, see J. Eddison, ed., *A Study in Spiritual Power* (Crowborough, U.K.: Highland, 1992).

71On these, see F. F. Bruce, "The Tyndale Fellowship for Biblical Research," *Evangelical Quarterly* 19 (1947): 52-61; Douglas Johnson, *Contending for the Faith: A History of the Evangelical Movement in the Universities and Colleges* (Leicester, U.K.: InterVarsity Press, 1979).

72Billy Graham has had a major impact on evangelicalism elsewhere. Australia is a particularly significant example. The mission of 1959 led to a reinvigoration of evangelical churches and institutions, especially in the Sydney area. See S. B. Babbage and

I. Siggins, *Light Beneath the Cross: The Story of Billy Graham's Crusade in Australia* (Kingswood, U.K.: World's Work, 1960). See also Ian Breward, *Australia: The Most Godless Place Under Heaven?* (Melbourne: Beacon Hill Books, 1988), pp. 77-78.

[73]See Arthur Pollard, "The Evangelical Revival: The Triumphant Phase, 1790-1830," *Churchman* 107 (1993): 254-66.

[74]Letter to *The Times,* dated August 15, 1955.

[75]In his *Fundamentalism and the Church of God* (London: SCM Press, 1957), Gabriel Hebert mounted a forthright yet inaccurate attack on the ideas of "conservative evangelicals in the Church of England" and "the Inter-Varsity Fellowship" (p. 10). This attack was decisively refuted by James I. Packer in his first major published work, *Fundamentalism and the Word of God* (London: Inter-Varsity Press, 1958), which remains a landmark of British evangelical writing.

[76]See Owen Chadwick, *Michael Ramsey: A Life* (Oxford: Oxford University Press, 1990), pp. 234-35. There is a brief reference to Ramsey's earlier views at page 92.

[77]James I. Packer, *A Kind of Noah's Ark? The Anglican Commitment to Comprehensiveness* (Oxford: Latimer House, 1981), p. 10. See also his earlier *The Evangelical Anglican Identity Problem: An Analysis* (Oxford: Latimer House, 1978), p. 5. Both these seminal papers can be obtained from the Warden, Latimer House, 131 Banbury Road, Oxford, England.

[78]*The Christian,* October 21, 1966.

[79]I hope to be able to provide an account of the importance of both James I. Packer and Latimer House to the evangelical renaissance in England in my biography of the former, which is due to be published in 1996.

[80]James I. Packer, ed., *Guidelines: Anglican Evangelicals Face the Future* (London: Falcon, 1967). At one point these papers were conceived as lectures to be delivered at the congress and published later. In the end they were published in advance, allowing full discussion of their themes and the establishment of a greater degree of consensus than might otherwise have been the case.

[81]Adrian Hastings, *A History of English Christianity, 1920-85* (London: Collins, 1986), p. 554. For the statement, see P. Crowe, ed., *Keele '67: The National Evangelical Anglican Congress Statement* (London: Falcon, 1967).

[82]Packer, *Evangelical Anglican Identity Problem,* p. 12.

[83]Ibid., p. 5.

[84]Hans Küng, "Against Contemporary Roman Catholic Fundamentalism," in *Fundamentalism as an Ecumenical Challenge,* ed. Hans Küng and Jürgen Moltmann, Concilium 1992/1993 (London: SCM Press, 1992), pp. 116-25; quote at p. 124.

Chapter 2: The Characteristics of Evangelicalism

[1]See George Gallup and Jim Castelli, *The People's Religion: American Faith in the 90's* (New York: Macmillan, 1989), p. 93.

[2]For details, see Alister E. McGrath, *The Intellectual Origins of the European Reformation* (Oxford: Blackwell, 1987), pp. 5-7.

[3]There is an enormous literature, which will be explored in this study. For a useful survey of more recent writings, see Edith Blumhofer and Joel A. Carpenter, *Twentieth Century Evangelicalism: A Guide to the Sources* (New York: Garland, 1990).

[4]What follows summarizes the influential set of "evangelical affirmations" set out in *Evangelical Affirmations,* ed. K. S. Kantzer and C. F. H. Henry (Grand Rapids, Mich.: Zondervan, 1990), pp. 27-38, using the format employed earlier by James I. Packer, *The Evangelical Anglican Identity Problem: An Analysis* (Oxford: Latimer House, 1978), pp. 20-23. George M. Marsden, "The Evangelical Denomination," in

Evangelicalism and Modern America (Grand Rapids, Mich.: Eerdmans, 1984), pp. vii-xix, identifies five defining characteristics, as follows: (1) the Reformation doctrine of the final authority of Scripture, (2) the real, historical character of God's saving work, (3) eternal salvation only through personal trust in Christ, (4) the importance of evangelism and missions, and (5) the importance of a spiritually transformed life. A similar list is provided in David W. Bebbington, *Evangelicalism in Modern Britain* (London: Unwin Hyman, 1989), pp. 2-17. For further discussion, see D. F. Wells and J. D. Woodbridge, eds., *The Evangelicals* (Nashville: Abingdon, 1975); Donald G. Bloesch, *Essentials of Evangelical Theology,* 2 vols. (San Francisco: Harper & Row, 1978-1979).

[5]See my own attempt to contribute to this process within Anglicanism by arguing for the construction of a "middle way" between fundamentalism and liberalism: Alister E. McGrath, *The Renewal of Anglicanism* (Wilton, Conn.: Morehouse, 1993).

[6]I. John Hesselink, *On Being Reformed,* 2nd ed. (Grandville, Mich.: Reformed Church Press, 1988), p. 101. As Hesselink points out (pp. 29-36), the Reformed tradition cannot be dismissed as "rationalistic" or "scholastic."

[7]For the synthesis of Calvinism and Pietism in the writings of Theodore J. Freling-hausen (1691-1748), see James Tamis, *Dutch Calvinistic Pietism in the Middle Colonies* (Leiden, Netherlands: Brill, 1967).

[8]James Houston, "Spirituality," in *Evangelical Dictionary of Theology,* ed. W. A. Elwell (Grand Rapids, Mich.: Baker Book House, 1984), p. 1046.

[9]Note the emphasis placed on the idea by Max Warren, *What Is an Evangelical?* (London: Church Book Room Press, 1944), p. 23. For a survey of the concept in Scripture, see R. T. France, "Conversion in the Bible," *Evangelical Quarterly* 65 (1993): 291-310.

[10]Kern Robert Trembath, *Evangelical Theories of Biblical Inspiration* (New York: Oxford University Press, 1987), p. 4.

[11]I use the word *belief,* following the lead of Packer in *The Evangelical Anglican Identity Problem.* By doing so I am in no way implying that they are (as in the secular sense of the term) mere assumptions, pulled, as it were, out of thin air. For evangelicalism, the six positions outlined are true, biblical and foundational—that is, "beliefs" in the biblical sense of the term, as something truthful and reliable that is to be believed, trusted and obeyed.

[12]For details of the various interpretations of the *sola Scriptura* principle, see Alister E. McGrath, *Reformation Thought: An Introduction,* rev. ed. (Oxford: Blackwell, 1993), pp. 140-55. For the high view of Scripture associated with the Reformation heritage, see the excellent study of W. Robert Godfrey, "Biblical Authority in the Sixteenth and Seventeenth Centuries," in *Scripture and Truth,* ed. D. A. Carson and J. D. Woodbridge (Grand Rapids, Mich.: Zondervan, 1983), pp. 225-50.

[13]For an evangelical assessment of the role of the Holy Spirit in biblical interpretation, see Clark H. Pinnock, "The Work of the Holy Spirit in Hermeneutics," *Journal of Pentecostal Theology* 2 (1993): 3-23.

[14]For a full discussion of this passage, see D. A. D. Thorsen, *The Wesley Quadrilateral* (Grand Rapids, Mich.: Zondervan, 1990).

[15]See further James I. Packer, *Fundamentalism and the Word of God* (London: Inter-Varsity Press, 1958), pp. 80-84; I. Howard Marshall, *Biblical Inspiration* (London: Hodder & Stoughton, 1982), pp. 40-47.

[16]A point stressed by Carl F. H. Henry in his magisterial *God, Revelation and Authority,* 6 vols. (Waco, Tex.: Word, 1976-1983), 4:140-61.

[17]Packer, *Fundamentalism and the Word of God,* pp. 78-79.

18Ibid., pp. 40-47.

19For an excellent discussion, with particular reference to assurance of salvation, see Randall C. Zachman, *The Assurance of Faith: Conscience in the Theology of Martin Luther and John Calvin* (Minneapolis: Fortress, 1993), pp. 210-23.

20W. Robertson Smith, *Answer to the Form of Libel* (Edinburgh: Douglas, 1878), p. 21.

21For various approaches to these questions within evangelicalism, see Bernard Ramm, *Protestant Biblical Interpretation: A Textbook of Hermeneutics,* 3rd ed. (Grand Rapids, Mich.: Baker Book House, 1970); Harold Lindsell, *The Battle for the Bible* (Grand Rapids, Mich.: Zondervan, 1976); James I. Packer, *Beyond the Battle for the Bible* (Westchester, Ill.: Cornerstone, 1980); Dewey Beegle, *Scripture, Tradition and Infallibility* (Grand Rapids, Mich.: Eerdmans, 1973).

22Alasdair MacIntyre, *Against the Self-Images of the Age: Essays on Ideology and Philosophy* (London: Duckworth, 1983).

23David L. Edwards, *The Futures of Christianity* (London: Hodder & Stoughton, 1987), pp. 416-17.

24The issue raised here is both complex and important and lies at the heart of evangelical reflection concerning how the gospel may be related to non-Western cultures, especially in the Third World. For the general theological issues, see Harvie M. Conn, *Eternal Word and Changing Worlds* (Grand Rapids, Mich.: Zondervan, 1984). Major evangelical assemblies that addressed such issues include the 1974 Lausanne Congress and the 1980 Consultation on World Evangelization held in Pattaya, Thailand.

25For some of the issues raised in relation to Christology, see Alister E. McGrath, *The Genesis of Doctrine* (Oxford: Blackwell, 1990), pp. 52-66.

26See McGrath, *Reformation Thought,* pp. 165-85. For an excellent study of Calvin's position, see B. A. Gerrish, *Grace and Gratitude: The Eucharistic Theology of John Calvin* (Minneapolis: Fortress, 1993).

27Stephen C. Neill, *Christian Faith and Other Faiths* (Oxford: Oxford University Press, 1961), p. 91.

28For major studies at various levels, see Murray J. Harris, *Jesus as God: The New Testament Use of "Theos" in Reference to Jesus* (Grand Rapids, Mich.: Baker Book House, 1992); Alister McGrath, *What Was God Doing on the Cross?* (Grand Rapids, Mich.: Zondervan, 1993); I. Howard Marshall, *The Origins of New Testament Christology* (Downers Grove, Ill.: InterVarsity Press, 1976); John Stott, *The Cross of Christ* (Leicester, U.K.: Inter-Varsity Press, 1986).

29*Ioannis Calvini opera quae supersunt omnia,* 59 vols. (Brunschweig, Germany: Schwetschke, 1863-1900), 9:815. "Mais fault que nostre entendement soit du tout arresté à ce poinct, d'apprendre en l'Escriture à cognoistre Iesus Christ seulement."

30See David Wenham, ed., *The Jesus Tradition Outside the Gospels* (Sheffield, U.K.: JSOT, 1984); more briefly, R. T. France, *The Evidence for Jesus* (London: Hodder & Stoughton, 1986), pp. 19-85.

31For a popular presentation of the grounds and consequences of this belief, see Alister McGrath, *Understanding Jesus* (Grand Rapids, Mich.: Zondervan, 1987). A new edition is available: *Jesus* (Leicester, U.K.: Inter-Varsity Press, 1994).

32Karl Barth, *Church Dogmatics,* 14 vols. (Edinburgh: Clark, 1936-1975), 2/2:52-53.

33See the helpful survey of Douglas Jacobsen and Frederick Schmidt, "Behind Orthodoxy and Beyond It: Recent Developments in Evangelical Christology," *Scottish Journal of Theology* 45 (1993): 515-41.

34See the telling study of Karl Menninger, *Whatever Became of Sin?* (New York: Hawthorn, 1973).

35For the full history of the development of this doctrine, see Alister E. McGrath, *Iustitia Dei: A History of the Christian Doctrine of Justification,* 2 vols. (Cambridge: Cambridge University Press, 1986).

36See the classic study of Ernst Wolf, "Die Rechtfertigungslehre als Mitte und Grenze reformatorischer Theologie," *Evangelische Theologie* 9 (1949-1950): 298-308. For further analysis, see Alister E. McGrath, "The Article by Which the Church Stands or Falls," *Evangelical Quarterly* 58 (1986): 207-28; Alister E. McGrath, "Der articulus iustificationis als axiomatischer Grundsatz des christlichen Glaubens," *Zeitschrift für Theologie und Kirche* 81 (1984): 383-94; Alister E. McGrath, "Karl Barth and the *Articulus Iustificationis:* The Significance of His Critique of Ernst Wolf Within the Context of His Theological Method," *Theologische Zeitschrift* 39 (1983): 349-61.

37Westminster Shorter Catechism, question 31.

38John Calvin *Institutes of the Christian Religion* 4. 2. 7. For an excellent analysis of this definition, see Edward A. Dowey Jr., *The Knowledge of God in Calvin's Theology* (New York: Columbia University Press, 1952), pp. 148-205.

39See R. M. Anderson, *Vision of the Disinherited: The Making of American Pentecostalism* (Oxford: Oxford University Press, 1980). For more recent developments, see Richard Quebedeaux, *The New Charismatics: The Origins, Developments and Significance of Neo-Pentecostalism* (New York: Doubleday, 1976).

40P. E. Hughes, "Editorial," *Churchman* 76 (1962): 131-35. This editorial was reprinted in pamphlet form and is estimated to have sold some thirty-nine thousand copies.

41For its impact on the ministry of David Watson, see Teddy Saunders and Hugh Sansom, *David Watson: A Biography* (London: Hodder & Stoughton, 1992), pp. 68-85.

42C. Peter Wagner, *The Third Wave of the Holy Spirit: Encountering the Power of Signs and Wonders Today* (Ann Arbor, Mich.: Servant, 1988).

43See Lewis B. Smedes, ed., *Ministry and the Miraculous: A Case Study at Fuller Seminary* (Pasadena, Calif.: Fuller Seminary, 1987).

44See *John Wimber: Friend or Foe?* (London: St. Matthias Press, 1990), which details the criticisms made of Wimber's theology at this time.

45See the useful survey of Henry H. Knight, "God's Faithfulness and God's Freedom: A Comparison of Contemporary Theologies of Healing," *Journal of Pentecostal Theology* 2 (1993): 65-89.

46See E. G. Rupp, "Word and Spirit in the First Years of the Reformation," *Archiv für Reformationsgeschichte* 49 (1958): 32-84.

47See the powerful exposé in M. Horton, ed., *The Agony of Deceit: What Some TV Preachers Are Really Teaching* (Chicago: Moody Press, 1990).

48Elsewhere, Copeland declares that "the believer is as much an incarnation as was Jesus of Nazareth": Kenneth Copeland, *Word of Faith* (Fort Worth, Tex.: Copeland, 1980), p. 14. Similar statements can be found in Kenneth E. Hagin, *Zoe: The God-Kind of Life* (Tulsa, Okla.: Faith Library, 1981).

49See Gordon Fee, "Some Reflections on Pauline Spirituality," in *Alive to God,* ed. James I. Packer and Loren Wilkinson (Downers Grove, Ill.: InterVarsity Press, 1992), pp. 96-107.

50An additional consideration, which can only be noted here, is that the growth of evangelicalism in Africa, with its traditional spirit-centered spiritualities, has led to a growing appreciation of the charismatic elements of the gospel; see A. Anderson, *Moya: The Holy Spirit in an African Context* (Pretoria: University of South Africa Press, 1991).

51A good balance of appreciation and criticism of the charismatic movement from a classical evangelical perspective may be found in James I. Packer, *Keep in Step with the Spirit* (Grand Rapids, Mich.: Revell, 1984).

[52]There are some important pointers, as well as a critique of some aspects of older Pentecostal theology, in James I. Packer, "Theological Reflections on the Charismatic Movement," *Churchman* 94 (1980): 7-25, 103-25. A revised version of these important articles can be found in Packer, *Keep in Step with the Spirit,* pp. 200-34.

[53]Alister E. McGrath, "Theology and Experience: Reflections on Cognitive and Experiential Approaches to Theology," *European Journal of Theology* 2 (1993): 65-74.

[54]Packer, "Theological Reflections on the Charismatic Movement," p. 119.

[55]Packer, "An Introduction to Systematic Spirituality," *Crux* 26, no. 1 (1990): 2-8; quote at p. 6.

[56]Søren Kierkegaard, *Concluding Unscientific Postscript* (London: Oxford University Press, 1941), pp. 169-224. Cf. P. L. Holmer, "Kierkegaard and Religious Propositions," *Journal of Religion* 35 (1955): 135-46.

[57]See the perceptive analysis of Waldron Scott, *Karl Barth's Theology of Mission* (Downers Grove, Ill.: InterVarsity Press, 1978).

[58]*Christian Century* 73 (1956): 848-49. This response was provoked by an earlier article by Niebuhr in the same journal: *Christian Century* 73 (1956): 640-42.

[59]For the background, see Marshall Frady, *Billy Graham: A Parable of American Righteousness* (Boston: Little, Brown, 1979); William G. McLoughlin, *Billy Graham: Revivalist in a Secular Age* (New York: Ronald, 1960).

[60]See John C. Bennett, "Billy Graham at Union," *Union Seminary Quarterly Review* 9 (May 1954): 9-14.

[61]*Christianity and Crisis* 16 (March 5, 1956): 18. On Niebuhr, see Richard Wightman Fox, *Reinhold Niebuhr: A Biography* (New York: Pantheon, 1985).

[62]Edward J. Carnell, "Can Billy Graham Slay the Giant?" *Christianity Today,* May 13, 1957, pp. 3-5. An earlier, less effective response may be found in his "Proposal to Reinhold Niebuhr," *The Christian Century,* October 17, 1956, pp. 197-99.

[63]*Christianity and Crisis* 16 (April 2, 1956): 40.

[64]See Stanley Grenz, *Revisioning Evangelical Theology: A Fresh Agenda for the 21st Century* (Downers Grove, Ill.: InterVarsity Press, 1992), which argues for the reign of God and the community of Christ being central integrative motifs for a renewed evangelical theology.

[65]There are some useful reflections in D. A. Carson, "Evangelicals, Ecumenism and the Church," in *Evangelical Affirmations,* ed. K. S. Kantzer and C. F. H. Henry (Grand Rapids, Mich.: Zondervan, 1990), pp. 347-85.

[66]For an excellent analysis, see Robert C. Walton, "A Mixed Body or a Gathered Church of Visible Saints: John Calvin and William Ames" in *Calvin: Erbe und Auftrag,* ed. W. van't Spijken, (Kampen, Netherlands: Kok Pharos, 1991), pp. 168-78.

[67]See Linden J. De Bie, "Saving Evangelical Catholicism Today," *New Mercersburg Review* 6 (1989): 11-21; Gabriel Fackre, "Evangelical Catholicity," *New Mercersburg Review* 8 (1990): 41-50.

[68]*Los Angeles Times,* December 22, 1990, sec. S, p. 1.

[69]Calvin *Institutes* 4. 1. 1.

[70]Ibid. 4. 1. 4. Note that Calvin's reference here is to the visible church.

[71]John Stott, *The Cross of Christ* (Leicester, U.K.: Inter-Varsity Press, 1986), p. 255.

[72]See Avery Dulles, *Models of the Church: A Critical Assessment of the Church in All Its Aspects* (Garden City, N.Y.: Doubleday, 1974).

[73]See Stephen Judd and Kenneth Cable, *Sydney Anglicans: A History of the Diocese* (Sydney: Anglican Information Office, 1987).

[74]Packer, *Evangelical Anglican Identity Problem*, p. 18.

[75]Kern Robert Trembath, *Evangelical Theories of Biblical Inspiration* (New York: Oxford University Press, 1987), p. 4.

[76]See R. Albert Mohler Jr., "Carl F. H. Henry," in *Baptist Theologians*, ed. T. George and D. S. Dockery (Nashville: Broadman, 1990), pp. 518-38. Mohler notes especially his association with Capitol Hill Metropolitan Baptist Church in Washington, D.C., during Henry's time as editor of *Christianity Today*.

[77]Packer, *Fundamentalism and the Word of God*, p. 48.

[78]For a discussion of these models, see Alister E. McGrath, *Christian Theology: An Introduction* (Oxford: Blackwell, 1994), pp. 281-94.

[79]Trembath, *Evangelical Theories of Biblical Inspiration*.

Chapter 3: The Appeal of Evangelicalism

[1]John Shelby Spong, *Rescuing the Bible from Fundamentalism* (San Francisco: HarperCollins, 1991), pp. 35-36.

[2]Leonard E. Sweet, "The 1960s: The Crises of Liberal Christianity and the Public Emergence of Evangelicalism," in *Evangelicalism and Modern America*, ed. George M. Marsden (Grand Rapids, Mich.: Eerdmans, 1984), pp. 29-45.

[3]An approach that is often discussed in evangelical circles on the basis of Anthony C. Thiselton's magisterial work *The Two Horizons: Hermeneutics and Philosophical Description* (Exeter, U.K.: Paternoster, 1980). For examples of both the difficulties and the opportunities that such "fusion of horizons" offers, see W. M. Swartley, *Slavery, Sabbath, War and Women* (Scottdale, Penn.: Herald, 1983).

[4]Adrian Hastings, *A History of English Christianity, 1920-1985* (London: Collins, 1986), p. 545.

[5]Ted Peters, *The Cosmic Self: A Penetrating Look at Today's New Age Movement* (San Francisco: HarperCollins, 1991).

[6]See John A. Hutchinson, *We Are Not Divided: A Critical and Historical Study of the Federal Council of Churches of Christ in America* (New York: Round Table Press, 1941); Henry J. Pratt, *The Liberalization of American Protestantism: A Case Study in Complex Organization* (Detroit: Wayne State University Press, 1972).

[7]Peter L. Berger, *A Far Glory: The Quest for Faith in an Age of Credulity* (New York: Free Press, 1992), pp. 10-11.

[8]Ibid., p. 12 (emphasis in original).

[9]Wade Clark Roof and William McKinney, *American Mainline Religion: Its Changing Shape and Future* (Brunswick, N.J.: Rutgers University Press, 1987), p. 242.

[10]On which see Alister E. McGrath, *Intellectuals Don't Need God and Other Modern Myths: Building Bridges to Faith Through Apologetics* (Grand Rapids, Mich.: Zondervan, 1993).

[11]The Reformation heritage of evangelicalism is an important controlling influence here; see Jan Koopmans, *Das altkirchliche Dogma in der Reformation* (Munich: Kaiser Verlag, 1955).

[12]Space permits me only to note the case of evangelical reflection on the "two natures" doctrine; see Douglas Jacobsen and Frederick Schmidt, "Behind Orthodoxy and Beyond It: Recent Developments in Evangelical Christology," *Scottish Journal of Theology* 45 (1993): 515-41.

[13]Robert Morgan, preface to *The Religion of the Incarnation: Anglican Essays in Commemoration of Lux Mundi*, ed. R. Morgan (Bristol, U.K.: Bristol Classical, 1989), p. xi.

[14]See Alvin Plantinga and Nicholas Wolterstorff, eds., *Faith and Rationality: Reason*

and Belief in God (Notre Dame, Ind.: University of Notre Dame Press, 1983).

[15]Karl Holl, "Johannes Calvin," in *Gesammelte Aufsätze zur Kirchengeschichte III: Der Westen* (Tübingen: Siebeck, 1928), pp. 254-84; quote at p. 267.

[16]An excellent example of a work that recognizes Edwards's importance is Robert W. Jenson, *America's Theologian: A Recommendation of Jonathan Edwards* (New York: Oxford University Press, 1988). For a more popular analysis, see Alister E. McGrath, "Jonathan Edwards," in *A Cloud of Witnesses* (Grand Rapids, Mich.: Zondervan, 1990), pp. 100-110.

[17]On the importance of the Reformed tradition for Western Christianity in general, see M. Welker and D. Willis-Watkins, eds., *The Future of Reformed Theology* (Grand Rapids, Mich.: Eerdmans, 1993).

[18]See David F. Wells, *No Place for Truth: Or, Whatever Happened to Evangelical Theology?* (Grand Rapids, Mich.: Eerdmans, 1993), which deserves careful study.

[19]James Barr, *Fundamentalism* (London: SCM Press/Philadelphia: Westminster Press, 1977); John Hick, ed., *The Myth of God Incarnate* (London: SCM Press/Philadelphia: Westminster Press, 1977).

[20]Hastings, *History of English Christianity,* pp. 650-51.

[21]Kenneth S. Kantzer, afterword to *Evangelical Affirmations,* ed. K. S. Kantzer and C. F. H. Henry (Grand Rapids, Mich.: Zondervan, 1990), pp. 513-23; quote at p. 522.

[22]Eugene B. Borowitz, "The Enduring Truth of Religious Liberalism," in *The Fundamentalist Phenomenon,* ed. N. J. Cohen (Grand Rapids, Mich.: Eerdmans, 1990), pp. 230-47; quote at p. 231.

[23]See McGrath, *Intellectuals Don't Need God.* At a more popular level, see Alister E. McGrath and Michael Green, *Springboard for Faith* (London: Hodder & Stoughton, 1993).

[24]Arie R. Brouwer, "The Real Crises at the NCC," *The Christian Century,* June 27, 1990, pp. 631-35.

[25]Yet denominationalism still exercises considerable influence within evangelical circles, as pointed out by J. M. Frame, *Evangelical Reunion: Denominations and the Body of Christ* (Grand Rapids, Mich.: Baker Book House, 1991).

[26]See David Martin, *Tongues of Fire: The Explosion of Protestantism in Latin America* (Oxford: Blackwell, 1990); David Stoll, *Is Latin America Turning Protestant?* (Berkeley: University of California Press, 1991).

[27]David Stoll, "A Protestant Reformation in Latin America?" *The Christian Century,* January 17, 1990, pp. 44-48; quote at pp. 46-47.

Chapter 4: A Loss of Vision?
[1]Gabriel Fackre, *Ecumenical Faith in Evangelical Perspective* (Grand Rapids, Mich.: Eerdmans, 1993), pp. 22-23.

[2]Timothy George and David S. Dockery, *Baptist Theologians* (Nashville: Broadman, 1990), p. 14.

[3]David F. Wells, *No Place for Truth: Or, Whatever Happened to Evangelical Theology?* (Grand Rapids, Mich.: Eerdmans, 1993), p. 128. On the social function of doctrine, see Alister E. McGrath, "Dogma und Gemeinde: Zur sozialen Funktion des christlichen Dogmas," *Kerygma und Dogma* 37 (1991): 24-43.

[4]Wells, *No Place for Truth,* p. 129.

[5]This point is made in relation to Anglican evangelicalism by Colin Buchanan, "The Role and Calling of an Evangelical Theological College in the 1980s," *Churchman* 94 (1980): 26-42.

[6]Leszek Kolakowski, *Main Currents of Marxism,* 3 vols. (Oxford: Clarendon, 1978).

7Ibid., 1:3.

8James I. Packer, *The Evangelical Anglican Identity Problem: An Analysis* (Oxford: Latimer House, 1978), p. 29.

9For some reflections, see Alister E. McGrath, *A Life of John Calvin: A Study in the Shaping of Modern Western Culture* (Oxford: Blackwell, 1990), pp. 195-218.

10See Peter Gay, *The Dilemma of Democratic Socialism: Edward Bernstein's Challenge to Marx* (New York: Octagon, 1979).

11For interesting reflections, see Michael Scott Horton, *Made in America: The Shaping of Modern American Evangelicalism* (Grand Rapids, Mich.: Baker Book House, 1991).

12See Alister E. McGrath, "The European Roots of Evangelicalism," *Anvil* 9 (1992): 239-48.

13David F. Wells, "The Nature and Function of Theology," in *The Use of the Bible in Theology: Evangelical Options,* ed. R. K. Johnston (Atlanta: John Knox, 1985), p. 177.

14See George M. Marsden, *Reforming Fundamentalism: Fuller Seminary and the New Evangelicalism* (Grand Rapids, Mich.: Eerdmans, 1987), p. 189. There was at first enormous resistance within fundamentalism to the RSV, due to its association with the mainline National Council of Churches.

15See the important comments of Packer, *Evangelical Anglican Identity Problem,* pp. 27-28.

16Interview published in *Modern Reformation,* July/August 1993, pp. 20-21; quote at p. 21.

17For the idea and its applications, see John Bowlby, *A Secure Base* (London: Routledge, 1988).

Chapter 5: The Quest for an Evangelical Spirituality

1Robert S. Ellwood, *Alternative Altars: Unconventional And Eastern Spirituality in America* (Chicago: University of Chicago Press, 1979).

2Karl Holl, "Johannes Calvin," in *Gesammelte Aufsätze zur Kirchengeschichte III: Der Westen* (Tübingen: Siebeck, 1928), pp. 254-84; quote at p. 267.

3This is illustrated neatly by William P. Abraham, representing the Wesleyan tradition within evangelicalism, who dismissed Carl F. H. Henry's massive *God, Revelation and Authority* as "over three thousand pages of turgid scholasticism": *The Coming Great Revival* (San Francisco: Harper & Row, 1984), p. 37.

4James I. Packer, "An Introduction to Systematic Spirituality," *Crux* 26 (March 1990): 2-8; quote at p. 3.

5There is a useful survey in Gordon James, *Evangelical Spirituality* (London: SPCK, 1991). Although the volume includes much interesting material, the only writers to be dealt with in the period subsequent to World War II are Martyn Lloyd-Jones and John Stott. A more perceptive analysis, drawing on developments in the last two decades, may be found in David Parker, "Evangelical Spirituality Reviewed," *Evangelical Quarterly* 63 (1991): 123-48, and James Houston, "Spirituality," in *Evangelical Dictionary of Theology,* ed. W. A. Elwell (Grand Rapids, Mich.: Baker Book House, 1984), p. 1046. There is also some useful material in Peter Adam, *Roots of Contemporary Evangelical Spirituality* (Nottingham, U.K.: Grove Books, 1988).

6Material here is taken from the *Los Angeles Times,* dated December 12, 1989, sec. B, p. 1.

7Donald E. Miller, "Bucking a Powerful Trend," in *All Saints Church Every Member Canvas 90* (Pasadena: All Saints Episcopal Church, 1990). See also his paper "Liberal

Church Growth: A Case Study," delivered at the Society for the Scientific Study of Religion, Salt Lake City, Utah, October 27-29, 1989.

[8]Owen Chadwick, "Indifference and Morality," in *Christian Spirituality: Essays in Honour of Gordon Rupp,* ed. P. N. Brooks (London: SCM Press, 1975), pp. 203-30.

[9]Jeanne Marie Bouvier de la Mothe, generally known as Madame Guyon (1648-1717), was a vigorous defender of the "quietist" doctrines of total indifference to everything, including the hope of salvation, and the practice of noncognitive meditation, in which the believer refuses to focus on definite ideas such as the nature of God or the life of Christ. Her concept of spirituality, especially as it is found in her *Moyen court et très facile de faire oraison* (1685), brings out the radically introverted associations of the term at this time.

[10]See the careful study of James M. Houston, "Reflections on Mysticism: How Valid is Evangelical Anti-Mysticism?" in *Gott Lieben und seine Gebote halten,* ed. M. Bockmuehl and H. Burkhardt (Basel, Switzerland: Brunner Verlag, 1991), pp. 163-81. Although clearly appreciative of mysticism, Houston draws attention to areas of concern that need to be addressed.

[11]Thus there is no entry on "spirituality" in D. McKim, ed., *Encyclopedia of the Reformed Faith* (Louisville, Ky.: Westminster/John Knox, 1992); the material relating to this theme is to be found under the entry "piety" (pp. 278-79).

[12]Gerhard Ebeling, *Lutherstudien II: Disputatio de homine, Text und Hintergrund* (Tübingen: J. C. B. Mohr, 1977), pp. 31-43.

[13]Robert M. Banks, "Home Churches and Spirituality," *Interchange* 40 (1986): 15.

[14]T. R. Albin, "Spirituality," in *New Dictionary of Theology,* ed. S. Ferguson and D. F. Wright (Leicester, U.K.: Inter-Varsity Press, 1988), pp. 656-58; quote at p. 657.

[15]John Waterhouse, "The Crisis of Evangelicalism," *On Being* 18, no. 2 (1992): 4-8; quote at p. 4.

[16]An example of the works that Waterhouse has in mind would presumably be Robert M. Banks, *All the Business of Life: Bringing Theology Down to Earth* (Sutherland, New South Wales: Albatross, 1987).

[17]James Davison Hunter, *Evangelicalism: The Coming Generation* (Chicago: University of Chicago Press, 1987).

[18]I explore this point, with particular reference to the neglect of the spirituality of the sixteenth-century Reformation, in Alister E. McGrath, *Spirituality in an Age of Change: Rediscovering the Spirit of the Reformers* (Grand Rapids, Mich.: Zondervan, 1994).

[19]An example is provided by Timothy Keller, "Puritan Resources for Biblical Counselling," *The Journal of Pastoral Practice* 9, no. 3 (1988): 11-44.

[20]James I. Packer, *A Quest for Godliness: The Puritan Vision of the Christian Life* (Wheaton, Ill.: Crossway, 1990).

[21]Billy Graham, *Peace with God* (Kingswood, U.K.: World's Work, 1954), pp. 152-54.

[22]John Calvin, *Institutes of the Christian Religion,* 2 vols (Grand Rapids, Mich.: Eerdmans, 1975), 1:37.

[23]For a full discussion, see W. Balke, "The Word of God and Experientia According to Calvin," in *Calvinus Ecclesiae Doctor,* ed. W. H. Neuser (Kampen, Netherlands: Kok Pharos, 1978), pp. 19-31; Edward A. Dowey, *The Knowledge of God in Calvin's Theology* (New York: Columbia University Press, 1952); T. H. L. Parker, *Calvin's Doctrine of the Knowledge of God,* rev. ed. (Edinburgh: Oliver & Boyd, 1969).

[24]The uncritical use of such psychological material in evangelical contexts has been documented by James Davison Hunter in his *Evangelicalism,* pp. 64-71, and also in his *American Evangelicalism: Conservative Religion and the Quandary of Modernity*

(New Brunswick, N.J.: Rutgers University Press, 1983), pp. 91-99.

25David Powlinson, "Integration or Inundation?" in *Power Religion: The Selling Out of the Evangelical Church?* ed. M. Horton (Chicago: Moody Press, 1992), pp. 191-218; quote at p. 200.

26Ford Lewis Battles, "God Was Accommodating Himself to Human Capacity," *Interpretation* 31 (1977): 19-38.

27Robert H. Schuller, *Self-Esteem: The New Reformation* (Waco, Tex.: Word Books, 1982).

28Joanna McGrath and Alister E. McGrath, *The Dilemma of Self-Esteem: The Cross and Christian Confidence* (Wheaton, Ill.: Crossway, 1992).

29See the seminal study of Daniel Benoit, *Direction spirituelle et protestantisme: étude sur la légitimité d'une direction protestante* (Paris: Alcan, 1940). Useful material may also be found in John T. McNeill, *A History of the Cure of Souls* (New York: Harper & Row, 1951).

30Edward C. Sellner, "C. S. Lewis as Spiritual Mentor," in *Traditions of Spiritual Guidance,* ed. L. Byrne (Collegeville, Minn.: Liturgical Press, 1990), pp. 142-61.

31Eugene H. Peterson, *A Long Obedience in the Same Direction: Discipleship in an Instant Society* (Downers Grove, Ill.: InterVarsity Press, 1980).

32Cheryl Forbes, *Imagination: Embracing a Theology of Wonder* (Portland, Ore.: Multnomah Press, 1989).

33Eugene H. Peterson, *Reversed Thunder: The Revelation of John and the Praying Imagination* (San Francisco: Harper & Row, 1988).

34James Houston, *The Heart's Desire: A Guide to Personal Fulfillment* (Batavia, Ill.: Lion, 1992); *The Transforming Friendship: A Guide to Prayer* (Batavia, Ill.: Lion, 1989).

35Houston, *Heart's Desire,* p. 156.

36Ibid., p. 151.

37See the recent reissue: James I. Packer, *Knowing God* (Downers Grove, Ill.: InterVarsity Press, 1993).

38Packer, "Introduction to Systematic Spirituality," p. 7.

39An excellent contribution here is Donald S. Whitney, *Spiritual Disciplines for the Christian Life* (Colorado Springs: NavPress, 1991).

Chapter 6: The Dark Side of Evangelicalism

1James I. Packer, in *Evangelicals Today,* ed. J. C. King (London: Lutterworth, 1973), p. 15.

2This theme is explored in depth in Joanna McGrath and Alister E. McGrath, *The Dilemma of Self-Esteem: The Cross and Christian Confidence* (Wheaton, Ill.: Crossway, 1992). This work will be of interest to any wanting psychological and theological guidance on this theme, especially persons who have been wounded by the types of preaching or counseling described above.

3See Randall C. Zachman, *The Assurance of Faith: Conscience in the Theology of Martin Luther and John Calvin* (Minneapolis: Fortress, 1993).

4Os Guinness, "I Believe in Doubt," in *Doubt and Assurance,* ed. R. C. Sproul (Grand Rapids, Mich.: Baker Book House, 1993), pp. 31-35; quote at pp. 31-32.

5Calvin *Institutes of the Christian Religion* 3. 2. 7.

6Ibid. 3. 2. 17. The issue of doubt in the theology of Luther and Calvin is discussed in Alister E. McGrath, *Spirituality in an Age of Change: Rediscovering the Spirit of the Reformers* (Grand Rapids, Mich.: Zondervan, 1994).

7See Os Guinness, *In Two Minds: The Dilemma of Doubt and How to Resolve It*

(Downers Grove, Ill.: InterVarsity Press, 1976).

[8]John Macquarrie, *Jesus Christ in Modern Thought* (London: SCM Press, 1990), p. 253.

[9]See Harold J. Lindsell, *The Battle for the Bible* (Grand Rapids, Mich.: Zondervan, 1976).

[10]Among the responses to Lindsell see especially Jack Rogers, ed., *Biblical Authority* (Waco, Tex.: Word, 1977); Jack Rogers and Donald K. McKim, *The Authority and Interpretation of the Bible* (San Francisco: Harper & Row, 1979); John Woodbridge, *Biblical Authority: A Critique of the Rogers/McKim Proposal* (Grand Rapids, Mich.: Zondervan, 1982); James I. Packer, *Beyond the Battle for the Bible* (Westchester, Ill.: Cornerstone, 1980).

[11]George M. Marsden, *Reforming Fundamentalism: Fuller Seminary and the New Evangelicalism* (Grand Rapids, Mich.: Eerdmans, 1987), p. 288.

[12]For general discussions of the points at issue, see Stephen B. Clark, *Man and Woman in Christ* (Ann Arbor, Mich.: Servant, 1980); Paul K. Jewett, *Man as Male and Female* (Grand Rapids, Mich.: Eerdmans, 1975); Gilbert Bilezikian, *Beyond Sex Roles: A Guide for the Study of Female Roles in the Bible* (Grand Rapids, Mich.: Baker Book House, 1985); Aída Besançon Spencer, *Beyond the Curse: Women Called to Ministry* (Nashville: Thomas Nelson, 1985).

[13]Timothy George, *The Future for Theological Education Among Southern Baptists* (Birmingham, Ala.: Beeson Divinity School, 1989), p. 11 (no pagination in original).

[14]Sinclair Lewis, *Elmer Gantry* (New York: Dell, 1954).

[15]*The Washington Post,* June 12, 1987.

[16]Max Weber, "The Sociology of Charismatic Authority," in *From Max Weber: Essays in Sociology,* ed. H. H. Gerth and C. Wright Mills (London: Oxford University Press, 1946), pp. 246-52. For an excellent analysis of the "power religion" movement, see Michael Scott Horton, *Power Religion: The Selling Out of the Evangelical Church?* (Chicago: Moody Press, 1992).

[17]Martin Luther, *Three Treatises* (Philadelphia: Fortress, 1973), pp. 12-14. I have modified the English translation of the German to bring out the modernity of Luther's language at vital points.

Chapter 7: Evangelicalism and the Future of Christianity

[1]I explore this issue in *The Renewal of Anglicanism* (London: SPCK/Wilton, Conn.: Morehouse, 1993).

[2]*The Truth Shall Make You Free: The Lambeth Conference 1988* (London: Anglican Consultative Council, 1988), resolution 43, p. 231.

[3]Ibid., resolution 44, p. 231.

[4]Ibid., p. 32.

[5]For an excellent survey, see V. Samuel and A. Hauser, eds., *Proclaiming Christ in Christ's Way: Studies in Integral Evangelism* (Oxford: Regnum Books, 1989).

[6]Kathryn Tanner, "Respect for Other Religions: A Christian Antidote to Colonialist Discourse," *Modern Theology* 9 (1993): 1-18.

[7]David L. Edwards, *The Futures of Christianity* (London: Hodder & Stoughton, 1987), p. 277. Edwards's liberal credentials are impeccable, as may be seen from his dialogue with John Stott: David L. Edwards with John Stott, *Essentials: A Liberal-Evangelical Dialogue* (London: Hodder & Stoughton, 1988); published in the U.S. as *Evangelical Essentials* (Downers Grove, Ill.: InterVarsity Press, 1989).

[8]Michael Green, *Acts for Today: First Century Christianity for Twentieth Century Christians* (London: Hodder & Stoughton, 1993), p. 38.

[9]For the context of this famous citation, see J. H. Barrows, ed., *The World's Parliament of Religions,* 2 vols. (Chicago: Parliament, 1893), 2:1254-55.

[10]See Anthony Brewer, *Marxist Theories of Imperialism: A Critical Survey* (London: Routledge & Kegan Paul, 1980). Lenin's pamphlet can be found reprinted in vol. 22 of *Collected Works,* 45 vols. (Moscow: Progress Publishers, 1960-1970).

[11]A further consideration here relates to the fact that Islam, like Christianity, is a missionary religion and is actively seeking to expand its influence in the West through conversion *(da'wah)* and territorial expansion *(dâr al-islâm);* see Larry Poston, *Islamic Da'wah in the West: Muslim Missionary Activity and the Dynamics of Conversion to Islam* (New York: Oxford University Press, 1992). Secular critics of Christian evangelism often suggest that Christianity is the only missionary religion; this is clearly not the case. Nor can Islam conceivably be thought of as "Western."

[12]Karl Rahner, cited in *International Bulletin of Missionary Research* 11, no. 1 (1987): 11.

[13]In his careful survey of the issue, Grant Wacker records his view that the "syncretistic inclinations" of liberals proved to be the "kiss of death" for their presence on the mission field; see Grant Wacker, "The Protestant Awakening to World Religions," in *Between the Times: The Travail of the Protestant Establishment in America, 1900-1960,* ed. W. R. Hutchinson (Cambridge: Cambridge University Press, 1989), pp. 253-77; quotes at pp. 267, 268.

[14]See Alister E. McGrath, *Iustitia Dei: A History of the Christian Doctrine of Justification* (Cambridge: Cambridge University Press, 1986), 1:4-16.

[15]Boyd Hilton, *The Age of Atonement: The Influence of Evangelicalism on Social and Economic Thought, 1785-1865* (Oxford: Oxford University Press, 1988).

[16]There is a perceptive analysis of the causes of evangelical neglect of social issues in John Stott, ed., *Issues Facing Christians Today* (Basingstoke, U.K.: Marshall Pickering, 1984), pp. 2-10.

[17]See C. Howard Hopkins, *The Rise of the Social Gospel in American Protestantism, 1865-1915* (New Haven, Conn.: Yale University Press, 1940); Robert Moats Miller, *American Protestantism and Social Issues, 1919-39* (Chapel Hill: University of North Carolina Press, 1960); R. C. White and C. H. Hopkins, eds., *The Social Gospel: Religion and Reform in Changing America* (Philadelphia: Temple University Press, 1976).

[18]See Joan Mansfield, "The Social Gospel and the Church of England in Australia," *Journal of Religious History* 13 (1985): 417-21.

[19]"Evangelical Affirmations," in *Evangelical Affirmations,* ed. K. S. Kantzer and C. F. H. Henry (Grand Rapids, Mich.: Zondervan, 1990), pp. 27-38; quote at p. 35.

[20]See Eberhard Jüngel, "Erwägungen zur Grundlegung evangelischer Ethik im Anschluan die Theologie Paulus," *Zeitschrift für Theologie und Kirche* 63 (1966): 379-90; Victor Paul Furnish, *Theology and Ethics in Paul* (Nashville: Abingdon, 1968).

[21]Carl F. H. Henry, *The Uneasy Conscience of Modern Fundamentalism* (Grand Rapids, Mich.: Eerdmans, 1947).

[22]Os Guinness, "Tribespeople, Idiots or Citizens? Evangelicals, Religious Liberty and a Public Philosophy for the Public Square," in *Evangelical Affirmations,* ed. K. S. Kantzer and C. F. H. Henry (Grand Rapids, Mich.: Zondervan, 1990), pp. 457-97; quote at pp. 459-60.

[23]Jerry Falwell, ed., *The Fundamentalist Phenomenon* (Garden City, N.Y.: Doubleday, 1981), p. 144.

[24]Ibid., pp. 184-85.

[25]Guinness, "Tribespeople, Idiots or Citizens?" p. 468.

[26]William A. Galston, *Liberal Purposes: Goods, Virtues and Diversity in the Liberal State* (Cambridge: Cambridge University Press, 1990), pp. 277-78.

[27]Guinness, "Tribespeople, Idiots or Citizens?" p. 471.

[28]Walter Wink, *Engaging the Powers: Discernment and Resistance in a World of Domination* (Minneapolis: Augsburg/Fortress, 1992), pp. 13-85.

[29]Cited by Milton Mayer, *They Thought They Were Free: The Germans, 1933-45* (Chicago: University of Chicago Press, 1955), p. 339.

[30]Wink, *Engaging the Powers,* p. 157.

[31]Os Guinness, *The American Hour* (New York: Free Press, 1992), pp. 414-15.

[32]See the important survey in Donald Hay, "Evangelicalism and Economic Issues," in *Evangelical Anglicans,* ed. R. T. France and A. E. McGrath (London: SPCK, 1993), pp. 120-33. Further studies of importance include John Gladwin, *God's People in God's World: Biblical Motives for Social Involvement* (Leicester, U.K.: Inter-Varsity Press, 1979); and Nigel Biggar, *Theological Politics* (Oxford: Latimer House, 1988).

[33]Harry Blamires, *Where Do We Stand?* (Ann Arbor, Mich.: Servant, 1980), p. 19.

[34]This danger is stressed by Paul Ramsey, *Who Speaks for the Church?* (Nashville: Abingdon, 1967).

[35]Charles W. Colson, *Kingdoms in Conflict* (New York: Morrow, 1987).

[36]See especially Guinness, "Tribespeople, Idiots or Citizens?"

[37]The origins of this evangelical belief are difficult to trace. As Peter Toon has shown, it is certainly present in English evangelical polemics of the first half of the nineteenth century. See Peter Toon, *Evangelical Theology, 1833-1856: A Response to Tractarianism* (London: Marshall, Morgan and Scott, 1979), pp. 141-70.

[38]Donald A. Carson, "Evangelicals, Ecumenism and the Church," in *Evangelical Affirmations,* ed. K. S. Kantzer and C. F. H. Henry (Grand Rapids, Mich.: Zondervan, 1990), pp. 347-85.

[39]Such as that I set out in Alister E. McGrath, *The Genesis of Doctrine* (Oxford: Blackwell, 1990).

[40]For a witty literary exploration of such themes by a leading English Roman Catholic novelist, see David Lodge, *How Far Can You Go?* (Harmondsworth, Middlesex, U.K.: Penguin, 1980).

[41]See David Martin, *Tongues of Fire: The Explosion of Protestantism in Latin America* (Oxford: Blackwell, 1990); David Stoll, *Is Latin America Turning Protestant?* (Berkeley: University of California Press, 1991).

[42]See the exploration of such issues in J. H. Armstrong, ed., *Roman Catholicism Today* (Chicago: Moody Press, 1994).

[43]See Carlos M. N. Eire, "Calvin and Nicodemitism: A Reappraisal," *Sixteenth Century Journal* 10 (1979): 45-69.

[44]See Dermot E. Fenlon, *Heresy and Obedience in Tridentine Italy* (Cambridge: Cambridge University Press, 1972).

[45]See Alister E. McGrath, "Religion," in *The Blackwell Companion to the Enlightenment,* ed. J. W. Yolton (Oxford: Blackwell, 1992), pp. 447-52.

[46]Leslie Houlden, in *The Myth of God Incarnate,* ed. J. Hick (London: SCM Press, 1977), p. 125.

[47]On these general themes see Diogenes Allen, *Christian Belief in a Postmodern World* (Louisville, Ky.: Westminster/John Knox, 1989); Thomas C. Oden, *After Modernity . . . What? Agenda for Theology* (Grand Rapids, Mich.: Zondervan, 1990).

[48]Details may be found in Matei Calinescu, *Five Faces of Modernity* (Durham, N.C.: Duke University Press, 1987); Terry Eagleton, *The Ideology of the Aesthetic* (Oxford: Blackwell, 1990); Kevin Hart, *The Trespass of the Sign* (Cambridge: Cambridge Uni-

versity Press, 1989); David Harvey, The Condition of Postmodernity (Oxford: Blackwell, 1989); Christopher Norris, *What's Wrong with Postmodernism?* (Baltimore: John Hopkins Press, 1990).

[49]For developments in Canada, see Michael Gauvreau, *The Evangelical Century: College and Creed in English Canada from the Great Revival to the Great Depression* (Montreal: McGill-Queen's University Press, 1991).

[50]An excellent example is provided by the nonevangelical archbishop of Melbourne, Australia: Keith Rayner, *We Have a Gospel to Proclaim* (Melbourne: Anglican Diocese of Melbourne, 1991), especially pp. 11-12, 30.

[51]Cited in H. Cohn, "The Territorial Princes in Germany's Second Reformation," in *International Calvinism, 1541-1715,* ed. M. Prestwich (Oxford: Clarendon, 1985), pp. 135-66; quote at p. 135.

[52]For an excellent case study focusing on Holland, see Andrew Fox, "The Intellectual Consequences of the Sixteenth-Century Religious Upheaval and the Coming of a Rational World View," *Sixteenth Century Journal* 18 (1987): 63-80.